BETTY FRIEDAN
THE SECOND STAGE

"IF YOU WANT TO KNOW WHERE THE WOMEN'S MOVEMENT IS NOW, READ THIS BOOK." —*Vogue*

"The underlying theme of this book—and it is a valid message—is that both men and women need to be free to discover their own 'personhood' and to build a new society on that discovery without preconceptions and in the absence of social compulsion."

—*The New York Times Book Review*

"Her understanding of the doubleness of things, her refusal to be conned by slogans, her insistence on psychological truth rather than political polemicizing, her insistence on seeing the feminist movement in historical perspective, her refusal, in all instances, to throw out the baby with the bathwater, make the reading of this book a supremely optimistic experience."

—*Erica Jong*

W9-BEO-749

The
Second Stage

Betty Friedan

A LAUREL BOOK
Published by
Dell Publishing
a division of
Bantam Doubleday Dell Publishing Group, Inc.
666 Fifth Avenue
New York, New York 10103

Some of the material in this book was originally published in a different form in *Family Circle, The New York Times Magazine, Redbook,* and *Woman's Day.*

ISBN: 0-440-20843-2

Reprinted by arrangement with Simon & Schuster, Inc.

Printed in the United States of America

Published simultaneously in Canada

February 1991

10 9 8 7 6 5 4 3 2 1

RAD

Acknowledgments

This book evolved slowly in my consciousness over the last ten years as I was involved in the exhilarating actions and the disturbing impasses of the women's movement, and as I was beginning to formulate, in my teaching, writing, and conversations with personal friends, the concepts of what I came to call the second stage. I started to systematize these ideas in the early and mid-seventies when, as visiting professor of sociology at Temple University, and then at Yale and Queens College, I decided not to teach "women's studies" but to call my courses "The Sex Role Revolution—Stage Two" and "Human Sex and Human Politics."

In 1979, when Abe Rosenthal invited me to lunch with the editors of *The New York Times* to discuss the deadlock on the Equal Rights Amendment, I shared some of my thinking on the larger implications and the future direction of feminism, which they urged me to publish. That same year I was asked by Sey Chassler, editor of *Redbook*, to formulate the new questions for the eighties for the young women and men now living in terms of the movement for equality which I had helped to start. I also shared my sense of the political urgency of these questions with other movement veterans on the board of the NOW Legal Defense and Education Fund, who asked me to convene a National Assembly on the Future of the Family in November, 1979.

While my original sense that we must move now into the second stage came from my personal questions and observations of the conflicts of the young and not-so-young women, and men, trying to live in terms of first-stage feminism, the emergence of full-scale backlash with and after the Reagan election in 1980, when I was halfway through this book, gave enormous political immediacy to my task.

I am deeply indebted to more people than I can name here for various kinds of help in formulating and substantiating my hunches; in helping me to arrange and taking part in the personal and group interviews on which this book is based; in deepening my research and leading me to other research converging on and illuminating my own; in sustaining me through my hesitations over articulating questions that would inevitably disturb some of my older feminist sisters even as they urgently needed to be articulated to help resolve the conflicts, doubts and fears of younger women and men; and for the work over and above the call of professional duty required to get this book out in time to meet the deadline now facing the women's movement in America.

Specifically, I am indebted to Cynthia Epstein and Jonathan Cole of the Center for the Social Sciences at Columbia University, where I have been Senior Research Associate for part of this period, and participant in the Program for Sex Roles and Social Change. This invaluable program, which was made possible by a grant from the Ford Foundation, served as catalyst and sounding board for my thinking about the second stage. Madeline Simonson devoted some of her lunch hours to help me technically. Susan Roberts gave fine research aid.

I am equally indebted to Sey Chassler, Sylvia Koner, Ann Mollegen Smith and Elizabeth Dobell of *Redbook*, who were extremely helpful in getting me to formulate these ideas in concrete terms; to Abe Rosenthal and Ed Klein of *The New York Times*, whose questions and reactions made me realize I had to write this as a book; to Muriel Fox, Gene Boyer, Stephanie Clohesy, Phyllis Segal and Laurie Goldstein of the NOW Legal Defense and Education Fund, who helped give these ideas a first tryout at the National Assembly on the Future of the Family and, as is the way with the women's movement, gave them far more substance and resonance than I could have done alone.

I am also indebted to Linda Bird Francke, Myrna and Paul Davis, Arthur Dubow, Judy and Avery Corman, Judy Bates, Emily Friedan and her friends in the Harvard Women's Coalition, Daniel and Jonathan Friedan and their friends, and all the others who shared their own thoughts with me and got others to do so. All the people, women and men, quoted in this book are real individuals, alive and well and living their problems in various parts of the country in ways that give me hope for the future. I have disguised their names and certain details to protect their privacy. I am only sorry I could not use more of those wonderfully rich interviews of women and men who gave me their time, but they all combined to form my own sense of the second stage.

Serendipity—in which I firmly believe—steered me, at just the right time, to the illuminating research of Susan Harding, Nancy Bennett, *et al.*, at the University of Michigan; Peter Schwartz and Lyn Rossner at Stanford Research Institute; Major William Ritch at West Point; Irving Levine and Joseph Giordano of the Institute for Pluralism and Group Identity of the American Jewish Committee; Dolores Hayden, Sheila Kammerman, Rosabeth Kanter and Bernard Lefkowitz.

I also want to thank my personal helpers who sustained me in various ways over the rough spots of this search: first of all, my indefatigable assistant, Nancy Hawley; Natalie Gittelson and the gitteldaughters, so generous with their inimitable critical and culinary talents; Millie Becerra of Inside Address, who typed and retyped this manuscript; Patricia King and the staff of the Schlesinger Library at Harvard; David White, who introduced me to Rilke; and Judith Garten, Joe Haggerty, John Pierrakos, Judith Rossner, Alex Ross, Bert Shaw, Syd and Annie Solomon, Harold Wit, Susan Wood, and all the members of my extended family of choice who cheered me through the dark winter of my writing. I am much more than professionally grateful for the support of my agent, Emilie Jacobson of Curtis Brown; for the sensitive editing of the lines of this manuscript by Paul Bresnick of Summit Books; and for the sustaining confidence and friendship of my editor and publisher, Jim Silberman, through the storms of these years. I hope that they all forgive me for the hard time I gave them, getting into and through *The Second Stage*, and that they will themselves enjoy the vistas I seek to open, personally and politically.

In preparing this book for the paperback edition, I have made a few corrections in the final half of Part One, "End of the Beginning." In the last chapter of the book, I have taken into account the foreboding economic and political developments of 1982, which force us to enter the second stage in reality now, no matter what our ideology. We know that we cannot stop here. We will not go back from this new place. Our hope now is simply to move on.

Cambridge, Massachusetts
June 1982

For my own children—
Emily, Jonathan, Daniel—
and for my extended family of choice.

Contents

Be patient toward all that is unsolved in your heart
And try to love the questions themselves.
Do not seek the answers that cannot be given you
Because you would not be able to live them
And the point is to live everything
Live the questions now
Perhaps you will gradually without noticing it
Live along some distant day into the answers.

—RAINER MARIA RILKE

Introduction

 On August 26, 1989, I flew to Seneca Falls, where in 1848 our foremothers (Elizabeth Cady Stanton, Susan B. Anthony and others) first met to declare their sentiments for women's rights.

In that historic place, on the seventieth anniversary of the right to vote, which was the goal of our foremothers, mothers and daughters who assembled to celebrate National Women's Equality Day faced the Supreme Court's retreat on the right of choice.

A year later, President Bush vetoed the parental leave bill and has threatened to veto national child-care legislation. The media has become increasingly traditional in their portrayal of women. It is clear that we must move, with urgency, to the second stage of feminism, which has been too long delayed.

**The Full Text of a Speech Given by
Betty Friedan at the National Women's Hall of Fame
on August 26, 1989
Seneca Falls, NY**

On August 26, 1970, nearly twenty years ago, on the fiftieth anniversary of women getting the vote, I called for a nationwide strike for equality. It was not a strike in the strictest sense, because we did not even know how big the women's movement was. We were just beginning to get organized. The organizations that I helped start—NOW, the National Women's Political Caucus, the National Abortion Rights Action League—had just begun. But it was clear that far beyond the reach of any one of these organizations there was strong identification with the cause of women's equality, the personhood of women, our own voice and our destiny. We had to make clear to ourselves and to the nation how strong we were, because the media, which should come as no surprise after all those years of perpetuating the feminine mystique, were trying to trivialize us as "bra burners." So I called for a nationwide women's strike for equality, and some of my sisters in NOW helped organize it. People from all walks of feminist life joined: the young radicals, who had not yet joined organizations like NOW, the traditional groups—old suffragettes, Junior Leaguers, the Women's Strike for Peace—the professional women, including Helen Gurley Brown and other magazine editors, and the women who just came out from the offices, museums, and hospitals where they worked. It was a miracle. It was the first nationwide demonstration of women since winning the vote. Fifty thousand of us marched in New York, comparable numbers in the other large cities, and in small towns. In East Hampton, we had a march on the beach. We said, "Don't iron while the strike is hot." We made the husbands bake the cakes for the cake sales. And we marched. What we marched for twenty years ago was our serious and real commitment to equality of opportunity in jobs and education, to our own political voice, to our right to safe access to abortion, and for child care. Then we began to organize in real earnest, and we changed our lives and the possibilities of life for the women who came after us.

And now it is twenty years since that explosion of the modern women's movement. Now our daughters have come of age. The daughters who grew up with those rights seemingly so sure, so secure, so visible, that they took it all for granted. The "I'm not a feminist, but . . ." generation. "I'm not a feminist, but I'm going to be an astronaut." "I'm not a feminist, but I'm going to law school." "I'm not a feminist, but I don't know yet whether I'll be a judge and head for the Supreme Court or for the Senate."

Today, after the Supreme Court's decision to take away our constitutional right to make the most private and basic of decisions about childbirth, after the erosion of the laws we won on sex discrimination in employment and education, after the dilution, diminution, and virtual cessation of affirmative action by the Bush administration, now, today, here in this nation, the younger generation, the daughter's generation, the "I'm not a feminist, but . . ." generation is rising to defend the rights we won. And on this day, from this place, from Seneca Falls, I call to the new generation, not only to join with the mothers, but to take this great unfinished revolution, this stalled movement of women to full equality —to take it to the next stage.

We are on the cusp today. The conventional wisdom has been that the daughters, the women under forty, the women born of the great baby boom, don't identify with feminism. This has been a great misconception, sown by the seeds of a new feminine mystique in the mass media. As you know, the feminine mystique is the name I gave twenty-five years ago to the image of women that came to us from the mass media then and was accepted by all the organs of sophisticated thought, and even by women themselves. The only image of women then was in sexual relation to man as his wife, mother, housewife, serving physical needs of husband, children, home, never a person herself. That image had wiped out the memory of the great feminist foremothers and their hundred-year struggle for women's rights. It made "career women" and "women's rights" and "feminism" dirty words that were not even heard anymore or in the consciousness of young women even at the best colleges. Each woman then, twenty-five years ago, just before *The Feminine Mystique* came

out, thought she was alone if, no matter how much she had
wanted that husband, those children, the home, the appliances, the wall-to-wall carpeting, the dishwasher, she wondered "Who am I?" She had the feeling the world was going
on without her. That she was alone. That no one else felt that
way. That something was wrong with her. That it was her
personal problem that she should confess in the confessional
or on the couch.

Then we realized we were not alone and we began to
name our own problems, and we broke through that feminine mystique. Once we said women are people, because the
personhood of women was what it was all about, then we
began to move, and move very fast indeed to demand our
human and American birthright, equality of rights, our own
voice in the decisions that control our destiny. We won the
laws on sex discrimination and got them enforced. We won
the affirmative-action programs. We fought the class-action
suits and we won them. We changed the language. And we
won from the Supreme Court the ruling, Roe versus Wade,
that the Constitution and the Bill of Rights—which had been
written over two hundred years ago of, by, and for the people
who were men—now had to be interpreted to guarantee the
basic right of a woman to control her body, to control her
reproductive process. Women had the right to decide for
themselves, according to the dictates of their own consciences, this basic decision of when, whether, and how many
times to bear a child, and therefore to have safe, legal, medical access to all forms of birth control, and if necessary, to
abortion. This right was basic to the personhood of women.

Then we had the ten years of Reagan and Bush and the
declaration of war on women's rights. The attempt to make
feminism a dirty word. The defeat of the Equal Rights
Amendment, and a continual, hysterical waving of a flag on
the issue of abortion by the forces that said they were for life.
The so-called pro-life forces were not for the life of women.
They were not for the right and the responsibility of women

to bring only wanted life into this world, life that could be supported and cared for. They were not for the right of children to have child care, and for women to be able to earn and fulfill their responsibilities both to work and to family. They waved the fetus as an object. They waved it in obscene ways in an attack on women's lives and on the personhood of women. They miscalled themselves pro-life. They miscalled themselves the silent majority. The polls showed that women of all generations who believed in equality and believed in choice were the majority, but sometimes even politicians don't believe the polls when there is extremism and hysteria on one side or the other, and powerful forces are fanning that extremism and hysteria.

Lately though, the new generation is coming up against the biological clock: having, yes, won the choice to have children, but not having good choices yet because the U.S. is in this obscene position of being the only advanced industrial nation, besides South Africa, without national policies on child care and parental leave. So, they've had to postpone having babies, sometimes until they are forty. And because they are having babies late, without adequate child care and parental leave, the new generation is having real difficulties combining home and work. And because the women's movement has been so stalled, forced to defend the rights we won long ago, and prevented by the politics of the Reagan era from advancement of social programs, and with no priority attention from either Democrats or Republicans to child care and parental leave—each women has, again, begun to see her own problem as personal, not political. "Having it all" has become a perjorative, as if she is not supposed to have it all—home and work. You see in the media the new traditionalism: a woman should put down her briefcase, pick up the baby, put on an apron, and go home again. But the economic reality is that it is not just the search for self-fulfillment that is forcing the great majority of American women of all ages, even when children are little, to work outside the home, but sheer economic necessity. Now it takes a two-paycheck family to buy a house or a condo and to pay for tuition and college bills. It is very hard for a single-parent paycheck, which is usually the woman's, to support a family today.

The politicians and the media have misinterpreted the problems women have been having in juggling career, family, and child care, and have assumed that women do not care anymore about their rights. They've misunderstood so badly that in this last presidential election campaign, while Bush openly campaigned against choice, the Democratic Party did not put up a fight. It didn't make an appeal for the women's vote. In fact, Bella Abzug and I had been working with some of the women leaders in this state on a political leaflet appealing to women's concerns. It was going to be issued on Eleanor Roosevelt's birthday. We wanted to warn women of the effect on the Supreme Court and on the rights that had been protected by the Supreme Court—such as tne right of privacy—if Bush won the election. But on tne Democratic side the advisers of Dukakis, including some women who had bought the new feminine mystique, would not let us make that warning. So it is not right to blame any one party for this terrible misunderstanding that has got us to where we are today. One party may be more responsible, but the other party let it happen. There is a lesson here for both political parties.

The Supreme Court issued the Webster decision in July. Not in law yet, but de facto, this gave the states the go-ahead to take away a woman's right to make this basic decision herself. The polls show that no matter what people think about abortion—and you have to recognize the complexity of values involved here, that it is not an easy question—the latest polls, Gallup and *The New York Times*, showed that 68 percent of the American people believe that it is nobody's business but the woman's; that it is not the government's business to make that decision. Since Bush's Justice Department went to the Supreme Court to reverse Roe versus Wade

in that Webster decision—the political landscape of this nation has begun to change. The politicians do not yet quite
understand, but they are dimly beginning to be aware. Because the "I'm not a feminist, but . . ." generation may have
taken the rights for granted—and who has ever heard of the
Supreme Court going back on a constitutional decision so
basic as that—but once they saw their own rights in real
danger, the daughters have risen to join the mothers.

If you were in Washington on the march, and saw the
great coalition of all the organizations that make up the wom-
en's movement—it was incredible, the number of daughters.
I marched with my daughter, who is a doctor, with her new
baby in the backpack. Many, many others were marching
with their daughters, too, and someone said, "My God, the
feminists have bred." It is now the feminist family that is
marching. The sons were there. I loved the sight of a little
eleven-year-old girl with a handwritten sign that said, "I was
a choice." The sons and the husbands and the lovers marched
too.

I came here on this little plane that the National Parks
Service was kind enough to send for me, because first I had to
open a rally in East Hampton, near my house in Sag Harbor,
where my friends and neighbors, and above all, our daughters—over a thousand strong—turned out in the ballpark to
demonstrate for choice. "The fight begins again," their banner said. And the daughters, sixteen-year-olds, nineteen-year-
olds, a Cornell student who is taking the year off for "students organizing students," sons of feminists, and women
that I would not even have called feminists, showed up for
this march. The woman who organized that, Linda Francke,
is now running for state assembly against a virulent enemy
of choice. This is happening all around this country.

There are already upsets astounding the politicians and
media pundits. In Escondido, California, the candidate that
was expected to win the congressional bi-election lost. Why?

Because that candidate was against choice. In Hilton Head, South Carolina, there were three candidates: one was against choice and that one is out; the other two are for choice and there is going to be a run-off. In Iowa, in Maine, in New Hampshire, in Florida, in the New Jersey and Virginia gubernatorial elections, candidates who have opposed choice are shivering in their boots. They are trying to say, "No, I really didn't mean it when I said I was against choice." They are trying to weasel like mad, but nobody believes them. In the New York mayoralty election, prosecutor Giuliani, the law-and-order man, tried to keep it a secret that he has a long record of being against choice, but women knew. Women wouldn't vote for him. The pollsters discovered that he couldn't possibly win because now 63 percent of the people are for choice as a basic women's right, and are going to vote that way. They are going to vote not in a single-issue sense, but because this is symbol and substance of all the issues having to do with woman's life and woman's commitment to life.

I know this is a bipartisan gathering, and I want to be a little bipartisan in my warning. The Republicans have outraged women. But the Democrats cannot take pro-choice women for granted. No matter how much a woman may have thought of herself as a Democrat, she is not going to vote for a Democratic candidate who is unclear, ambivalent on choice. Governor Cuomo, thank heavens, understands this. Now, he has said he will uphold choice in this state, despite what the Supreme Court does. He will not let women of New York be victims of this kind of backward, repressive thinking. Other governors should follow suit. But they would misunderstand also if they thought that this was just a single-issue vote. They now know that the people who believe in choice, the women and the men, are dead serious about it. They now know that these people represent the mainstream and the real majority—no longer silent—and that the people who have been bombing abortion clinics are the violent extremists, and that they had better get into the mainstream if they want to be reelected. But I wonder if they are still too bemused by that feminine mystique, by the ten years of false-speak, news-speak that made feminism a dirty word, to misunderstand how broad the commitment to life is on the part of the women and men who mobilized for choice.

I would say this to my fellow Democrats who control both houses of Congress: You will be held accountable. You will be held accountable on your vote on Patricia Schroeder's bill for the birth-control research that has been prevented in this country and that could make abortion obsolete one day. You will be held accountable for your vote, and your leadership, and your making a priority of the child-care bill that is an utter necessity if women today in America are going to be able to meet their responsibility to children and family and work. You will be held responsible for adopting into law, this session of Congress, parental leave. So women can have good choices about having children, and women and men can take the leave that is necessary to bond with their new children, because life does not end at birth—human life only begins at birth. You must show real responsibility to life.

At a rally where I spoke recently in Long Island, Lloyd Cutler, a distinguished former presidential advisor in Carter's White House, said to me and to the other women, "You make a mistake if you just put this in terms of women's individual right, as if it is some selfish thing. It is in terms of the good and the need of society that we say that women should not be forced to bring into this world a life for which they cannot be responsible." Because every child that is born unwanted, unloved—a baby born to babies, parents that can't bring it up, can't support it, mothers lacking in prenatal and postnatal care—every such child is going to be a burden on society, and even a threat to society. It is in the largest sense of social responsibility that we now move to the second stage of this women's movement, because this is the moment to

move for the lives of women and for the choice, the autonomy, the freedom, and the equality of women. We have the
opportunity now to keep the door open for the new generation, and to turn the politics of this nation around.

Of the younger generation, 71 percent believe that there is
a need for a strong women's movement. I say to the leaders of
the organizations that I helped start, and to the whole coalition that comprises the women's movement today, that this is
the moment for the new generation. This is the moment
when that is more important than your organization's power,
or your power in your own organization, or your organization's treasury, or even the rhetoric that served you well ten
years ago. There must be a listening and an involvement and
a dialogue with the daughters, and a grooming of the daughters and a handing on of the torch to the daughters.

And you daughters, don't wait for them. If you do not find
in any organization of the women's movement attention to
your real needs, start your own. Start your own, or better,
join any one of them, *and transform it.* But the next stage of
the women's movement is not women against men. There are
sons and husbands and fathers that really want to play a role.
It is true, women are doing twice as much housework as
men, still. But twenty years ago they were doing ten times as
much housework as men. We cannot ask for miracles in one
generation. Now, I think that by the time they share fifty
percent of the housework, we will share fifty percent of the
leadership—of the new movement. But meanwhile, maybe
we ought to think of bringing men in, in more than token
numbers, because the next stage will and can be men as well
as women. We have to have a lot of open thinking about this.

We have to really mean it about choice. To be able to
responsibly choose to bring children into the world. We have
to get beyond the male model of the workplace now. We have
to be able to talk of our own values again. The values of love
and care and nurturing, to which women have been social-

ized. We did not move for equality only to get a few jobs that only men had before. We did not move to equality to exchange our old frustrations as housewives for the strokes and the heart attacks that are making the men die too young. We moved for a personhood for woman and an equal voice in our society, but if it was worth fighting for, we have to be true to our own basic values as women; the values of nurturing and of life, to which we subscribe.

In this historic place, I call the organizations, I call the daughters, I call the mothers no longer burned out, rising to defend the right for their daughters, I call in a new way the sons and the lovers and the husbands to a new place, a new stage of the women's movement: the most life-affirming revolution that ever was, this great unfinished revolution, knowing that when we take this new step there will be the power to turn the values of this nation away from selfish material greed and back to the largest interests of life again. Move!

PART I

End of
the Beginning

1 End of
the Beginning

I did not intend to write another book on the woman question. I have already started a major new quest that is taking me way beyond my previous concerns, opening strange doors. I am tired of the pragmatic, earthbound battles of the women's movement, tired of rhetoric. I want to live the rest of my life.

But these past few years, fulfilling my professional and political commitments, and picking up the pieces of my personal life, for which the women's movement has been the focus for nearly twenty years, I have been nagged by a new, uneasy urgency that won't let me leave. Listening to my own daughter and sons, and others of their generation whom I meet, lecturing at universities or professional conferences or feminist networks around the country and around the world, I sense something *off*, out of focus, going wrong, in the terms by which they are trying to live the equality we fought for.

From these daughters—getting older now, working so hard, determined not to be trapped as their mothers were, and expecting so much, taking for granted the opportunities we had to struggle for—I've begun to hear undertones of pain and puzzlement, a queasiness, an uneasiness, almost a bitterness that they hardly dare admit. As if with all those opportunities that we won for them, and envy them, how can

3

they ask out loud certain questions, talk about certain other
needs they aren't supposed to worry about—those old needs
which shaped our lives, and trapped us, and against which
we rebelled?

• In California, in the office of a television producer who
prides himself on being an "equal opportunity employer," I
am confronted by his new "executive assistant." She wants to
talk to me alone before her boss comes in. Lovely, in her late
twenties and "dressed for success" like a model in the latest
Vogue, she is not just a glorified secretary with a fancy title in
a dead-end job. The woman she replaced has just been promoted to the position of "creative vice-president."

"I know I'm lucky to have this job," she says, defensive
and accusing, "but you people who fought for these things
had your families. You already had your men and children.
What are we supposed to do?"

She complains that the older woman vice-president, one
of the early radical feminists who vowed never to marry or
have children, didn't understand her quandary. "All she
wants," the executive assistant says, "is more power in the
company."

• A young woman in her third year of Harvard Medical
School tells me, "I'm going to be a surgeon. I'll never be a
trapped housewife like my mother. But I would like to get
married and have children, I think. They say we can have it
all. But how? I work thirty-six hours in the hospital, twelve
off. How am I going to have a relationship, much less kids,
with hours like that? I'm not sure I can be a superwoman.
I'm frightened that I may be kidding myself. Maybe I can't
have it all. Either I won't be able to have the kind of marriage
I dream of or the kind of medical career I want."

• In New York, a woman in her thirties who has just been
promoted says, "I'm up against the clock, you might say. If I
don't have a child now, it will be too late. But it's an agonizing choice. I've been supporting my husband while he gets

his Ph.D. We don't know what kind of job he'll be able to get. There's no pay when you take off to have a baby in my company. They don't guarantee you'll get your job back. If I don't have a baby, will I miss out on life somehow? Will I really be fulfilled as a woman?"

Mounting the barricades yet again in the endless battle for the Equal Rights Amendment—in Illinois, at the national political conventions—I also sensed a political bewilderment, a frustration, a flagging, finally, of energy for battle at all. It is hard to keep summoning energy for battles like ERA, which, according to all the polls and the public commitment of elected officials and political parties, should have been won long ago; or for the right to choose when and whether to have a child, and thus to safe, legal, medical help in abortion —won eight years ago and decreed by the Supreme Court more basic than many of the rights guaranteed in the Constitution and the Bill of Rights as it was written of, by and for men—only to be fought over and over again, until even the Supreme Court in 1980 took that right away for poor women.

I sense other victories we thought were won yielding illusory gains; I see new dimensions to problems we thought were solved. As, for instance, the laws against sex discrimination in employment and education, and the affirmative action programs and class-action suits that have given women access to professions and executive jobs held only by men before. Yet, after fifteen years of the women's movement, the gap between women's earnings and men's is greater than ever, women earning on the average only fifty-nine cents to every dollar men earn, the average male high school dropout today earning $1,600 more a year than female college graduates. An unprecedented majority of women have entered the work force in these years, but the overwhelming majority of women are still crowded into the poorly paid service and clerical jobs traditionally reserved for females. (With the divorce rate exceeding 50 percent, it turns out that 71 percent of divorced women are now working compared to only 78 percent of divorced men; the women must be taking jobs the men won't touch.)

What will happen in the eighties as inflation, not just new aspirations, forces women to keep working, while unemployment, already reaching 7.8 percent, hits women the worst? Growing millions of "discouraged workers," who are no longer counted among the unemployed because they have stopped looking for jobs, were reported in 1980, two thirds of them women.

It becomes clear that the great momentum of the women's movement for equality will be stopped, or somehow transformed, by collision or convergence with basic questions of survival in the 1980s. Is feminism a theoretical luxury, a liberal or radical notion we could toy with in the late soft age of affluence, in the decadence of advanced capitalist society, but in the face of 10 percent inflation, 7.8 percent unemployment, nuclear accident at home, and mounting terrorism from Right and Left abroad, something we must put aside for the grim new realities of economic and national survival? Or is equality itself becoming a question of basic human survival?

I go home to Illinois, to march with nearly 100,000 for ERA on Mother's Day in Chicago, and touch base with relatives and old friends in Peoria, where I was born and grew up. Main Street is deserted, shadowed by massive layoffs, the first in forty years, at the big Caterpillar tractor plant. An aging saleswoman with dyed red hair helps me buy a white skirt to wear for a final lobbying effort in Springfield. She can't understand why, with the Republican Governor and the Democratic President supposedly committed to the ERA, it doesn't get ratified. "I'll never again vote for a man who does me dirty on ERA," she says. "I have no alternative. I'm on my own now, four daughters to support. It's a question of survival." She and I remember our childhood, during the Depression, in Peoria, when married women weren't allowed to take or keep jobs as teachers.

Yet, despite the months of ceaseless lobbying by such saleswomen, by teachers and housewives from towns like Peoria, and Chicago and its suburbs, by nuns camping in a trailer under Lincoln's gaze at the foot of the state capitol, by women executives in their suits and fedoras, carrying briefcases, by union members and Junior Leaguers in their summer dresses and pumps; despite the outpouring of NOW veterans from other states, organized better than I've ever seen them; and despite the hundreds of thousands of mailgrams, postcards, petitions—the Illinois legislature refused for the eighth time, in June 1980, to ratify the Equal Rights Amendment.

The papers that day were full of black riots in Miami, terrorist bombing in Italy. "What are we going to do with our rage?" asked a usually cheerful Peoria mother, the NOW leader in my hometown, who looks like a Pillsbury bakeoff ad. "I can't see us throwing bombs—yet."

That same month, in the state of New York, where I live now, a so-called "Equitable" Divorce Reform law was passed. Under this law a woman who has been a housewife for many years, or has not earned as much as her husband, will have to pay lawyers, appraisers and accountants to "prove" on ten counts the "equitability" of her contribution to their marriage. She has to prove this in economic terms in order to receive on divorce a decent share of whatever property or other assets were accumulated during the marriage, even if the house is in her name. The rhetoric of "women's lib" was used to justify the granting to such a divorced wife only "maintenance," as for an automobile, to be cut off, after one or two years of "rehabilitation," however long she might have been a housewife, however ill-equipped to earn, however unstable her job. The legislators ignored the census figures revealing 8 million female-headed households in 1979, a 46 percent increase since 1970, half existing on less than $10,000 a year, one third on less than $7,000.

Unless the Equal Rights Amendment gets ratified, the

courts of my state, according to the precedent of other states with such divorce laws, will divide the assets of marriage on 20-80 percent or 30-70 percent lines, favoring the husband. The main supporters of this bill were lawyers—including women lawyers—who would make money from it. The two NOW women who had driven me to Albany in a futile attempt to halt passage of this law had themselves been housewives, divorced after twenty and twenty-eight years of marriage. One, recently laid off from the clerical job she'd finally found, was worried that she'd lose her house now. The other, who'd given up her own accounting trade to help her accountant husband during her housewife years, was back on her own as an accountant now, making $21,000 a year compared to her husband's $250,000.

In that same period, I got a phone call asking me to speak at a "March Against Pornography," which was being billed by the media as the new frontier of feminism. I found myself snapping, "I'll be out of town." It seemed irrelevant, wrong, for women to be wasting energy marching against pornography—or any other sexual issue—when their very economic survival was at stake.

Also about that time, I found myself walking out in the middle of the monthly lunch of the Women's Forum, our "new girls" equivalent of the old boys' network, unable to sit through another corporate bigwig's tips on how women can get "real power" in the executive suite. Was this what the women's movement was all about?

Even in that "new girls" network of the women who've broken through to the executive suite and enjoyed the tokens of professional and political equality, I sense the exhilaration of "superwomen" giving way to a tiredness, a certain brittle disappointment, a disillusionment with "assertiveness training" and the rewards of power. Matina Horner, the high-powered president of Radcliffe, calls it a "crisis of confidence."

An older woman in Ohio reflects: "I was the first woman

in management here. I gave everything to the job. It was exciting at first, breaking in where women never were before. Now it's just a job. But it's the devastating loneliness that's the worst. I can't stand coming back to this apartment alone every night. I'd like a house, maybe a garden. Maybe I should have a kid, even without a father. At least then I'd have a family. There has to be some better way to live. A woman alone . . ."

A woman who works in a bank in Chicago says: "My husband takes more responsibility for the children now than I do. He also does all the cooking. I don't feel guilty. I just feel sorry that I don't see more of the children. A job is not the end. Larry used to make a lot more money than I do but he hated what he was doing. I didn't see why it always had to be on him. It was exciting to get my job. The hard part is staying when you discover it's just a job, that you really don't like what you're doing."

In August 1980, my own college, Smith, fountainhead of feminism, held a gruelingly intensive three-week management-training program for "Women on the Way Up" at big corporations such as Xerox, Time, Grumman Aerospace, Digital Equipment, Chase Manhattan, Pfizer and General Motors. These women decided they "did not need assertiveness training—and moved on to power," a General Electric woman executive was quoted (*New York Times*, August 18). "None of us is suffering discrimination," said another. Almost unanimously these women dismissed the "soft stuff" such as "women's issues" and "managing multiple commitments" in home and office as "a waste of time." They feverishly studied corporate finance, marketing, accounting and other "hard, practical skills" such as reading a balance sheet, from early morning till late at night. Only one participant-observer, trained in psychology, described these women as practicing "massive denial."

I read in the "Hers" column in *The New York Times* that an ambitious woman journalist of my acquaintance, a fervent feminist, was forced to take to her bed for six months by some mysterious joint disease that may or may not have been related to her rather extreme "workaholic" obsession. But even she was shocked when a "workaholic" woman friend and neighbor was "too busy" to stop off and buy her a carton of milk on her way home from work. She now blames feminism for the loss of the traditional "caring" that women had for women, as well as for men and children. On a larger national scale, an ominous increase of lung cancer and heart attacks recently reported among younger women is also being blamed on the women's movement.

Of course, the women's movement has for some years been the scapegoat for the rage of threatened, insecure housewives who can no longer count on husbands for lifelong support. Recently I've been hearing younger women, and even older feminists, blame the women's movement for the supposed increase of male impotence, the inadequacy or unavailability of men for the "new women." Some even suggest that the recent explosion of rape, "battered wives," "battered children" and violence in the family is a reaction to, or by-product of, feminism.

The women's movement is being blamed, above all, for the destruction of the family. Churchmen and sociologists proclaim that the American family, as it has always been defined, is becoming an "endangered species," with the rising divorce rate and the enormous increase in single-parent families and people—especially women—living alone. Women's abdication of their age-old responsibility for the family is also being blamed for the apathy and moral delinquency of the "me generation."

Can we keep on shrugging all this off as enemy propaganda—"their problem, not ours"? I think we must at least admit and begin openly to discuss feminist denial of the importance of family, of women's own needs to give and get love and nurture, tender loving care.

What worries me today is the agonizing conflicts young and not-so-young women are facing—or denying—as they come up against the biological clock, at thirty-five, thirty-six, thirty-nine, forty, and cannot "choose" to have a child. I fought for the right to choose, and will continue to defend that right, against reactionary forces who have already taken it away for poor women now denied Medicaid for abortion, and would take it away for all women with a constitutional amendment. But I think we must begin to discuss, in new terms, the choice to *have* children.

What worries me today is "choices" women have supposedly won, which are not real. How can a woman freely "choose" to have a child when her paycheck is needed for the rent or mortgage, when her job isn't geared to taking care of a child, when there is no national policy for parental leave, and no assurance that her job will be waiting for her if she takes off to have a child?

What worries me today is that despite the fact that more than 45 percent of the mothers of children under six are now working because of economic necessity due to inflation, compared with only 10 percent in 1960 (and, according to a Ford Foundation study, it is estimated that by 1990 only one out of four mothers will be at home full time), no major national effort is being made for child-care services by government, business, labor, Democratic or Republican parties—or by the women's movement itself.

Another troubling sign: When President Carter proposed registering young women as well as men for the draft, it was clear that most young women, and a lot of older feminists, as well as middle Americans generally, would oppose such a draft of women. Phyllis Schlafly seized on the draft, of course, to sow new hysteria against the ERA. But I got long-distance calls from young women across the country, blaming the women's movement for a draft they didn't want. What becomes of the feminist axiom that equal rights and opportunity have to mean equal responsibility? Did the women's movement really mean equal opportunity for women to fire ballistic missiles in another Vietnam?

·   ·   ·

When I think back to the explosion of the women's movement at the opening of the decade—thousands of women marching down Fifth Avenue on August 26, 1970, in that first nationwide women's strike for equality, carrying banners for "Equal Rights to Jobs and Education," "The Right to Abortion," "24-Hour Child Care," "Political Power to the Women"—our agenda then seemed so simple and straightforward.

But on August 26, 1980, the women's movement was too tired from these endless, never finished real battles for equality to mount a nationwide symbolic march. NOW leaders were exhausted by their eighth unsuccessful attempt to get the ERA ratified in Illinois. The march of nearly 100,000 on Mother's Day, 1980, in Chicago, astounding in these days of apathy, greater than any Presidential candidate could summon, did not budge the Illinois state legislature.

Political power to the women? "Make policy, not coffee," we had said, organizing the National Women's Political Caucus in 1971, to get women elected to office, seated as delegates in the national conventions, with a voice in the political process commensurate to our 52 percent of the population.

So, in 1980, the only battle against right-wing control of the Republican convention in Detroit was put up by women, and men, too, who protested in vain against repudiation by the Republican platform of their half-century endorsement of the Equal Rights Amendment. And the Republicans pledged instead to name only judges who would prosecute abortion as murder. Would Republican women then repudiate Reagan or keep their mouths shut and vote against their own interests as women? After all, just one state had ratified the ERA under the Democratic President who had said only "Life is not fair" when federal funding was barred for poor women needing abortion.

In 1980, women, comprising 49 percent of the delegates to the Democratic convention, put into the platform, over the brass-knuckled opposition of the Carter machine and the indifference of Kennedy's, an uncomfortable plank barring party money or technical support to any Democratic candidate who was not committed to ERA. By an overwhelming roll-call vote, that convention affirmed the right to choose for women of all income levels, including federal aid for poor women needing abortion. Would Carter run with this? No, but at least women had succeeded in flushing the unseen enemy out of the shadows of reaction, in both parties, and had made ratification of the Equal Rights Amendment and every woman's right to choice in childbirth and access to abortion major issues in the Presidential election.

Shall we admit that some women who had been elected to Congress, or City Hall, or named to posts in the White House or near-cabinet level as a result of the women's movement, operated during that exhilarating, unprecedented battle of women on the Democratic convention floor as witting agents of the male political machine, trying to make us compromise or withdraw those feminist teeth? At a 3 A.M. meeting, Sarah Weddington, who came to fame arguing the historic abortion case before the Supreme Court, tried in vain to make the women's coalition bow to her boss in the White House and accept his compromise on ERA and abortion. Eleanor Smeal, the beleaguered president of NOW, said to me, "You can't count on any woman, once she gets some power, not to sell other women out."

Even within the women's movement there are new questions that should be faced about power. Before, and after, that shining hour of feminist unity on the Democratic convention floor, leaders of some organizations in the women's movement were spending as much energy in fighting each other and jockeying for money and power to shore up their own organizational machines as they were on ERA and abortion.

I share certain misgivings with other feminist leaders. Florence Howe, an educator who has been leading the battle for women's studies these ten years, is surprised that women delegates stood firm against the Carter whips to the degree they did. "We fought to get in the mainstream. Once inside,

who wants to risk being out again? I'll admit that I feel isolated now, in the women's studies ghetto. I miss the stimula-
tion of being part of my field."

"Maybe the women's movement is the mainstream now,"
says Bella Abzug, who lost her own safe seat in Congress
while trying to parlay her championship of women into the
Senate and Mayoralty of New York. Fired as head of the
President's Advisory Committee on Women when she insisted that inflation, unemployment and the federal budget
were women's issues, she was now trying to start a new
women's power base, "outside" the framework of existing
feminist or political organizations. For a moment she glowed
with power again, exercising her shrewd political skills in
managing the women's caucus floor whip operation at the
Democratic convention.

But on August 26, 1980, only five hundred turned out to
march on Fifth Avenue. The many hundreds of thousands of
women for whom such a march ten years ago had been the
cutting edge of feminist consciousness were in some different
place now. A few women chained themselves to the fence
outside Republican National Headquarters in Washington.
President Carter signed a proclamation at the White House,
and Mayor Koch of New York, in proclaiming "Women's
Equality Week," said he would not be bound by that plank
women wrote into the party platform. I stayed home on
Long Island, and marched with my neighbors and friends
and our daughters to a village green, honoring our own history. But it is a mistake to try to make history repeat itself.

This uneasy sense of battles won, only to be fought over
again, of battles that should have been won, according to all
the rules, and yet are not, of battles that suddenly one does
not really want to win, and the weariness of battle altogether
—how many women feel it? What does it mean? This ner-
vousness in the women's movement, this sense of enemies
and dangers, omnipresent, unseen, of shadowboxing enemies
who aren't there—are they paranoid phantoms, and if so,

why do these enemies always win? This unarticulated malaise now within the women's movement—is something wonderful dulling, dwindling, tarnishing from going on too long, or coming to an end too soon, before it is really finished?

Though the women's movement has changed all our lives and surpassed our dreams in its magnitude, and our daughters take their own personhood and equality for granted, they—and we—are finding that it's not so easy to *live*, with or without men and children, solely on the basis of that first feminist agenda. I think, in fact, that the women's movement has come just about as far as it can in terms of women alone. The very choices, options, aspirations, opportunities that we have won for women—no matter how far from real equality —and the small degree of new power women now enjoy, or hunger for, openly, honestly, as never before, are converging on and into new economic and emotional urgencies. Battles lost or won are being fought in terms that are somehow inadequate, irrelevant to this new personal, and political, reality. I believe it's over, that first stage: the women's movement. And yet the larger revolution, evolution, liberation that the women's movement set off, has barely begun. How do we move on? What are the terms of the second stage?

In the first stage, our aim was full participation, power and voice in the mainstream, inside the party, the political process, the professions, the business world. Do women change, inevitably discard the radiant, inviolate, idealized feminist dream, once they get inside and begin to share that power, and do they then operate on the same terms as men? Can women, will women even try to, change the terms?

What are the limits and the true potential of women's power? I believe that the women's movement, in the political sense, is both less and more powerful than we realize. I believe that the personal is both more and less political than our own rhetoric ever implied. I believe that we have to break through our own *feminist* mystique now to come to terms with the new reality of our personal and political experience, and to move into the second stage.

All this past year, with some reluctance and dread, and a strange, compelling relief, I've been asking new questions and listening with a new urgency to other women again, wondering if anyone else reads these signs as beginning-of-the-end, end-of-the-beginning. When I start to talk about them, it makes some women, feminists and antifeminists, uncomfortable, even angry.

There is a disconcerted silence, an uneasy murmuring, when I begin to voice my hunches out loud:

The second stage cannot be seen in terms of women alone, our separate personhood or equality with men.

The second stage involves coming to new terms with the family—new terms with love and with work.

The second stage may not even be a women's movement. Men may be at the cutting edge of the second stage.

The second stage has to transcend the battle for equal power in institutions. The second stage will restructure institutions and transform the nature of power itself.

The second stage may even now be evolving, out of or even aside from what we have thought of as our battle.

I've experienced before the strange mix of shock and relief these hunches arouse. It happened twenty years ago when I began to question the feminine mystique. It happened before when I put into words uncomfortable realities women had been avoiding because they meant we'd have to change. Even the makers of change, self-proclaimed revolutionaries, women no less than men, resist change of the change that has become their security, their power.

If we put these symptoms I have hinted at to the test of full consciousness—as I intend to do in this book—facing clearly, openly, publicly what they mean, will we find that the women's movement is, in fact, harboring some incurable cancer, dooming it to imminent death? Inconceivable—never has the women's movement, and the movement of women in the largest sense, seemed stronger, more endurable, irreversible. Three generations of women, millions upon millions, in this and other lands, are living, moving, changing, frantically grasping a new life, or trying to hold on to life, in terms of feminism.

I and other feminists dread to admit or discuss out loud these troubling symptoms because the women's movement has, in fact, been the source and focus of so much of our own energy and strength and security, its root and support, for so many years. We cannot conceive that it will not go on forever the same way it has for nearly twenty years now. But we can't go on denying these puzzling symptoms of distress. If they mean something is seriously wrong, we had better find out and change direction yet again—as much as we ourselves resist such change now—before it is too late.

"How can you talk about the second stage when we haven't even won the first yet?" a woman asks me at a Catholic college weekend for housewives going back to work. "The men still have the power. We haven't gotten enough for ourselves yet. We have to fight now just to stay where we are, not to be pushed back."

But that's the point. Maybe we have to begin talking about the second stage to keep from getting locked into obsolete power games and irrelevant sexual battles that never can be won, or that we will lose by winning. Maybe only by moving into the second stage, and asking the new questions —political and personal—confronting women and men trying to live the equality we fought for, can we transcend the polarization that threatens even the gains already won, and keep alive the national commitment to women's rights, equal opportunity and choice through this time of economic turmoil and reaction.

There's almost a religious feeling many women share about the women's movement that keeps us from asking these questions. A sacredness, a reverence, an awe, a pride beyond arrogance and an incredulous humility that we who made this movement share truly as sisters, overriding our ideological differences and power battles: the grandiose heroics of knowing that in our own lifetime we have changed history more basically than women ever before, and more than most men; the grounding certainty that the women's movement "changed our whole lives," and the very terms by which the new generations of women and men approach life.

But the women's movement didn't start with heroics, or even with the political rhetoric of revolution. For me, as for most others, it started with facing the concrete, mundane personal truth of my own life and hearing the personal truth of other women—the "problem that had no name" because it didn't quite fit the image of the happy suburban housewife we were all living in those days—that image of woman completely fulfilled in her role as husband's wife, children's mother, server of physical needs of husband, children, home. That image, which I called the "feminine mystique," bombarded us from all sides in the fifteen or twenty years after World War II, denying the very existence in women of the need to be and move in society and be recognized as a person, an individual in her own right.

We broke through that image. So for nearly twenty years now, the words written about and by and for women have been about women's need to be, first of all, themselves . . . to find themselves, fulfill themselves, their own personhood . . . to free themselves from submission as servants of the family and take control of their own bodies, their own lives . . . to find their own identity as separate from men, marriage and child-rearing—and to demand equal opportunity with men, power of their own in corporate office, Senate chamber, spaceship, ballfield, battlefield, at whatever price. Organizing the women's movement, we broke through the barriers that kept women from moving, working, earning and speaking in their own voice in the mainstream of society. For nearly twenty years we have been pressing our grievances against men in office and home, school and field, in marriage, housework, even sex.

I remain committed to these unfinished battles. We had to do what we did, to come out of the shadow of the feminine mystique, and into our personhood, as women. We had to fight for our equal opportunity to participate in the larger work and decisions of society and the equality in the family that such participation entails and requires. This was the essence of the women's movement—the first stage. It happened, not because I or any other feminist witch somehow seduced otherwise happy housewives by our words, but because of evolutionary necessity. Women could no longer live out an eighty-year life span as childbearers, wives and mothers alone. For function, identity, status in society, and their own economic support, women—for the first time in history freed from passive, necessary submission to their role as breeders of the race—were forced by the longer span of their lives to take their own place, as individuals in society.

The feminine mystique was obsolete. That's why our early battles were won so easily, once we engaged our will. It was, is, awesome—that quantum jump in consciousness. A whole new literature, a new history, new dimensions in every field are now emerging, as the larger implications of women's personhood and equality are explored. The women's movement, which started with personal truth, not seen or understood by the experts, or even by women themselves, because it did not fit the accepted image, has, in the span of a single generation, changed life, and the accepted image.

But the new image, which has come out of the women's movement, cannot evade the continuing tests of real life. That uneasiness I have been sensing these past few years comes from personal truth denied and questions unasked because they do not fit the new accepted image—the *feminist* mystique—as our daughters live what we fought for. It took many centuries of social evolution, technological revolution, to disturb "the changeless face of Eve." That immutable, overshadowing definition of woman as breeder of the race, once rooted in biological, historical necessity, only became a mystique, a defense against reality, as it denied the possibilities and necessities of growth opened by women's new life span in advanced technological society.

•   •   •

Such is the accelerated pace of change today that it may take only a few years for the feminist image to harden into a similarly confining, defensive mystique. Does our feminist image already leave out important new, or old, dimensions of woman's possibility and necessity? I think the problem here is somehow to disentangle the basic truth of feminism from *reaction*—not just reaction against feminism, but the half-truth of *feminist reaction*. For insofar as the new feminist mystique is defined by reaction against the old feminine necessity, it could suppress important parts of our personhood—breeding a new "problem that has no name." It will not take long for younger daughters to rise against a mystique that does not truly open life for women. In another pendulum swing of reaction they could turn their backs again on the necessary, unfinished true battles of feminism, as some of us turned our backs on the life-serving core of feminine identity, along with the distorting, confining mystique.

At the Harvard commencement in June 1980, class speaker Diana Shaw criticized the feminists who had paved the way for her graduation from that venerable arrogant university on equal terms, with the same diploma, as men. "Contemporary feminism," she said, "has taught us to reject the values conventionally associated with our sex. We are expected to pursue the male standards of success, while remaining 'feminine' according to male standards."

Her words hit a sensitive nerve in one of those earlier feminists, Ellen Goodman, who graduated from the same college, when Radcliffe women were separate from and not quite equal to Harvard men, class of 1963, the year *The Feminine Mystique* was published. "We were to be the first generation of superwomen," she writes *(Washington Post*, June 7, 1980).

We were the women who would—in fact, should—
have dazzling careers and brilliant, satisfied husbands,
and remarkable, well-adjusted children.

The half-formed feminism of the early 1960's . . . taught us that to find fulfillment we would have to fit in—fit in to family life . . . fit in to career ladders . . . fit in to our husband's goals . . . fit in to the basic ideas of womanhood. . . .

Through the 1970's, we argued about what kind of equality we wanted. Did we want equal access to the same system or the power to change it? Can you change the system only by becoming a part of it? Once you are in it, does it change you instead?

We discovered that it is easier to fit in than to restructure. When the "male" standard is regarded as the "higher" one, the one with the most tangible rewards, it is easier for women to reach "up" than to convince men of the virtues of simultaneously reaching "down."

It has proved simpler—though not simple, God knows—for women to begin traveling traditional (male) routes than to change those routes. It is simpler to dress for success than to change the definition of success. . . .

"I'm suffering from feminist fatigue," writes Lynda Hurst, a columnist on the *Toronto Star*, in a new non- or antifeminist sheet started in Canada in June 1980 called *Breakthrough*. "After the last dazzle of the [feminist] fireworks, there was deeper darkness. You are perhaps more enslaved now than you have ever been."

She says defiantly:

I've been letting sexist cracks slip past with barely a shrug. I haven't read *Ms*. magazine in months. I can sleep nights without worrying about my lack of a five-year career plan. I can even watch "I Love Lucy" reruns without tsk-tsking over the rampant sexism of the Ricardo marriage.

Don't get me wrong. It's not the women's move-

ment I'm fed up with. . . . It's the "feminist" label—
and its paranoid associations—that I've started to resent. I'm developing an urge to run around telling people that I still like raindrops on roses and whiskers on
kittens, and that being the local easy-to-bait feminist is
getting to be a bore.

I'm tired of having other people (women as well as
men) predict my opinion on everything from wedding
showers to coed hockey. . . .

I don't want to be stuck today with a feminist label
any more than I would have wanted to be known as a
"dumb blonde" in the fifties. The libber label limits
and shortchanges those who are tagged with it. And
the irony is that it emerged from a philosophy that set
out to destroy the whole notion of female tagging.

I write this book to help the daughters break through the
mystique I myself helped to create—and put the right name
to their new problems. They have to ask new questions,
speak the unspeakable again, admit new, uncomfortable realities, and secret pains and surprising joys of their personal
truth that are hard to put into words because they do not fit
either the new or old images of women, or they fit them
disconcertingly.

These questions come into consciousness as personal ones,
each daughter thinking maybe she alone feels this way. The
questions have to be asked personally before they become
political. Or rather, these simple, heartfelt questions I've
been hearing from young women all over the country this
past year seem to me to indicate a blind spot in feminism that
is both personal and political in its implications and consequences. The younger women have the most questions:

"How can I have it all? Do I *really* have to choose?"

"How can I have the career I want, and the kind of marriage I want, and be a good mother?"

"How can I get him to share more responsibility at home?

Why do I always have to be the one with the children, making the decisions at home?"

"I can't count on marriage for my security—look what happened to my mother—but can I get all my security from my career?"

"Can I make it in a man's world, doing it the man's way? What other way is there? But what is it doing to me? Do I want to be like men?"

"What do I have to give up? What are the tradeoffs?"

"Will the jobs open to me now still be there if I stop to have children?"

"Does it really work, that business of 'quality, not quantity' of time with the children? How much is enough?"

"How can I fill my loneliness, except with a man?"

"Do men really want an equal woman?"

"Why are men today so gray and lifeless, compared to women? How can I find a man I can really look up to?"

"How can I play the sex kitten now? Can I ever find a man who will let me be myself?"

"If I put off having a baby till I'm thirty-eight, and can call my own shots on the job, will I ever have kids?"

"How can I juggle it all?"

"How can I put it all together?"

"Can I risk losing myself in marriage?"

"Do I have to be a superwoman?"

Among ourselves, the mothers, I also sense new uneasiness, new questions even harder to put into words lest they evoke those old needs, long since left behind, by us who fought so hard to change the terms of our own lives:

"I have made it, far beyond my dreams. If I put everything else aside, I can see myself as president of the company in ten years. It's not impossible for a woman now. But is that what I really want?"

"My marriage didn't work. I value my independence. I don't want to get married again. But how can I keep on taking care of my kids and myself, on what I earn, and have any kind of life at all, with only myself to depend on? All I do is work to pay the bills."

This is the jumping-off point to the second stage, I believe: these conflicts and fears and compelling needs women feel about the choice to have children now and about success in the careers they now seek—and the concrete practical problems involved (which have larger political implications). I believe daughters and mothers hold separate pieces of the puzzle. I think of my own uneasiness, being called "mother" of the women's movement—not because of modesty, but because of the way I felt about being a mother altogether. An uneasiness, an unsureness, a fear about being a mother because I certainly didn't want to be like my mother. How many generations of American women have felt like that? Until recently I've sensed that same uneasiness with my daughter, an agonizing love-fear-dread, as we see ourselves in each other and do not want to see the pain of it.

With my own daughter now, and so many others, I sense that we have begun to break some seemingly endless vicious cycle. "Another one like me!" "Don't let me be like her!" What we did, we had to do, to break that cycle. But it is not finished yet. It won't be finished until our daughters can freely, joyously choose to have children. They, and we, are beginning to be afraid—and some of our fears are false shadows of dangers past, and some are presently real—because the cycle we broke, and have to embrace again, is basic to life.

From their new place, the daughters can deny their fears and confusions until exaggerated dangers and unrecognized real problems turn them back. The daughters can't make a map from their own experience alone—they might not even recognize the same old traps, dead ends, that we had such a hard time finding our way out of, or the feel of firm ground we were looking for. They never knew the necessity that drove us. But the daughters cannot get their map from us because they truly start from a different place, that assumption of their own personhood and semblance of equal opportunity we won.

Daughters moving ahead where mothers could not go may be, in fact, not so much in danger of being trapped as their mothers were as they are in danger of wasting, avoiding life in unnecessary fear. But even the map we piece together from our bridged experience as women—our daughters and ourselves, moving proudly now as women through the first stage, breaking the chains that kept us out of man's world—is not enough for the next stage. For women may be in new danger of falling into certain deadly traps that men are now trying to climb out of to save their own lives. We can't traverse the next stage and reembrace the cycle of life as women alone.

I have been hearing from men this past year warning signs of certain dead ends for women. Surprising clues of the second stage can be found in the new questions men are asking.

• A Vietnam veteran, laid off at the auto plant where he thought he was secure for life, decides: "There's no security in a job. The dollar's not worth enough anymore to live your life for. I'll work three days a week at the garage and my wife will go back to nursing nights, and between us we'll take care of the kids."

• A man on his way up in a New York bank quits to sell real estate on the tip of Long Island for part of his groceries, and to grow the rest himself. "I asked myself one day whether, if my career continued going well and I really made it up the corporate ladder, did I want to be there, fifteen years from now, with the headaches of the senior executives I saw being pushed off to smaller offices, their staff, secretaries, status taken away, or having heart attacks, strokes. Men who had been loyal to the company twenty-five years, it consumed their whole lives—to what end? Did I want to live my life to wind up like them?"

• A hotshot MBA in Chicago balks at the constant traveling

and the sixty-to-eighty-hour weeks he is expected to work, assigned to troubleshoot an aerospace company in Texas. "I'm supposed to leave Sunday night and get back Friday. My wife and I are getting to be strangers. Besides, I want to have a family. There are other things I want in life besides getting ahead in this company. But how can I say I won't travel like that when the other guys are willing to? They'll get ahead, and I won't. How can I live for myself, not just for the company?"

• A sales engineer in New Jersey, struggling to take equal responsibilities for the kids now that his wife has gone to work in a department store, says: "For ten years now, all you hear is women talking about what it means to be a woman, how can she fulfill herself as a woman, even forcing men to talk about women. It's over, the man sitting down with his paper, the wife keeping the kids out of his way. The women's movement forced us to think it through—the presumption that the house and the children were the women's responsibility, the shopping, the cooking, even if both were working. Now you're going to see more men asking, What am I doing with my life, what about my fulfillment, what does it mean being a man? What do I have but my job? I think you're going to see a great wave of men dropping out from traditional male roles. Our sense of who we are was profoundly based on work, but men are going to begin to define themselves in ways other than work. Partly because of the economy, partly because men are beginning to find other goodies at the table, like the children, where men have been excluded before. Being a daddy has become very important to me. Why shouldn't she support the family for a while and let *me* find myself?"

Are men and women moving in opposite directions, chasing illusions of liberation by simply reversing roles that the other sex has already found imprisoning? Maybe there are some choices we, they, don't want to face, or shouldn't have to face. Maybe they are not real choices—not yet, not the way society is structured now, or not ever, in terms of basic human reality. Do we have to transcend the very terms of these choices in the second stage?

I think we can only find out by sharing our new uncertainties, the seemingly insoluble problems and unremitting pressures, our fears and shameful weaknesses, and our surprising joys and strengths as we each have been experiencing them, the daughters, ourselves, and the men, as we begin to live the equality we fought for. Even though we know it's not really all that equal yet, even if we have some new thoughts about what equality really means—for women and men. We had better admit these feelings, or more and more women and men will lose heart and say they do not want equality after all.

I know that equality, the personhood we fought for, is truly necessary for women—and opens new life for men. But I hear now what I would not let myself hear before—the fears and feelings of some who have fought our movement. It is not just a conspiracy of reactionary forces, though such forces surely play up and manipulate those fears.

Do we deny certain painful feelings, certain yearnings, certain simple needs—for fear we will drown in them, be trapped again in the weakness, the helplessness, the terrible dependence that was women's lot before? Does our need to deny that fear in ourselves make us unable to recognize its reality in other women, whom we turn into our enemies? If we suddenly suggest that old experiences supposedly irrelevant or distracting to new women are, in fact, more important than we wanted to admit—experiences like motherhood, which the old feminine mystique and the new enemies of equality claim are the only importance for women—do we thereby deny the importance, the necessity and the real liberation for women in the gains won in these twenty years of the women's movement: the opportunities our daughters now enjoy to move in the world, and earn, and have some power and voice in its big decisions? Would we, or the daughters, or even the men want to go back?

That is the fear, of course. That is why we do not want to face new questions, new tests. But if we go on parroting or denouncing or defending the clichés of women's liberation in the same old terms until they harden into a new mystique, denying the realities of our personal experience and the new problems, *then* we are in real danger of going back. *Then* we invite a real backlash of disillusioned, bitter women—and outraged, beleaguered men, who could, in confusion, blame our necessary but incomplete movement toward equality for the emotional scars of generations of pathology bred by inequality. We could confuse (and forfeit) liberation, for women and men, with the pains of transition, or the extremes of reaction that our silence locks us into.

There is a danger today in feminist rhetoric, rigidified in reaction against the past, harping on the same old problems in the same old way, leaving unsaid what's really bothering women and men in and beyond the new urgencies of personal economic survival. For there is a real backlash against the equality and the personhood of women—in America, as in Islam and the Vatican. Dangerous reactionary forces are playing to those unadmitted fears and yearnings with the aim of wiping out the gains of equality, turning women back to the old dependence, silencing women's new voice and stifling women's new active energy that threatens their own power in ways we do not yet clearly understand. In the name of the family, they would destroy the new equality that gives the family strength to resist dehumanizing forces that are emerging in the seeming impotence of capitalist America, in the resurgence of fundamentalist religion, in neofascism and in autocratic communism, and in the chaos of the Third World. We must ask new questions or we could lose, in the economic and emotional turbulence, the measure of equality that is essential to strengthen human life—and the future of the family. We could mistake, subvert, and betray the truly life-strengthening possibilities opened by the women's movement.

There is no going back. The women's movement was necessary. But the liberation that began with the women's movement isn't finished. The equality we fought for isn't livable, isn't workable, isn't comfortable in the terms that structured our battle. The first stage, the women's movement, was fought within, and against, and defined by that old structure of unequal, polarized male and female sex roles. But to continue reacting against that structure is still to be defined and limited by its terms. What's needed now is to transcend those terms, transform the structure itself. Maybe the women's movement, as such, can't do that. The experts of psychology, sociology, economics, biology, even the new feminist experts, are still engaged in the old battles, of women versus men. The new questions that need to be asked—and with them, the new structures for the new struggle—can only come from pooling our experience: the agonies and ecstasies of our own transition as women, our daughters' new possibilities, and problems, and the confusion of the men. We have to break out of feminist rhetoric, go beyond the assumptions of the first stage of the women's movement and test life again— with personal truth—to turn this new corner, just as we had to break through the feminine mystique twenty years ago to begin our modern movement toward equality.

Saying no to the feminine mystique and organizing to confront sex discrimination was only the first stage. We have somehow to transcend the polarities of the first stage, and even the rage of our own "no," to get on to the second stage: the restructuring of our institutions on a basis of real equality for women and men, so we can live a new "yes" to life and love, and can *choose* to have children. The dynamics involved here are both economic and sexual. The energies whereby we live and love, and work and eat, which have been so subverted by power in the past, can truly be liberated in the service of life for all of us—or diverted in fruitless impotent reaction.

How do we surmount the reaction that threatens to destroy the gains we thought we had already won in the first stage of the women's movement? How do we surmount our own reaction, which shadows our feminism and our femininity (we blush even to use that word now)? How do we transcend the polarization between women and women and between women and men, to achieve the new human wholeness that is the promise of feminism, and get on with solving the concrete, practical, everyday problems of living, working and loving as equal persons? This is the personal and political business of the second stage.

2 The Half-Life of Reaction

 Before we can come to grips with the practical problems of living, working and loving in equality in the second stage, we have to understand and transcend the reaction against the family that characterized and distorted the first stage of the women's movement. Otherwise, the modern women's movement could fizzle out in the same stalemate and backlash that aborted the early struggle for women's rights after the winning of the vote in 1920.

Reviewing the history of the original feminist movement and why it failed to alter the lives of most American women, historian William O'Neill, in his book *Everyone Was Brave*, concluded that the trouble was rooted in the movement's unwillingness to tackle the problems of the family. Most of the early American feminists were either young single women opposed to marriage and family or else married professional women who didn't have children or preferred to concentrate on loftier issues, such as the vote. They assumed that winning suffrage would automatically usher in equality and purify society. Yet, wrote O'Neill, since the masses of American women were married or wanted to be, the only way that equality between the sexes could have been achieved was through a "revolution in domestic life" that would reconcile the demands of family and career—a revolution that the first feminists never attempted. And that is why the original feminist movement collapsed after the vote was won in 1920.

Over two million strong in the heyday of their equivalent of NOW, the early feminists' dreams and passions were buried in memory by the backlash of the feminine mystique, as most American women continued to marry, have children, and work briefly before marriage, and in national or domestic emergencies—while a few "exceptional" women had "careers," forgoing marriage or motherhood. Like ghosts of their own truncated dream, the early suffragette leaders grew old and died, a final fiery bitter few living on in Washington in the old house, now a National Historic Landmark, that was headquarters of the National Woman's Party, making a nuisance of themselves with Congressmen about the Equal Rights Amendment, which they had introduced in 1922. Women's rights became an embarrassing dirty joke in Washington, and in the national memory, until we broke through the feminine mystique and began the modern women's movement, nearly fifty years later, starting over from scratch, it seemed.

A few years ago it looked as if the modern women's movement might suffer the same fate as its historical predecessor. The popular (and unpopular) image of the modern feminist was that of a career "superwoman" hellbent on beating men at their own game, or of a young "Ms. Libber" agitating against marriage, motherhood, the family, sexual intimacy with men, and any and all of the traits with which women in the past pleased or attracted men.

That bra-burning image, and other phenomena of "sexual politics" in general, distorted the main thrust of the women's movement for equality and gave its enemies a powerful weapon. For it played into the fears and violated the feelings and needs of a great many women, and men, who still look to the family for security, love, roots in life. And it may have led other women, especially younger women, who ardently embrace the new opportunities and the feminist goal of self-realization, to deny those other needs.

In earlier years I used to blame that bra-burning image on the media or on fringe extremists who did not speak for the women's movement. They were an embarrassment we had to endure, to keep up that solid front of sisterhood. The media did exaggerate the extremist note, but it is necessary now to examine the personal truth of the women who were preaching the most extreme rhetoric of women's lib, and those for whom that note resonated, seductive or threatening. The very extremity of the reaction, and the rage and fear it reflects and elicits, have to be understood now, so that we can transcend reaction and move on to the real work of the second stage, as the first feminists did not.

As long as women remain locked in reaction, they will continue to swing between extreme versions of one half-life or another—the feminine mystique or its feminist reversal—never transcending the terrible split that has tormented women for so long, never embracing the fullness of life that is open to women now, in love and work, as it never was to women before. Or rather, as long as women remain locked in reaction to what was, they will be obsessed with false fears and unreal options instead of confronting the new problems that have to be solved in Stage Two.

It seems to me you can trust feminists—or any other "ists" for that matter—only when they speak from personal truth in all its complexity. Such truth is never black or white. The image of "women's lib" as being opposed to the family was encouraged by women locked in violent reaction against their own identity—in those days when a woman was defined not as a person in herself, but as someone else's wife or mother, defined by her service role in the family as less than a person, "just a housewife," even when she worked outside the home. That feminine mystique had to be broken through so that we might be able to demand and be taken seriously in our demand for equal rights and opportunities in the world.

The anger we felt, then, was real enough. But the rhetoric we used to assert our personhood denied—or somehow omitted, skipped over after so many years of overemphasis—other elements of our personal truth.

For instance, the founding mothers of NOW in 1966 averaged more than two children apiece. Kay Clarenbach took care of her three kids in a Quonset hut after World War Two while her husband went to Columbia University on the GI Bill. After her kids went to school, she went back and got her own degree in Wisconsin, where they now lived, and then headed its Continuing Education program. Muriel Fox, high-powered public relations executive, brought her two children along to NOW's founding conference in Washington in 1966, and her surgeon husband put them to bed in the hotel while she stayed up all night getting out our first press release. All the years I was working on *The Feminine Mystique*, I would blithely stop writing when my little daughter came home from school, or my boys were in a Little League or basketball game, or to make a martini when my husband got home, fix dinner, argue, go to the movies, make love, join an expedition to the supermarket or a country auction on Saturday, organize a clambake on the beach at Fire Island, take the kids over the battlefield at Gettysburg, or camping on Cape Hatteras—the stuff of family life. We took all that for granted. But that was supposed to be all of a woman's life, in those days of the feminine mystique. That image had to be corrected. The thrust then, when we started the women's movement, had to be "action to break through the barriers that kept women from participating in the mainstream of society." That meant breaking through the housewife image. Even the demand for equal pay was subverted by that image of women in terms of family—she didn't need the money because she had a husband to take care of her.

I resorted to a rather extreme metaphor at that time, likening the "trap" of the suburban housewife to a "comfortable concentration camp." But even then I realized that it was our fear of risking ourselves in the world that made us cling to the trap. The Statement of Purpose of NOW, as I drafted it, demanded "full equality for women, in truly equal partnership with men." It demanded equality, not only in office, classroom, government and church, but in marriage and the family. It forswore "enmity to men"; men were members of NOW from the very beginning.

Around 1969, when that anti-man, anti-family, bra-burning image of "women's lib" was built up in *Newsweek* and *Time* cover stories exaggerating the antics of the most extremist voices in the movement, I remember the helpless feeling shared by the founding mothers of NOW: "But that's not what we meant, not at all." For us, with our roots in the middle American mainstream and our own fifties' families, equality and the personhood of women never meant destruction of the family, repudiation of marriage and motherhood, or implacable sexual war against men. That "bra-burning" note shocked and outraged us, and we knew it was wrong— personally and politically—though we never said so, then, as loudly as we should have. We were intimidated by the conformities of the women's movement and the reality of "sisterhood is powerful," as we never would have been by "the enemy."

But in the late sixties and the seventies, young radical women, scarred early by the feminine mystique, and without firm roots in family or career, gave vent to their rage in a rhetoric of sexual politics based on a serious ideological mistake. And they, and later daughters who based personal and political strategies on their distortion, locked themselves and the movement into a reaction that perpetuates, in reverse, the very half-life they were reacting against.

Consider, for instance, the personal reality of some of those valiant women who produced fantasies of mounting Amazonian armies against men, wrote SCUM manifestos (Society for Cutting Up Men), or would shock and titillate suburban matrons at meetings of the League of Women Voters and the National Conference of Christians and Jews by proclaiming, "All married women are prostitutes," and

"Only honest prostitutes are heroines." Consider the ones who said women would never be free unless the family was abolished and women forswore motherhood and sexual intercourse with men. "Let babies be bred in test tubes!" they cried. Or they created elaborate rationales reducing every relation of man to woman, and the military and economic depredations of the nation, to rape. The rhetoric ranged from the ridiculous (the members of the consciousness-raising group deciding that if they go home and sleep with their husbands, from now on they must be "on top"; the belief that masturbation or sex with a woman was superior to any "submission" to man's penis) to the sublime (the high preaching of the new feminist theologians against every manifestation of "God, the father," or Mary Daly's image of man as vampire who feeds "on the bodies and minds of women . . . like Dracula, the he-male has lived on woman's blood"). "The personal is political" was the motto: not shaving your legs or underarms, refusing to go to the beauty parlor or wear makeup, not letting him pay the restaurant bill or hold the door open, not making his breakfast or dinner, or washing his socks.

It is easy today for critics to single out the most ludicrous fulminations of radical feminists, and thus to dismiss the entirety of the women's movement and its message as antifamily. Jean Bethke Elshtain, a Massachusetts political scientist, can easily document the case against the women's movement for "mean-spirited denunciations of all relations between men and women and . . . contempt for the female body, for pregnancy, childbirth, child-rearing." She need only cite the following: Man is portrayed as "the oppressor" in Kate Millett's *Sexual Politics;* he is driven by "metaphysical cannibalism" (Ti-Grace Atkinson); he is a "natural predator" (Susan Brownmiller). Pregnancy is "the temporary deformation of the body for the sake of the species," and the fetus is a "parasite," an "uninvited guest" (Shulamith Firestone). Ms. Elshtain could find plenty of feminists who reduced heterosexual sex to "using people, conning people, messing up people, conquering people, exploiting people" (as she put it in "Feminists Against the Family," *The Nation*, November 17, 1979). She found others who treated love itself as a "pathological condition," a "mass neurosis" which must be destroyed. Indeed, there was a time when women like Shulamith Firestone (or before them, Simone de Beauvoir) portrayed motherhood as "a condition of terminal psychological and social decay, total self-abnegation and physical deterioration."

Such rhetorical extremes gave vent to personal rage smoldering under the excessive, self-denying "smotherlove" of countless women who took Dr. Spock literally in that era: the suburban wife whose husband roamed freely in the world and was promoted and rewarded and ate those expense-account lunches while she ate peanut-butter sandwiches with her kids; her younger sister who bought that feminine mystique so completely that she gave up her education at nineteen to get a "nothing" job and put him through medical school (blinding herself to the probability that when he finished his residency, he would leave her for some bright, ambitious intern). "All I wanted was to get married and have four children. I love the kids and Bob and my home. There's no problem you can even put a name to. But I'm desperate. I'm a server of food and putter-on of pants and a bedmaker, somebody who can be called on when you want something. But who am I?" (from *The Feminine Mystique*).

The rhetoric of sexual politics resonated and dignified the mundane, daily buried rage of countless "happy" suburban housewives and sweetly efficient secretaries, nurses and stewardesses. But its origin was the extreme reaction of the "chicks" and "earth mothers" of the radical student movement of the sixties against their own situation in the so-called revolutionary counterculture where, in fact, the feminine mystique reached its apogee.

The position of women in that hippie counterculture was, as a young radical black male leader preached succinctly, "prone." Tom Hayden and others might like to forget it now, but those early male leaders of the radical student movement and counterculture of the sixties, white and black, were more blatantly male chauvinist pigs than their conservative fathers. From the communes of Haight-Ashbury and Big Sur and Vermont to the seized and trashed academic fortresses of Harvard and Columbia, women were supposed to wash the pots and pans and cook the spaghetti and be good girls at the mimeograph machine—the "woman trip"—while the men made the revolutionary decisions, smoking their pot around the commune fire and taunting "the pigs" under the television lights.

And when these radical "chicks" were finally infected by our first feminist stirrings, and saw through the feminine mystique in the radical movement itself, and introduced their resolutions for "women's liberation" at Berkeley or Cornell, the radical young men just laughed. So the women walked out of the larger radical "movement" and formed their separate "women's lib" groups—like black separatism, right? No men allowed; man was the *enemy*.

Their personal truth as women in the counterculture or radical student movement of the sixties was doubly humiliating when viewed through the lens of revolutionary equality: the ideology of class warfare they had learned to apply to oppressed races and masses, black, brown and pink.

They made a simple, though serious, ideological error when they applied the same political rhetoric to their own situation as women versus men: too literal an analogy with class warfare, racial oppression. It was heady, and made headlines, to vent the venom earlier directed against "whitey" or "boss finks" against *men*—your own man and the whole damn sex—and use all that sophisticated Marxist jargon to make a new revolutionary case for destruction of "the patriarchal nuclear family" and the "tyranny" of sexual biology as the source of all oppression. The media seized on the rhetoric. A "revolutionary in every bedroom" was both sexier and less threatening to vested economic and political interests (it was not political at all, merely personal) than the mainstream actions of the women's movement: breaking through sex discrimination in employment, professions, education, the church; gaining women some measure of the economic independence and self-respect they so desperately needed, control over their own bodies and reproductive process and simple, nonhumiliating police protection against rape.

Even at that time, many of us saw the extremist rhetoric of sexual politics as a pseudo-radical cop-out from the real and difficult political and economic battle for equality for women in society—which would provide a new basis for equality in the family, and for marriage, motherhood and sexual love without martyrdom, masochism and denigration of women. We never thought this revolution could be won in the bedroom. The sexual politics was an acting-out of rage that didn't really change anything. When women's position in society changed, sex would take care of itself. Woman's situation with respect to man or the family was *not* the same as that of the worker and boss, the black race and the white. From the totality of our own experience as women—and our knowledge of psychology, anthropology, biology—many feminists knew all along that the extremist rhetoric of sexual politics defied and denied the profound, complex human reality of the sexual, social, psychological, economic, yes, biological relationship between woman and man. It denied the reality of woman's own sexuality, her childbearing, her roots and life connection in the family.

But our voice was drowned out, for a time, in the media, and even in the movement itself, by the more strident, titillating, angry and less politically risky message of sexual politics. And those books *sold*. For they expressed that rage long buried in women out there. It was easier to fulminate against the male chauvinist pig in your own bedroom and liberate yourself from the missionary position than to take the test for law school, get the union to fight for parenting leave or lobby the state legislature to ratify the Equal Rights Amendment.

Remembering, now, it seems to me the reaction was the most extreme—and deceptive—for those of us who had been, and maybe still were, the most dependent on men. I remember one particularly beautiful and seductive young woman, in those early days, who had quit school at eighteen to marry a successful executive, wearing her fluffy silver fox coat on our first picket lines, and *coming on*, reflexively, to the reporters and politicians she then viciously berated for treating her like a "sex object." When she wrote her treatises, exhorting women to take up arms and kill those male oppressors, she herself was living on alimony.

Another, preaching the doctrine that for women to wear eye makeup, nail polish, a bra or a dress was to sell out to the enemy, hid behind *Vogue* while she had her own hair streaked at Kenneth's. One who had pronounced categorically that "all married women are prostitutes," outdoing the other sisters in her consciousness-raising group in invectives against the male chauvinist pigs, was so devastated when her own husband, a successful lawyer, left her that she dropped her feminist activities, joined a singles club and a computer-dating service, and came back to the group three months later with a new "fiancé." My own brave words in the early days of the women's movement hid a certain abject terror of making it on my own, in the last days of my self-destructive marriage.

The concrete, personal immediacy of the women's movement, the fact that its doctrines were rooted in and immediately applied to the stuff of daily life, was its unique political power—and its danger. For the reactive rhetoric of sexual politics, distorting or denying certain painful or taken-for-granted realities of women's life, hardened into a ritual feminist mystique that triggered an even more distorted and virulent antifeminist reaction. When extremists—both feminists and antifeminists—perpetuate the myth that equality means death to the family, other women, especially younger women, have a hard time figuring out what their real options are, and their own real feelings.

So Phyllis Schlafly and Marabel Morgan make a lot of money pursuing their own careers, going around the country lecturing to women that they don't need equal rights, just husbands to support them (which they'll allegedly stop doing when the Equal Rights Amendment is passed). But Phyllis Schlafly is herself taking advantage of the equal opportunity she says other women don't need, getting her law degree at a prestigious university which never would havē admitted a middle-aged woman like herself before the women's movement. And Marabel Morgan admits to *Time* magazine that she herself no longer has time to deck her naked body in Saran Wrap, ostrich feathers, black-lace garter belt and baby-white boots, in the manner she prescribes to all those insecure women who pay her for lessons on how to meet their tired husbands at the door, cooing, "I crave your body," to keep them from straying and to keep themselves supported in the style they'd like to stay accustomed to. Marabel Morgan's ability now to contribute her own money to that support may be assumed to be as enticing to her own husband as the Saran Wrap, which in real life does not seem to keep those husbands from straying. Lecturing in Texas recently, several months after Marabel Morgan ran one of her "Total Woman" courses, I heard from some psychologists of the devastation to women, who had flogged themselves on to new depths of self-degradation and denial with those ostrich feathers and Saran Wrap maneuvers, when their husbands, in fact, did run off (maybe faster?) with the younger "chicks" from the office.

Reaction is dangerous in its denial of reality. The underlying reality is no different for the bitterest feminists than for the most stridently fearful defenders of the family. None of us can depend throughout our new long lives on that old nuclear family to meet our needs for nurture, love and support, but all of us still have those needs. The answer is not to deny them, but to recognize that equality makes it possible, and necessary, for *new* kinds of family. The answer is to recognize, strengthen or create new family forms that can sustain us now—and that will change, as our own needs change, over time.

But it is not easy to free ourselves from the reaction against past dangers which makes some women so strongly fearful now of marriage or motherhood—and some women fearful of equality, and their own selves, now denying real weakness, now real strength.

As, for instance, Ellen Willis, a fine young feminist writer, in "The Family: Love It or Leave It" (the *Village Voice*, September 17, 1979) fears the very notion of family as "reactionary family chauvinism." She writes:

> When I talk about my family, I mean the one I grew up in. I have been married, lived with men, and participated in various communal arrangements, but for nearly all of my thirties—I have lived alone. . . . Compromises that might once have seemed reasonable or simply to be expected, felt stifling. A rebellious community of peers supported me in wanting something other than conventional family life; feminist consciousness clarified and deepened my ambivalence toward men, my skepticism about marriage. . . . Over the years family boosters have subjected me to my share of hints that I'm pathetic, missing out on real life, or that the way I live is selfish and shallow.

In response to such criticism, Willis admits to "flaunting my independence and my freedom from the burdens of parenthood while implying that I see through their facade of happiness to the quiet desperation beneath."

She had married early, out of weakness. "While I had rebelled against the idea that a woman needs a man to run her life . . . what I was really fighting more often than not was my own worst impulses to give in, give up and be dependent."

Eventually, Willis goes on, "some balance had shifted. I

was on my own in a way I had not been before. . . . I was strong enough to love a man and preserve my identity." But she castigates herself for even "thinking about marriage in a very different spirit" as "a sure sign that backlash was getting to me." Her "vulnerability" as a single woman whose income has not kept up with inflation, her hunger for "the sustenance I have always gotten (and mostly taken for granted) from the family I grew up in; the intense bonds of affection and loyalty; the acceptance born of long intimacy; the power of 'we' "—even the reluctant admission that "I want a mate, or so I believe, and possibly a child"—makes her terribly "uneasy" that she might succumb to "the aggressive resurgence of family chauvinism."

For this young radical feminist, the family is "rooted in the assumption of male authority over dependent women and children, the sexual double standard and the traditional exchange of the husband's financial support for the wife's domestic and sexual services. . . . The family is still the main source of women's oppression and the main focus of feminist politics."

Reaction is the blind spot both feminists and antifeminists share about the family, locked in the past. Is the family, in fact, so dependent on women's inequality and denial of self that Phyllis Schlafly and Marabel Morgan, in their accurate recognition of women's deep-rooted feeling about marriage and the family, have to deny the reality of the strong self-hood and freewheeling, rewarding careers they both personally enjoy, while Ellen Willis and other radical feminists, in their accurate perception of the importance of women's autonomy and self-realization, have to deny the reality of their own and other women's deep personal needs for intimacy and family support?

Perhaps these fears themselves are the main problem now —making us cower behind these masks of blind reaction, resisting the tests of evolving life, at our own needless loss, and peril. For there is evidence already that the new sense of

equality and strength of self women are achieving may be
better, for women's own health and the strength of the family, than the old abject dependence.

There are also new conflicts, stresses and problems beyond reaction. Whatever their ideological fix, as more and
more women do, in fact, face these tests of life—seizing, or
forced by economic necessity to seize, new opportunities in
job or profession, dealing with the realities of the families
they already have, or making those new choices, to have a
baby, or not—the picture that emerges is something quite
different from either feminine or feminist mystique, integrat-
ing, in new forms, elements recognizable from both. The reality is richer, the problems and the pleasures more complex,
interesting, reassuring, surprising, the pains not as unendurable as those fears bred by blind reaction which keep some
feminists and antifeminists from risking new life tests.

"The worst problem for women today is trying to juggle
it all," said a thirty-eight-year-old lawyer in Chicago, mother
of two. "Wanting to get ahead in your career, wanting to
have a perfect marriage and really be with your husband,
wanting to do all the right things about your kids, and not
giving up any of it. The guilt, because you can't really do all
these and do each one perfectly."

Why does she feel she has to be superwoman? Of course,
there are the actual, practical problems of juggling home,
children, job. But why do so many women make those problems more difficult than they have to be? What is keeping us
from devising and demanding new practical solutions? Could
there be a kind of *female* machismo?

Why did so many of our mothers have that grim set of the
mouth, that all-patient, all-suffering, all-disapproving perfect
control that made us feel inadequate before we even began
making dinner, cleaning the kitchen, dressing the kids—and
made us such suckers for those guilt-inducing TV commer-
cials? That control, that perfection demanded of home and
children, that insistence that she be always *right*, was her

version of machismo—her supervirtuous equivalent of male
strength and power, which she used to counter or mask her
vulnerability, her economic dependence, her denigration by
society and denigration of herself. Inauthenticity was bred
into women by weakness. Lacking male power in society,
which was the only power recognized then, she got her
power in the family by manipulating and denying the feelings of men and children, and her own real feelings, behind
that mask of superficial, sweet, steely rightness. (The unmasking of the inauthentic paragon of female virtue has preoccupied generations of novelists and dramatists, from *Craig's
Wife* and *The Little Foxes* to the Mary Tyler Moore role in
Ordinary People.)

That *perfect* marriage, *perfect* house, *perfect* control of children—so hard for daughters today to emulate—also hid some
bitter negative feelings about that housewife-mother state of
selfless service. Like all dependent people, women couldn't
express, even to themselves, the rage such self-denying virtue
almost had to breed, and to mask. They took it out on themselves and covertly on husbands and children. The more
powerless and envious her state, the more intense her buried
rage, the more guilt over that rage, the more rigid the perfection and control over family and home required to mask
those shameful feelings.

The explosion of rage that marked the women's movement focused a conscious and extreme reaction against almost every aspect of that housewife-mother service role,
equating it all—female sexual biology, motherhood, cooking,
clothes—with the powerlessness, the denial and denigration
of self, the lack of freedom, adventure and control over their
own destiny, and the absence of recognized value, respect,
reward that daughters sensed in their mother's experience, or
their own. Some women remain imprisoned by that reaction,
merely shifting their focus from home and family to job or
career, exchanging one half-life for another.

But now that daughters are not boxed in as their mothers
were—now that they have that independence and identity

their mothers yearned for, through those skills that society values and rewards—they can, and must, transcend the imprisoning bonds of reaction. Do they still need that complete power and perfect control over family and home, as their mothers did? How much of it is really necessary for the well-being of children, family and happy home—how much for her own sense of power and control? Does she really still need or want female machismo in family and home or can she afford now to give it up?

How much of that superwoman demand of herself in the office comes from denying real aspects of herself and satisfactions of life: the identity and power that women did find in family and home, and that women still need for their own sense of authenticity? Do women locked in excessive reaction against female powerlessness—*or* female machismo—deny themselves certain real strengths as women, and become doubly passive and acquiescent to the excessive rigidities of masculine careerism, exchanging that despised female powerlessness for today's ever more desperate male powerlessness, under that uniform of success?

This is not to deny the realities of job and professional competition in a shaky economy, and the remaining barriers of insidious sex discrimination in every field, and the fact that standards on the job were set in terms of men who had wives to take care of all the details of life. But it's somehow necessary to *transcend reaction*— instead of continuing to play out that superwoman game, in home and/or office—in order to cope with these realities, personally and politically. Or else could we exhaust the energy necessary to restructure home and work, to make equality livable, for women and men, in the sheer fatigue, bitterness and lonely disillusionment of women discovering they can't make it as superwomen, and retreating in dismay from equality itself?

In Florida, the first week in April 1980, the governor in his opening message to the state legislature included a ritual call for ratification of the Equal Rights Amendment, but most of the newspapers didn't even report it. Even feminist leaders seemed to have lost heart. They told me privately that there was no hope at all for ERA in their state. The governor's support was phony, and everyone knew it.

When the young woman picked me up at the little Gainesville airport to keynote the "Accent on Women" week she'd organized at the university, I felt hopeful nevertheless. Early feminists may have become burned out, women in their thirties and forties were tired and preoccupied, trying to balance new job responsibilities with home and kids, but here was a new generation eagerly seizing the opportunities we'd won for them, with new energy to finish the job.

She was slim, dark, assured, a sorority girl, and very ambitious. She talked like a professional lecture agent, telling me how this program was arranged, discussing other speakers she planned to invite down there in the fall—Cronkite, Kissinger. In fact, she confessed, she'd already been offered a job when she graduated, by the top lecture agent in the East. But her boyfriend was at law school in Miami. The job was in Boston. It was a dream come true, to get offered a job like that.

I had to interrupt her because we were almost at the auditorium, and I needed some briefing on the campus situation regarding ERA. Of course, it was brilliant strategy to have the "Accent on Women" week just as the legislature was opening. What actions could they take? She looked at me in utter amazement. "I'm not for ERA," she said. "I don't want to think about discrimination against women, and I don't have to. That's all over. I've never been discriminated against. All I have to think about is myself."

I was appalled. "But this good job you've been offered," I said, "do you think that's just because of your own ability? I don't care how smart you are, a Florida sorority girl twenty years ago, even ten years ago, wouldn't even have thought of trying to get a job like that, much less have the offers you're mulling over now."

I scrapped my outline of Stage Two problems. These

young women in Florida (where Stage One is obviously not completed, with the state legislature balking at ratification of the ERA, and even feminists giving up the battle) were taking for granted opportunities that might not be open to them, after all, if the economic downturn worsened, and the reactionary forces now blasting ERA decided to get rid of existing laws against sex discrimination—reserving the jobs and the seats in the law schools for men. I told them about my own childhood during the Depression, when married women weren't allowed to keep jobs as teachers. I remembered, and told them about, my first visit to their university, over eight years ago, when women were not allowed in Blue Key, the university honor society, which was considered the cradle of Florida politics. All the bright, ambitious young men who intended to be lawyers, businessmen, and go into Florida politics got their first experience and contacts by speaking and politicking in Blue Key. For men only—as were politics and business itself.

Senator Edmund Muskie, then a Presidential candidate, was the speaker at the Blue Key banquet. And because there were the beginnings of women's movement unrest on the Gainesville campus, I had been invited down to speak at an alternate "separate but not equal" banquet for the girls. We all left that banquet and marched on the Blue Key affair, and Muskie and Presidential politics notwithstanding, demanded in the full glare of television lights that women be admitted, once and for all, to Blue Key. The sorority girls, then, were very scared, but they did it.

And now women are members, and even officers, of Blue Key, I understand. And sorority girls are confident that if they don't take those job offers in Boston and New York and Atlanta, they have all kinds of job possibilities and political futures, right there in Florida now. Only, they had better pay their dues, and get the ERA ratified in their own state, or those opportunities could just vanish.

And then I did go on and talk about the new kinds of problems they would face, if they were going to be able to use those opportunities that even Southern sorority girls were now excited about—and also get married and have children, as Southern sorority girls, at least, still seemed to want to do. (My young eager-beaver hotshot who wasn't for the ERA had told me, rather defiantly, that the past week she had taken part in the university beauty contest.)

Driving me to the airport the next morning, she said, a little hesitantly, "You know, you kind of shifted my brains last night. Talking about these new problems, and not having to be superwomen. I *will* get to work on ERA. I just didn't want to think about it. Ever since junior high, I've been ambitious. I didn't even want to go to the senior prom. I was the first woman president of this club and that, in high school, my church, here at college. But I really do love my friend in Miami. And I want a job like the one I've been offered in Boston, and every time I try to think of how I can do both, I feel sick to my stomach. So I didn't even want to hear about things like ERA anymore."

She asked me if I disapproved of her for entering the beauty contest. She wasn't quite sure why she had done it herself. It was just that after all these years of concentrating on "ambition," and proving she was "as good as the boys" in those games and clubs, she kind of enjoyed getting all dressed up and putting on eye makeup. She thought it might be a "fun" experience to enter the beauty contest—not necessarily to win it, but just to be a part of it. I told her that when the women's movement had originally demonstrated against the Miss America beauty contest, it was because it symbolized a kind of denigration of women generally, defining them not as people but as if they were *just* those measurements—36-24-36. But now that women could feel like people—and move in society as people, be seen and treated as people—they might *enjoy* being beautiful even more. I told her that on August 26, 1970, when we marched in that great nationwide strike for equality, and ERA passed Congress—the first nationwide action of women after the fifty years of silence since winning the vote—even hardnosed male reporters noted,

"All women looked beautiful on that march." She smiled at me, handing over my suitcase at the airport: "I'd feel beautiful, marching like that in Florida next year."

At a recent luncheon meeting in New York of an exclusive group of the top women who had made it in the city's businesses and professions, instead of listening to experts tell them how to invest their money or break into the "old boys' network" of real power, they decided to let down their hair and compare notes on their own "success."

Said the vice-president of a large corporation: "For seventeen years, all I've lived for is that company. Because we wanted so much to get up there, we had blinders on for everything else in life except finally making it on the board. My glamorous career! I hit some deep spiritual crisis, or something, but it wasn't satisfying to me any more. I have to find the center of my own being. I am not just my vice-presidency, my title in that company. It's like a long time ago, when I realized I'm not just my husband's wife, I'm a person. Now I realize I've traded off too much for my career, traded off my family—too much. At one point power and influence were the most important things to me, and I was going to tap into power and influence through that company. Now I'll keep my job and do it well, as I kept on being my husband's wife. But I want my own center, and to tap into some higher, different power. It's a real spiritual crisis, when you reach that plateau and you realize you've gone as far as you can go in that company, that industry, and all those trimmings and trappings you'd been working for all these years, that's all there is. I think women are asking these questions quicker than men, though men are asking them now, too, and the women after us will do it at an even younger age."

Celia, at thirty-six, is a lawyer in a large Wall Street law firm:

"I had no problem getting into law school or into my firm. I'm invited back to my law school as a role model, to tell the young women—who are nearly half the class now—how to integrate one's profession with family life. I see more and more young women deciding it can't be done—that the only way to resolve the conflict is to avoid it by not having children. But to me we have come to a sad state when the best and brightest women choose not to bring children into the world as the price for getting ahead in law.

"You go from law school to a large firm where, if you work your ass off, you become a partner between the seventh and ninth year, and if you don't, you're a failure. And to become a partner, you work nights, weekends—your work comes first. I'd run home to have dinner with the children, read to them, put them to bed, run back to the office and work till midnight. I alternated weekends and vacation weeks with my husband, so we never had time together. And for eleven years I never had a minute to myself.

"To be honest, unless women demand alternatives that don't exist now, I'm not sure we can have it all. Do you *have* to have it all at once? You are afraid to take the risk of what might happen if you don't take the opening. And how long can you wait to have children? But if women try to get all their emotional satisfaction from work—and pay an emotional price even men don't pay—women may be more disillusioned with their jobs than men are after a few years. The trouble is, we won't get these changes until men want them too."

Carol, at twenty-six, is going to be a surgeon:

"I don't want to be a superwoman, the way women in medicine were expected to be—twice as good as a man, and if they want kids, that's their problem. The other day a woman being interviewed for a cardiology fellowship at our hospital was asked to sign a paper promising not to get pregnant. She got right up and walked out. They realized suddenly it wasn't legal to do that any more, and they tried to get her back. The chief resident, a man who's not particularly a feminist, thought it was great that she walked out.

"A lot of the women in my class still go meekly along with the superwoman act, and they get upset when I raise questions. Every woman who finished her residency last year got pregnant, had her baby in December and is now back working full time.

"When one of the coolest superwomen quit because she couldn't take it, the rest got panicky. What is necessary is for medical training to change, to really work for *women and men* with little kids. Men in medicine, working one hundred and ten hours a week, have to be supermen, too. It's very hard to say at seven o'clock at night, 'My kids are waiting for me.' The man in the lab next to me leaves his lights on so they won't know he goes home to eat with his kids. Some of the men in my class are choosing fields like pathology, which have regular hours, so they can be with their kids. I think men have been missing out on something. Why am I so eager to jump in and do it their way?"

Reaction—which keeps looking for female identity according to old models, male and female, in pendulum either/or swings between home and job—doesn't change the rules (or pay the bills) or give a firm core of identity, in this unpredictably changing society.

A woman now twenty-nine tells me, "I got married at nineteen and had a baby because I wanted to stay home. But I began to resent my husband and his work. I separated from him and got a job selling cars and trucks, which everyone said a woman couldn't do. It was scary and exciting, being on my own, proving I could do what women hadn't done before. I won a cash prize, salesman of the month, selling the most vehicles. But after a while I'd had it. It was boring as hell being around cars eight hours a day, and I didn't feel the need to prove myself any longer. So I went back to my husband, to a different relationship that keeps changing. I got pregnant again. I don't need to prove any longer that I can do something women didn't do before."

Said a young woman MBA, gearing for the Young Presidents Club: "I know my only security as a woman now is what I achieve myself. Maybe I'm sacrificing personal relationships for that security. But whatever I make for myself is permanent security; relationships come and go. The saddest thing in the world to me are women in their forties, like my mother, who thought marriage was their security and suddenly she's a forty-eight-year-old divorced woman with no skills, nothing."

I talk to two daughters. The sister who reacted against the "powerlessness" of her mother by becoming a trial lawyer now envies her sister's power as a mother. And that sister is "liberating" herself to become an accountant.

The first sister now complains: "I loved being a trial lawyer. Two years ago I was willing to play squash, even football, to make it as a partner. When I got pregnant, my husband and I both got depressed; it would interfere with our careers. I had an abortion. Today, it's not so exciting, just being a cog in the corporate machine. I envy my sister with the three-year-old child and her boy going on six."

The second sister, who reacted against her lack of "power" and "value" as a housewife, is earning hard money now as an accountant, but is caught in the superwoman bind, not willing to give up that other power.

"I kept complaining about my husband's not doing enough in the house. Why did I always have to be the one to take the kids to the doctor? I Xeroxed contracts, splitting every chore in half—Monday night he's on, I'm off. Tuesday, vice versa. But when he was the one who bought the kids new socks and took them for their booster shots, I fell apart. It's hard to give up being the real parent, the one really responsible for the children and the house, the important one —to share it, and not just have him help."

Eleanor "chose" to stay home because she didn't really like her job—and didn't want to risk trying and failing at a better one. Her husband had no choice but to carry the whole economic burden. She compensated by elaborating her housewife-mother burden until it imprisoned them all in escalating reactions.

"Ten years ago, when we had a child, I felt required to be there all the time, a perfect mother, a perfect wife, an inspiration to my photographer husband, to entertain well, dress well, be on committees. I told my husband I might as well quit my job so I could stay home with the baby and be able to go on trips with him, too. I didn't know Phil counted on my salary, that it made a real difference.

"Phil had a dream we were on a bicycle built for two. He was in front and I was holding on behind and he was pedaling hard. We were both supposed to pedal. Every once in a while I'd stop pedaling and hug him, and it was nice but he'd say, 'You aren't pedaling.' The strain of pumping up the hill by himself was too much.

"So I spent several years putting all my energy in his career, taking over the details, the arranging, the billing, and I became a completely invisible woman and got very resentful. The invitations to professional meetings, the notices, never mentioned me.

"Then I started doing this cookbook, and I sold it. And I cleared out the spare room and made it my office instead of working at the dining-room table, which I always had to clear off for company meals. But for a long time it was like struggling to get out of a paper bag. I thought the problem was all my household chores. It was, a little bit, but not really. To get my own work done entails Phil's sharing these things I assumed as my entire responsibility, and teaching my son how to cook. So what if I come back at the end of the day and don't find the kitchen as neat as I left it?

"This mutual involvement in his ambitions is tricky. The fun was in the striving, and there was no risk of failure for me. It's only when he's made it that you realize all the credit, the accomplishment, is his, and you're supposed to be satisfied with a few pats on the head. You get resentful. But if you're married to someone who makes it, you don't want to start over at the bottom yourself. You're afraid to fail, so you do nothing. But I don't want to be a dilettante. We can't afford it now, with inflation. I'm looking for a real job. Not taking those risks is more frightening to me now than failing."

The breakthrough against sex discrimination has made a real difference for women, but it can't really be enjoyed and its real tradeoffs and implications for family and work assessed and solidified, in institutional terms, as long as women are still locked in the personal timidities, and the excesses, of either feminist or antifeminist reaction. So Irene, at forty, feels it's already too late for her.

"I was a secretary at the TV station. When the manager quit, I asked for the job and was told point-blank I couldn't have it because I was a woman and would get pregnant and they wouldn't be able to count on me. That was in 1963. At the time I didn't even realize it was discrimination. They said, 'You're terrific, Irene. Could you train this twenty-two-year-old guy we're hiring from the business school?' So I lost interest and quit to have a baby. When I read that a woman was made chairman of the board at NBC, I almost had a heart attack. That's the difference, and it's been only sixteen years.

"So, as a housewife, I started selling at a dress shop afternoons, started buying for them; then they wanted to put me in charge of a branch shop. They wanted me to work full time, but it makes me feel too stretched. I feel guilty not being home when the children get home from school, not being available to play golf with my husband on Saturday. If you're a woman, you're to be the comfort of the world—that's how I was raised. When the children come home at three, they're full of their day. But when you don't get home till five-thirty, and ask, 'What happened today?' they answer, 'Nothing.' You miss too much. It's all very well to tell yourself it's the quality of the time, not the quantity—but how much is *enough?*

"Still, it makes me mad—makes me feel like a child—

when I have to ask my husband for money. It bothers me that I could never be really independent on the money I make. My mother was always dependent on my father and so fearful of life. She is lost now without him. It frightens me, the thought of being dependent like my mother, though I have a very happy marriage. I get so upset, listening to battered wives on television, women with no options. It improves your sense of self-worth when you don't depend on your husband for everything good in life, when you can get it for yourself. I'm trying so hard to treat my daughter equally with my son. I don't want her to have the fears that paralyzed my mother and that I've always had to fight. I want her to have real options."

The psychological timidities and excesses of reaction that stem from women's self-hate had their roots in economic reality—and collide anew with economic reality in the U.S. today.

Tina, twenty-seven, a former radical feminist and "revolutionary artist" who now earns her living as a secretary, reacted against her mother's self-hate by joining the women's movement, and is now expressing her reaction *against* the women's movement.

"It was wonderful in the beginning, consciousness-raising, discovering you were not alone. But as I went on, it supported qualities of weakness in me. A woman growing beyond problems that paralyzed the rest of us was accused of acting like a man.

"My mother passed on her own self-hate to me. In the women's movement my self-hate went underground. It wasn't politically correct to want to feel feminine. I acted strong, tough, but I was denying a lot of softness in myself. The women's movement made me ashamed of my need to feel beautiful as a woman. It was not only that I rejected the woman's role, in its worst sense. I didn't think I could function as a woman in the real world. I fantasized myself as an artist, tough, an outlaw rejecting the whole American culture.

"I came into the women's movement because I wasn't treated right by the men in the radical movement, but I was treated in much the same way by the honchos in the women's movement. I've had enough of being told the right way to live as a feminist.

"It's a step forward for me to make my own living as a secretary, honestly confused about where I go from here, instead of calling myself an artist—which gave me a career I could talk about at a dinner party but left me in constant anxiety about paying the rent. Being married used to give women that easy out—you don't have to decide who you are, what you want to do with your life. Well, there isn't any alternate culture for me to live in as a feminist revolutionary. At least, I pay my own rent now. But when I ask myself, Where do I go from here? I look at that big sign on the office wall 'Equal Opportunity Employer' and I have to laugh. No matter how good a job I do as a secretary—which is the real work most women have to do to pay the rent—it's a dead end."

Aware of our own reaction against that housewife image, some leaders of the women's movement have been talking a lot lately about the real value of work women have traditionally done as nurses, secretaries—or housewives. There are some important new questions for economists here. But for women facing economic reality today there are dangerous illusions of personal choice.

Mary, my neighbor, is whistling in the dark: "If you stay home now, it's because you want to. I'm the first to admit I've ridden on the wave of the women's movement. But I think it's wrong when women who want to stay home while their children are little have no independence.

"I like the idea of the wife's having the equivalent of a salary. It's degrading to feel completely dependent. What would the work you do cost if he had to pay for it? It's real

work. Still, certain things just go along with life. I don't
think I should be paid for mothering. But we've both chosen
that I should stay home with the kids, work outside less than
full time, so if I got divorced, I'd expect compensation that
recognizes that choice. Maybe a percentage of the income for
every year should be put into a separate account for the wife.
It should be hers, not something she has to ask for."

But what money is left over, after paying for the necessities of life in these days of inflation, in any one- or even two-
income family? Economic reality cuts across both feminine
and feminist mystiques. The fear of ending up like women
they all know who looked to marriage for security and ended
up alone and desperate, has forced a lot of young women
today, married or not, to look for security in careers. It will
no longer be economically possible to live by the feminine
mystique—or, for that matter, the feminist mystique. For, on
new and more equal terms now, won't women as well as men
find it better, for economic as well as emotional survival, to
pool resources, live on two incomes, not just one—and share
the housework?

Can women earn enough to be really secure unless they
get ahead in the jobs and professions now controlled by men,
and do it the same way as the men, playing by their rules? If
so, won't they become as narrow as the men, whose whole
identity has too often been defined by their jobs? Are there
real options, alternate life styles that can pay the rent? Why
should the service jobs traditionally held by women, increasingly important to the economy, earn so little money? Why
can't all jobs and professions whose rules until now have
been set by and for men be more flexibly structured?

Sheer economic need, exposed and escalated with undeni-
able urgency by inflation, gives most women in the 1980s,
married or single, no choice but to work. And if the job market continues to shrink, who is going to assure that the jobs
now open to women will stay open in the 1980s? Who can be
sure that the barriers of sex discrimination won't be raised
again in the current political climate—particularly if young

women believe the problems have all been solved, or if, from their own crisis of confidence, they repudiate the necessary promise of equal opportunity for the illusion of domestic retreat?

If we don't get the Equal Rights Amendment, can women who want to stay home with their children or women who have been staying home have any semblance of real financial security? Until the ERA is part of the Constitution, women can't be sure of getting equal credit for their contribution as homemakers in a divorce settlement or of getting equitable social security payments—much less a "salary" for taking care of their husbands and children.

How many women today "choose" not to have children because they simply can't afford to stop working or because they can't count on adequate child-care facilities? But can women, any more than men, now find their total fulfillment, identity, security, in jobs and careers as they have been constituted by and for men?

Evelyn, the first woman newscaster in her state, has just been fired, at thirty-seven, after a career that other women fantasize about. To everyone's surprise, she is not devastated. She is, in fact, stripping wallpaper from an old house she has just bought, by and for herself.

"Women are in a different place now. It's been a bitch, these thirteen years, for me, the first woman they ever hired. Now I look at all these younger women coming in on a crest because the movement made the companies hire women. They don't have to be twice as good as the men anymore. I had to do it without any support.

"When you've had to fight your way in and up, every inch, nothing handed to you, it does something to you. We opened the doors for them, they can just walk in, they think women have no problems anymore. That's not true, but they can negotiate now, for terms they want or need, whereas I had to feel beholden, grateful they even hired me because I was a woman.

"The practicalities of liberation—that's what women have to deal with now. The movement got us to where we are, but now how do we live with it? We've broken through to get these jobs women never had before. How many of us, how long, on whose terms? What do you do about life, children, men, loneliness, companionship, the need to have a real home —things no one thought about when we were so obsessed with liberating ourselves? Women in the next decade have to find solutions for the practical problems, niches for themselves that feel more comfortable. We've gone through the metamorphosis. We're not worms anymore, but we're not butterflies yet either."

And so, new questions have to be asked about women's experience today that may have been hidden or unanticipated by feminist assumptions. These questions couldn't be asked before—and experts, including feminists, can't answer them yet—because women simply didn't have the same choices before.

We may face questions that seem to have no answers today, because the answers involve choices we don't want to make. Beware of that growing dismay that the choices we sought in the sixties and seventies are not so simple as they once seemed. Beware of that return of nostalgia for the simple days when women had no choices. In the fear, and even actual resentment, of the hard choices women face today, beware of the temptation to believe it is even possible, much less desirable, to go back.

We have to ask these new questions to free ourselves from unnecessary conflicts before we can solve other, real problems that we have been evading by sustaining illusions of choice where none exists. It is dangerous for women—or experts or politicians or leaders of women—to kid themselves that there is any real choice that can evade the complex problems women face today in making a new life pattern of family, love and work.

For instance, confusing the current national discussion of

the endangered family—and of women's rights to jobs, Social Security and child-care aids—is the illusion that it is possible for women to choose not to work outside the home. The idea that it is still possible for young women today to choose to be lifelong, full-time housewives—to look for their whole security, identity, satisfaction, status and support in marriage and motherhood—lurks underneath much that is written today about women, the family and children, even by sophisticated young women caught up in uncomfortable conflicts between the feminine and feminist mystiques, such as Linda Sexton in *Between Two Worlds: Young Women in Crisis* and Ellen Goodman in *Turning Points*.

If there is a dangerous denial of reality among some feminists locked in reaction—the ones who would deny their own need as women to love or to have children, as Ellen Willis does—there is an equally dangerous denial of reality among those who preach, or secretly believe, that women could solve a lot of complex new problems—from their own emotional fatigue, having to be superwomen on the job and at home, to male impotence, to national unemployment and inflation—by simply "choosing" not to work, to go back home again.

The unreality of much of the talk and thinking about women today in terms of "choice" worries me. If that sense of "either/or" choice was dangerous for women in my generation of the feminine mystique, it is even more dangerous in its denial of reality for women today. That is clearly evident in the conflicts young women now suffer as they reach their late thirties and cannot "choose" to have a child. I don't envy young women who are facing or denying that agonizing choice we won for them. Because it isn't really a free choice when their paycheck is needed to cover the family bills each month, when women must look to their own jobs and professions for the security and status their mothers once sought in marriage alone, and when these professions are not structured for people who give birth to children and take responsibility for their parenting. The superwomen who are trying to "have it all," combining full-time jobs or careers with having children, for whom they still are expected to assume full responsibility, do, in fact, endure such relentless pressure that their younger sisters may not even dare to think about having children.

Even such excellent new discussions of this conflict as Marilyn Fabe and Norma Wikler's *Up Against the Clock* assume it is a simple either/or choice. Feminists like Fabe and Wikler say women can solve it by simply choosing, without guilt, *not to have children*—if only they can get rid of their mothers' expectations (the remnants of the old feminine mystique) that they can't fulfill themselves as women, or will somehow miss out on life, if they don't have children. But isn't motherhood, the profound human impulse to have children, more than a mystique? Is it as lightly denied, by women or men, as much current discussion assumes? On the other hand, the new attacks on feminism, in the name of the family—from Selma Fraiberg (*Every Child's Birthright: In Defense of Mothering*), who says women except those as affluent as herself who can afford full-time nurses and governesses must give up their jobs for full-time mothering, to Jean Elshtain, who blames feminists for encouraging women to work, or even to ask for new child-care arrangements and flexible job hours because it will prevent other women from choosing full-time motherhood (which they assume is a much better "choice" for women and the family than most jobs)—deny the realities of economic survival today, the psychological and economic bottom line, which, in fact, prohibits such "choice" for most women now.

In the U.S., as in all industrialized nations today, an increasingly greater majority of women work outside the home, not just because they want to "fulfill themselves" and assert their independence, but because they must, to survive. They are single and responsible for their own support, divorced and usually responsibie for most or all of their children's support, or married and responsible for part of their families' support because one paycheck is not enough.

Yet the U.S. is one of the few advanced nations with no national policy of leaves for maternity, paternity or parenting at all, no national policy encouraging flexible working arrangements and part-time and shared jobs, and no national policy to provide child care for those who need it. Though most mothers as well as fathers now have to work outside the home, part or full time, the U.S. is spending less on child-care programs now than it did ten years ago. In the name of "preserving the family"—by which they mean that obsolete, traditional family in which mothers, by necessity or choice, stayed home and were supported as housewives by breadwinning fathers—Presidents, both Democratic and Republican, and even distinguished bodies of scholars such as the Carnegie Commission on Children, investigating the crisis of the American family, have ignored the need for such services, which are now available to parents at all income levels in countries much poorer than ours, with a sliding scale of fees according to a family's ability to pay.

So the question is still treated as the individual woman's "choice"—if she "chooses" to have a child, it is her responsibility to take care of it. Of course, her husband is supposed to help now, share the parenting. But even if he is willing, eager to help, the "choice," the responsibility, is still hers.

The new questions weight that "choice" so heavily that it is no wonder more and more young women say they don't want to have children: "Can we afford for me to stop working?" "Do I have to be a superwoman?" Etc.

But there is another compelling life urge that makes itself heard, drowning out these worrisome questions, as women hit thirty, thirty-five: "Will I miss out in life if I don't have children?"

And if she has the child, and her man is eager, or at least willing, to share as much responsibility as he can (or she will let him) she might ask, "Do I want him to be the important one with the children?"

And then, harassed, when the child comes down with a bug once again at school, and they call her at the office, and

she can't get hold of the baby-sitter, she wonders, rushing out
—she'll come back later and finish the report, if the baby-
sitter comes, after she takes Bobby's temperature, after she
talks to the doctor, or when Ralph gets home—but she wonders, "Is it worth it, working full time, always feeling so
stretched, for the money I earn?"

And, finally, she might ask, as a new question, "Why can't
I just stay home, be a mother, and enjoy it?"

And if, in desperation, she quits her job, and *does* stay
home, very soon she will face the reality of that no-win
choice: "I feel a pressure to go back to business. Even if
you're doing what you want to do, mainly taking care of your
own kids, more and more you're the odd woman out. Besides,
Jack is beginning to treat me some way I don't quite like. As
if he resents my staying home, but doesn't dare say so. The
pressure on him is terrible. He's not crazy about his job. His
new boss is really riding him, but we can't afford for him to
quit. If he gets fired, we won't be able to keep the house.
We're a month behind on the mortgage as it is. It was a hassle, working and the house and the two kids, but I'm getting
scared, just staying home."

These new problems, paradoxically, seem most urgent for
the very women, now in their twenties and thirties, who
stand to benefit most from the new opportunities we struggled for. We who fought for choices women never enjoyed
before can't help here. These new problems are not abstract
and theoretical—they are the concrete, practical, everyday
problems of really living, working and loving as equal persons with men. But our experience is their insurance policy
—with all the unsolved problems, and all the pressure and
the hassle, women cannot and should not want to go back.

For there is startling evidence that for women in general,
the changes brought about by the women's movement have
been liberating and life-opening beyond anyone's dreams.
The results of two important mental health studies (one conducted in 1954, one in 1959–62, and both repeated in the

1970s) show an unprecedented and totally unpredicted improvement in the psychological well-being of women, on a massive scale.

Twenty years ago women's mental health in every age group over twenty was so much worse than men's that the famous sociologist Jessie Bernard had concluded that marriage was good for men but was driving women crazy. Now, twenty years later, women's mental health seems to have become as good as men's or even slightly better.

In 1954, according to the classic Midtown Manhattan Longitudinal Study directed by Drs. Leo Srole and Anita Kassen Fischer of Columbia's College of Physicians and Surgeons, one out of every five women (or 21 percent) age forty to forty-nine was psychologically "impaired," compared with only 9 percent of men—and the ratio was worse for women in their fifties. In 1974 only 8 percent of women in their forties were "impaired," compared with 9 percent of men— and the ratio was better for women in their fifties. Women who once would have suffered increasing despair and the feeling their life was over as they hit forty were finding a new sense of self-worth and opportunities for growth. The deterioration that women used to suffer, decade by decade, after that early peak in their twenties (impairment rates were based on many measures of mental health, such as psychosomatic symptoms, insomnia, nausea, nervous breakdown, feelings of despair, "Sometimes I wonder if anything is worthwhile," etc.), and which was taken for granted as "normal" aging in women, no longer seemed to occur. Investigators found this a dramatic and startling change, and it was happening only among women.

The second important study, conducted by the National Center for Health Statistics on a cross-section of 6,672 adults from the entire U.S. population in 1959–62 and repeated in 1971–75, also showed that women over forty were less likely to report a nervous breakdown (or the feeling that one was about to happen) than women of that age in the early 1960s. Men showed no such improvement. Consequently, the director of that study, Dr. Harold Dupuy, concluded that the dramatic improvements for women over forty could be attributed to the women's movement, and the increased choices it gave to women. As Dr. Dupuy put it: "Before, too many women were in hopeless situations they couldn't get out of."

The National Center study showed, however, that younger women were experiencing more signs of psychological stress than women in their twenties and thirties had in the 1950s and early 1960s, and were slightly more likely to feel on the edge of "nervous breakdown" than young men. And, as they approached age thirty-five to thirty-nine, nearly one out of three women in the 1970s reported an actual or impending "nervous breakdown" compared with only 23 percent of women that age in the previous decade.

Dr. Dupuy felt these signs of stress in younger women were due to the same liberating new "choices" which were, in fact, improving lifelong psychological well-being for women. He told me: "Now younger women feel more pressure and expectations beyond just simply getting married. Even if they get married, they still have to make their own life, they still have to figure out what they are going to do in life. Men always knew they had to do that. When the women find themselves, I think they will be better off. I think they have a better set of options than women used to have. They may not be the psychological beneficiaries of the change yet —they have no role models, no patterns to follow, as men do. But having these options is like an insurance policy. Freedom is always better than servitude. It may not always feel like it at the time, but it is. Independence has to be a strong value for women's mental health. But they still have economic problems and marriage problems, and they have to work it all out for themselves."

The improvement in mental health seemed related to something more basic than the numbers of women working. In the Midtown Manhattan Study, nearly 60 percent of the women now in their forties and fifties were working, 41 percent of women in their sixties. But it went beyond the mere fact of jobs. For in the national study, both housewives and working women in their forties and fifties showed that new psychological well-being, and that new pressure in their thirties. The younger working women suffered slightly more signs of "stress"; the housewives slightly more "nervous breakdown" or its verge.

Drs. Srole and Fischer summed it up: "The daughters who are hitting forty now are much better off than their mothers, but the sons aren't better off than their fathers, and brothers and sisters are now equal [in psychological health]. Equality in general is good for mental health. Getting out of poverty, out of dependence, having some control over your own life, some measure of autonomy, independence and mastery of your life is good for people. That's the basic change for women."

The scientists who conducted these studies were especially impressed that women now working were so much better off psychologically after forty, compared to their housewife predecessors, notwithstanding the stress of dual responsibility, for both job and home. Clearly, for women of my generation, most of whom were married and focused on children and home in their twenties and thirties, it was revitalizing, a fountain of health, as we moved to new self-respect and put new energies and new talents to use in our forties and fifties, directing our energies outward, even against tough obstacles, instead of inward, against our own bodies, as despairing women used to do after the early peak of marriage and childbearing.

But what about the younger women, who show so much new stress or impending "nervous breakdown" in their late thirties? The superwomen trying to have it all, looking for security, status, power and fulfillment in full-time jobs and careers in the competitive ratrace, like men, and trying to hold on to that old security, status, power and fulfillment women once had to find solely in home and children. Or giving up, in midstream or in advance—because who can live as that kind of superwoman?—and "choosing" to go back again and stay home, despite the economic and nervous strain. Or "choosing" not to marry or have children, and therefore seeking all identity, status, power and fulfillment in job or career—embracing, more single-mindedly than most men now, that obsessive careerism that has made so many men die prematurely of stress-induced heart attacks and strokes.

There are dangerous signs. Dr. Alexander Leaf, chief of Medical Services at Massachusetts General Hospital, tells me more young women than ever before are being admitted with heart attacks, though hard data are not yet available nationally. And now the cancer experts, alarmed at the great increase in lung cancer among women, discover that as more young men stop smoking, more young women are starting. Stress? Or "You've come a long way, Baby"? What price women's equality, if its beneficiaries, by trying to beat men at their own old power games and aping their strenuous climb onto and up the corporate ladder, fall into the traps men are beginning to escape, forgoing life satisfactions basic for men and women, foreshortening their own lives, in impossible combination of the patterns that trapped their mothers and their fathers—or, faint-hearted, in fear of failure, retreating to a false security in the home that would be more of a trap for them, in terms of today's economic realities and real possibilities for women, than it ever was for their mothers?

Some of the new questions that have arisen in the wake of the first stage of the women's movement come from defensive reaction against past pain in women's lives; some seem practically unanswerable in terms of social arrangements as they are right now—and women's terrible need to please, to be perfect. Such need makes a woman too slavish a follower of *both* old role models.

The real question, the basic question, has still to be asked: Must—can—women now meet a standard of perfection in the workplace set in the past by and for men who had wives to take care of all the details of living and—*at the same time*—meet a standard of performance at home and as mothers that was set in the past by women whose whole sense of worth, power and mastery had to come from being perfect, all-controlling housewives and mothers?

From the experience of women in their thirties and forties to whom I have been talking, who have been juggling, trying to put it all together, in the last ten years, or making first one choice, then another—and from the experience of women now in their twenties, facing hard choices, refusing to choose, or on the verge of retreating to impossible, no-win choices again—I get a sense that these new questions have to be pressed further, and new alternatives demanded from society, to give women real choices, easier to work, love, live with. There may be various paths and choices possible for women today, with different tradeoffs and payoffs, in different patterns at different times, rather than that single pattern of lifelong full-time wife and mother, or lifelong male-career pattern, or even a simple combination of those two confining and possibly obsolete patterns.

Women's new experience has to lead to further questions to create new standards at home and at work that permit a more human and complete life not only for themselves but also for men. It may be that women's new experience, if we listen to it honestly, with all its dilemmas—instead of retreating in reaction or panic to women's old half-life, or its reversal, aping men's—will converge on new economic and emotional crises, and new technological possibilities in society, and will answer men's new questions in surprising ways.

There is a reconciling of seeming opposites that has to take place now, a dialectical progression from thesis-antithesis (feminine mystique-feminism) to synthesis: a new turn in the cycle that brings us back to a familiar place, from a different vantage. In the second stage, the path that Ibsen's Nora walked to find herself in the world after she slammed that door takes her full circle back—but it's no longer to a Doll's House.

3 The Family as New Feminist Frontier

 The new frontier where the issues of the second stage will be joined is, I believe, the family: that same trampled, bloody ground which the enemies of feminism are now supposedly defending against deathly siege. There are real and powerful emotional and economic stakes in that battle to which feminists have been strangely blind, to our personal and political peril.

On the economic bottom line, after nearly twenty years of the women's movement, it becomes clear that most women are still saddled with the work they used to do in the family (serving the physical needs of children, men, home) in addition to their hard new "male" jobs, at a price of fatigue and stress only superwomen can endure. Or they are facing economic misery in divorce and the loss of whatever power they had through that "female" family role—devalued and sometimes even replaced by other women who got into the men's world and sometimes took away their husbands.

On the emotional bottom line, younger women are shortchanging their own personhood, perpetuating old dilemmas or engaging in the wrong power battles because of their blind spot about the family. Even if women do not lose heart for the battle, as they surely will, there is no way out of the deadlock, the impasse, if we keep on fighting, even thinking, in terms of women alone, or women against men.

Was it all an illusion, women's movement toward equality —since no matter what we have done or are doing, it's still a men's world, and they call the shots? Not quite, not any longer. But the bridge we have to cross to live that equality we fought for is *the family*.

It is hardly new for women to be concerned with the family, I realize. But weren't feminists supposed to be liberating themselves *from* the family? Wasn't the women's movement supposed to be trying to destroy the family with the Equal Rights Amendment? And isn't the family, after all, supposed to be the last bastion of conservatism? Would the women's movement be surrendering, then, to the forces of reaction by reembracing the family, or would it truly be entering a new stage?

I believe that feminism must, in fact, confront the family, albeit in new terms, if the movement is to fulfill its own revolutionary function in modern society. Otherwise it will abort or be put on history's shelf—its real promise and significance obscured, distorted, by its denial of life's realities for too many millions of women. Locked into reaction against women's role in the family of the past, we could blindly emulate an obsolete narrow male role in corporate bureaucracy which seems to have more power, not understanding that the power and the promise of the future lie in transcending that absolute separation of the sex roles, in work *and* family.

The producer of the news show was a competent, seasoned professional in her late thirties, and rather obviously in the late stages of pregnancy. After the broadcast, she walked me to the elevator. "I never intended to get married and have kids," she said. "I wasn't interested in marriage and children at all. That was my mother's whole life. Ever since I can remember, she's been telling me, 'Don't do what I did. Have a career, *do* something with your life. Don't depend on anyone else.' I've been steadily moving up at the station, and I also have my own business on the side, marketing window shades. But a few years ago . . . well, I knew I'd always be able to take care of myself, but I was missing something. I was scared of getting married, though John and I had been living together for several years, and I liked it. But I was scared of giving up my independence. As if I might die or something.

"Then I began to be obsessed about having children. Every woman my age is agonizing about that, whether they admit it or not. After all those years of proving I could do these jobs as well as any man, I began to feel something very strong about being a woman. I realized that I did want to have a child. I won't be able to keep on in this job and run my other business, too, but if I didn't have a child for that reason, I'd feel like they had won."

Who were "they"? Well, men. No, not men in particular, or even in general. But some masculine thing, against which she felt she was affirming herself as a woman.

"All the younger women in my office are driving themselves nuts about whether to have a baby," said a magazine editor in her forties who'd had her own babies very young and had fought the feminist battles of the sixties and the seventies to break into the job world and to discover her own identity independent of her marriage and motherhood. Now a successful editor, and a beaming mother, as her lively daughters move from love of horses to science and boys, she says, "We didn't have that choice. We never thought of *not* having children. I don't envy them. Thinking back to the way I felt ten, fifteen years ago, if I'd had the choice I probably wouldn't have had children. I'd have put it all into my career. And think what I'd have missed!"

What is it we keep struggling against and for, back and forth, all of us daughters of mothers, mothers of daughters, daughters struggling to be-or-not-to-be mothers? This editor herself, in rebellion against her mother, became a mother too young. Struggling then, in conflict over her own motherhood, she rebelled against her dependence on her husband and left her marriage, in desperate ambition for a career.

Successful now in that career, fiercely independent, twice divorced and determined never to marry again, but knowing that she would have missed much if she had not been a mother, she has begun to write powerful poems about her mother and her own motherhood.

The *personhood of women*, that's what it's really all about, first and finally, I say now to younger women, trying to separate the essence of the women's movement from the rhetorical chaff of "women's lib." The personhood of women—and real equality, for women and men. Twenty years ago, breaking through the feminine mystique, it seemed as if the personhood of women meant only what a woman does and is, herself, not as her husband's wife, children's mother, housewife, server of her family. So, some of my feminist sisters react with a disconcerted sense of betrayal when I say we will come to a dead end if we keep on talking in terms of women alone. But I hear such sullenness from some younger women who now are living their personhood as women as if this somehow excludes all those emotions, capacities, needs that have to do with having babies, mothering children, making a home, loving and being loved, dependence and independence, softness and hardness, strength and weakness, in the family.

Joan of Arc said, facing the flames, "All that I am I will not deny." To deny the part of one's being as woman that has, through the ages, been expressed in motherhood—nurturing, loving softness, and tiger strength—is to deny part of one's personhood as woman. I am not saying that everyone has to be a mother to "fulfill" herself as a woman. I fought for women's right to choose, and I am still fighting for it in 1981 as the courts and the politicians, from the President down, are cynically appeasing reactionary forces who deny poor women exercise of that right, and by law or Constitutional Amendment threaten to force all women back to passivity to biological fate, or be prosecuted for murder for abortion, and even some forms of birth control.

The right to choose is crucial to the personhood of woman. The right to choose has to mean not only the right to choose not to bring a child into the world against one's will, but also the right to have a child, joyously, responsibly, without paying a terrible price of isolation from the world and its rewarded occupations, its decisions and actions. Women can choose motherhood now without paying the price of physical mutilation and shortening of life that women had to pay generations ago, but that choice is still weighted by the price of psychological mutilation, stunting of talents and economic disaster that too many women paid, even in my generation.

Part of the conflict over motherhood today—and part of the conflict that feminists feel about the family and that younger women will feel about feminism, if it has to keep denying the power of the impulse to love, motherhood, family—is a hangover from the generations when too great a price was paid. But part of the conflict is realistic: the price of motherhood is still too high for most women; the stunting of abilities and earning power is a real fear, because professions and careers are still structured in terms of the lives of men whose wives took care of the parenting and other details of life. The point is that *equality*— the rights for which women have been fighting for over a century—was, is, necessary, for women to be able to affirm their own personhood, and in the fullest sense of choice, motherhood. The point is, the movement to equality and the personhood of women isn't finished until motherhood is a fully free choice.

I have known for a long time that what drove me to tangle with the tortuous questions, to take on the uneasy, almost inconceivable mission of the women's movement, and what drives me now, at the zenith of that movement and in the face of its remarkable accomplishments, to wrestle anew with its assumed direction, is the simple driving need to *feel good* about being a woman, about myself as a woman, to be able to affirm who I really am—*All that I am I will not deny*. Not only in my secret heart of hearts, but in the reality of evolving life, in the world. My own mother, so many of our mothers, and their mothers, had good reason not to feel good about being women. They had a lot of real reasons, in the world slipping behind us, to envy that power of men, of which the penis was the symbol.

That freighted choice of motherhood is far behind most feminist and antifeminist leaders today, middle-aged women in middle-class America (or England, France, Italy), with our complex current problems of marriage, divorce, late-starting, escalating or stagnating careers, economic survival, husband's heart attacks or retirement, teenage rebellion, bravado of new single identity, unadmitted loneliness or the dreariness of supposed sexual adventure.

Our daughters, in the compulsion and challenge of their new career choices, are *surprised* when the power of that other choice now—the to-be-or-not-to-be of motherhood—hits them with an agonizing indecision. They discover it as some blessed possibility we kept from them or were too blighted, perverted to appreciate. Or, having learned some lesson we didn't realize we had passed on to them so well, they simply forgo that choice, with only the excessive energy expended in denying any urge to motherhood hinting at the possible power of that urge, in practical conflict now with career.

But they, the daughters, do not know the incalculable costs, the weights and burdens—and power and glory—which were built into that business of motherhood, when women had no choice. Anatomy is no longer destiny for these daughters in the same way as for Freud's women, but surely that very choice of motherhood is basic to their identity as women today, even though it no longer has to, or even can, define it totally.

Franny, a daughter who *has* other choices now, sits beside me on a winter beach and tells me why she cannot consider marrying Mike, the man she has been living with and loving these four years.

"Next year, when he gets his Ph.D., there's no telling

what kind of job he can get, there's so little opportunity for anthropologists now. He'll have to take anything halfway good—Maine, Nebraska, Utah—and there's no guarantee at all there will be any job in my field. I saw what happened to my mother when she gave up her career and concentrated on the house, and us kids, and helping my father. I saw the spark dulling in her and the bitterness grow. It destroyed their marriage, really. So, look at her now, divorced, lucky to get any kind of job at fifty, not even enough money to make a halfway good life as a woman alone. I don't want to end up like my mother. I don't even want to think about having kids myself."

And if Franny finally exorcises that phantom dread and has a baby (by natural childbirth, with her husband drilling her in the breathing as sophisticated young couples choose to share that experience today), will she suffer the same pain that wracked her mother or the mothers before her? Her very choice to have children changes the sociobiological reality, though that choice itself is still shadowed by her mother's pain. How do we grasp the tortuous double helix of our evolving female identity as it is passed on to daughters from the mothers before them, as immutably as the DNA and RNA, in terms of the irreversibility of the changes?

The grandmothers, who had no choices—no pill, no IUD or diaphragm, no professions open—made the best of their necessities. Most took what life offered them, a few rebelled, or secretly burned. The mothers swung between the drastic choice defined by the feminine mystique—no longer biological necessity, though still socioeconomic configuration—and it was a no-win choice—for the majority who bought the feminine mystique and were trapped by suburban motherhood, and for the minority who refused to buy, the first career women, the "freaks" who forswore marriage and motherhood to be lawyers, doctors, scientists, women's college presidents. Those few who combined motherhood and professions were "exceptional," and had, indeed, to be superwomen. Or they had to settle for second best in career, and/or were oppressed by terrible conflicts and guilts in their relationship with husband and children.

That was, and is, both the image and the reality that shadows the perceptions of daughters today, who face a different set of choices, in part because of the women's movement. That shadow also blinds the movement in its denial of the power of family and motherhood as a positive, desired and desirable choice for women, in a new and different historical context. Or rather, those shadows leave daughters, and women's movement strategists, blind or confused as to their real personal needs and choices, or the political steps still to be taken, or completed, to give them real choices.

For women to live their personal lives as a political scenario as some radical feminists tried to do (man as enemy, motherhood and family as oppressors of women, sexual surrender to the enemy as betrayal of self, treason to women) surely violates basic human needs for intimacy, sex, generation. It also vitiates will and energy for real political changes. But the feminist insight that the personal is political remains. In fact, personal, family life in the idealized past has been more political than men would like to believe, precisely because of the inequality, the imbalance of power between men and women in society.

It is historical, political reality that women at one time had no control over their reproductive process, no real choice about motherhood, except the nunnery, for Catholics, or a pariah spinsterhood. It is historical, political reality that when motherhood was woman's only function, status and identity, as well as her biological necessity, it kept her, or was used as an excuse to keep her, from education or opportunity to use her abilities in the mainstream of our evolving society. The inequality of woman, her second-class status in society, was in historical reality linked to that biological state of motherhood.

The change in woman's historical, political reality is that motherhood—which was once her necessity and passive destiny, and which confined, defined, used up her whole life

—is now no longer necessity, but choice, and even when chosen, no longer can define or even use up most of her life. So the women's movement, both the first century of struggle which led to the vote and the modern women's movement, focused on breaking through the barriers that kept woman from moving, earning and having her own voice in the advanced, rewarded work of modern society, dominated by men. That's where the power was.

But, as the historian Carl Degler has shown (in *At Odds, Women and the Family in America from the Revolution to the Present*, 1980)—and as psychologists and sociologists document incessantly, in praise or blame—the major movement of American women to get some power, before and during this century, was *through the family*, using and controlling the power that sexuality and motherhood gave them. And sexuality, motherhood, which used to be women's only sources of power, are still awesome powers indeed—and no man or woman who grew up in a family and has suffered or longed for or taken joy from another's touch can deny this, even if it has never been measured, or can be measured, by fractions or multiples of the dollar.

In history, as recorded in male terms, the intricacies and costs of this transaction have never been spelled out. Only psychologists, sociologists, psychoanalysts, poets, novelists and playwrights have shown the costs—in the pathological, powerful motherhood of the silver cord, and Philip Wylie's "momism," and the termagants abraded by Sophocles in fear of whom the ancient Greek men sought young boys as lovers; or the obsessively loved-hated Jewish mother (or her Italian, Mexican or Irish counterpart) who followed her son into the bathroom and to college; or Tennessee Williams' sweet southern belle who cannibalized her impotent son; or the modern mothers of "battered children." The costs are spelled out in the case histories of all the children smothered by the love-hate of the mothers who had to live through them, and of all the men exhorted to impossible, insatiable, never satisfied demands for status, glory and power by the women who had to meet their own needs for power and glory through them. As mothers, then as wives, women had only one powerful weapon over men: to give, or deny, that loving touch; to foster, by denying, that insatiable need for love in them, which became their need for power and glory-violent deeds, for Nielsen or Dow Jones ratings. And was sometimes transmuted into man's insatiable cruelty, in revenge, rape and even murder of women, children and the weak.

It is only recently that social historians and then the women's movement itself broke through history's sex blindness and uncovered the evolving history of women, and the family, beneath the dates and statistics of battles, currency, kings and revolutions. So we know now that the family, the role of men, women and children within it, and its relation to the economy is not a constant but has evolved in the context of the evolution of technology and society. When the common work of men and women, as peasants in the fields of Europe, or tilling the soil and riding the wagon trains west in America, or running the mom-and-pop stores, was transformed by the industrial revolution, man's role became increasingly defined by his new technological work in industry and professions in the city, and woman's by that old menial private domestic work in the home, with the children. In that modern world of sharply differentiated, unequal sex roles, where men had all the new power, the slow-building, conscious movement of women for equal rights in man's world—from Mary Wollstonecraft to Seneca Falls, Susan B. Anthony to NOW—was paralleled by the much more pervasive and effective movement of women for power in the family, over the children, over sexuality, the home.

The very importance of children, family, the home that is a constant of our consciousness today is based not only on the real needs of men and children for nurturing and loving care and the "complementary," "female" abilities of women—but also on the needs of women, equally real and basic to the human condition, for mastery, power, assertiveness, security and control. And evolving self-realization for us all. When woman was denied access to satisfaction of those needs in society as a person in her own right, she made home and the family into a vehicle for her power, control, status and self-realization. As Degler shows, American women's long movement for control and power, in and through the family, developed throughout the nineteenth century, and then came into conflict with women's new needs—economic and psychological—to move and earn and act in man's world, in the twentieth century. The family, which in a certain sense *was* women's power base (as Phyllis Schlafly and Marabel Morgan well understand), then became her Frankenstein monster.

We all carry in our own personal history the evidence of this heritage. My own feminism somehow began in my mother's discontent, forced to quit as woman's page editor of the Peoria newspaper when she married my father. Three children, one harassed businessman husband and an eight-room house were not enough for her energies, as great as mine, though she ran the Sunday school one year, the Community Chest the next, played endless games of bridge and mah-jongg, shopped for things no one needed, kept my father feeling continually inadequate and on the edge of bankruptcy because no matter how much he made, it wasn't enough for her.

She couldn't wait for me to get into junior high school to try out for the school paper. Her bitterness at having to depend on her husband for an allowance—her maneuvers, hiding the bills she charged, secretly trying her hand at gambling to recoup her debts and losing more, until she had to confess, causing terrible battles that shook our house at night —became our necessity to earn our own money, not to have to depend on any man. She was not a happy housewife. Her ulcerating colitis, which forced her to bed in sickening agony for days at a time, only subsided when my father's heart trouble and premature invalidism and death made it necessary for her to take over and run his business.

Then why did I, despite a superior education not available to her, give up psychology fellowships and feel almost relieved when I was fired from a newspaper job during my second pregnancy? I was determined to be "fulfilled as a woman" as my mother was not. My own conscious feminism began in later outrage at that mistaken either/or choice that the feminine mystique imposed on my generation. But I was, in fact, fired from my job as a reporter when I became pregnant. And there was no contract category or law against "sex discrimination" under which I could have taken such a grievance to my union, the Newspaper Guild. My mother had no real choice. Most of us let ourselves be seduced into giving up careers in order to embrace motherhood full time, and, we thought, lifelong. Then, sooner or later, we felt trapped. It wasn't easy to get back into the increasingly competitive rat race at forty or beyond—or, for those who, at the height of the feminine mystique, gave up college to put their husbands through law or medical school, and then had to ask, for the first time, at thirty or thirty-five, with the children already off to school, or in the crisis of divorce, the question, "What can I do myself?" when they had no confidence and no marketable skills.

But the secret of the house of my own childhood, and of so many others in America, the secret that we later underplayed or denied because it was somehow at odds with our feminism, was the feared, hated, overweening power of woman as mother, in that family, that home—the power my mother had no choice but to assume. I, too, had no choice but to assume it—no matter how much I, like most daughters until recently, did not want to be like my mother.

The real power, the rewarded power, was in that society outside the home, from which our mothers were barred and from which we retreated, not understanding the reality of their discontent, nor wishing to share it, not daring to know until later that we had to break down those bars. But we surely knew, and wanted to share, the reality of that other power—the accepted status and identity, the sense of belonging and the simple satisfaction that women did enjoy in the home. It was only later, in retrospect, when it was distorted by mistaken rhetoric, or unforeseen outcomes for which we did not want to claim responsibility, that we saw it as a trap. But the real bitterness women felt when they had to get out of that trap clouded the perception of the daughters.

Personal choices and political strategies of women today are distorted when they deny the reality of either set of needs: woman's need for power, identity, status and security through her own work or action in society, which the reactionary enemies of feminism deny; and the need for love and identity, status, security and generation through marriage, children, home, the family, which those feminists still locked in their own extreme reaction deny. *Both sets of needs are essential to women, and to the evolving human condition.* (They have been denied in different ways by men, as we will see later.)   The enemies of feminism insist that woman's move to equality, self-realization and her own power in society is destroying the family, which they feel is woman's real locus of power. Many feminists insist that the family was, and is, the enemy, the prime obstacle to woman's self-realization. There are pieces of the truth in these interlocking fears, shadows of conflicts that were insoluble in the past. I believe that the first stage, woman's movement to equality and her own personhood, was, in fact, necessary for the survival and economic/emotional health of the family, and that the second stage can, and must, transcend these conflicts. For I believe, from all we know of human psychology and history, that neither woman nor man lives by work, or love, alone: the absolutely powerless, the denigrated, the self-abnegating ones are too hungry for power, too lacking in self, to love and nurture; the loveless crave power because they lack both love and self. The human self defines itself and grows through love *and* work; all psychology before and after Freud boils down to that.

Why are some women so afraid, on either side of this conflict, to put to the test of personal reality our own needs for power in the world *and* for love and family?

Behind the ambivalent sensitivities that cause many women to flinch at the women's movement as a threat to the family, or to flail at the family as enemy of women's very self, lie generations of built-up frustration and conflict for which men and children inevitably have paid a price. The denigration of women and denial of opportunity and power in the world, which the women's movement exposed and fought, was the basis, in the past, of that enormous, compensating defensive and offensive buildup of women's power and pedestal in home and family.

But the ambivalent hysteria about the family today is also the tortuous end result of those needs which for all of us, as children, were necessarily satisfied or denied, magnified or distorted, within the family structure. The power of those needs, and the pathological consequences of their distortion or denial, has occupied a century of psychological researchers and therapists. But until recently the separate, unequal sex roles of men and women were taken for granted as a necessary, universal, functional norm of the family. They were not recognized or studied as a possible source of the pathology.

When women were totally defined as housewife-mothers, nurturers, servants of the family, and when home and children were totally "women's world," the case histories of psychologically wounded children and men almost by definition had to point to the omnipresent mother (or the absent father) as villain. The benign-destructive masks of pseudo- and real power that women acquired in the modern American family, hiding their socioeconomic dependency, are not so easy even now to give up, or see through. The scars that female power in the family left on both women and men create some of the exaggerated fears women experience as they now confront the reality tests of the very different kind of family their own move to equality has made possible—and necessary. As some of us fear the test of equality, others fear the test of the family, the way it really is now—or can be—when women don't have to find their whole power in it, or give up their own identity as equal persons to marry and bear children.

For women caught in the middle in the transition to equality, some of the fears and resentments are not easy to acknowledge. I think of women of my own generation and personal acquaintance who have spent thirty and more years married to businessmen, lawyers, doctors, writers, artists who are now successful. They all started out poor and struggling. She was his sounding board for every sentence he wrote, she kept the accounts, got the books from the library, made the plane reservations, in addition to the usual cooking, the children, the decorating, and the entertaining that everyone recognizes as part of his success. Or she filed the pictures, kept track of payments. Or was virtually full-time office-nurse-receptionist as doctor's wife. She had no separate life of her own—"He'd follow me even to the bathroom to read his last page aloud." Some of us who later became writers, artists, lawyers as women on our own, or with husbands preoccupied with their own careers, are not joking when we fantasize how much better we might be able to do ourselves "with such a wife."

Suddenly, after thirty years, the husband leaves this symbiotic marriage for a younger woman on her own way up, someone who is familiar with those same battles he fought—his equal. It turns out that the thirty-year wife-nurturer has only a few thousand dollars in the bank in her own name. Under the new divorce law, will her housewifely contribution of thirty years entitle her to equal share of their house, cars, whatever stocks he's bought (wherever he has put them)? No longer the eminent writer's wife, she will not share his future royalties. Will she even be invited to the parties?

The other women are appalled. They feel shaky. One suggests to her husband that maybe the house should be put in her name, since he's older, not in the best of health—though heaven forbid that he should die first! He smiles and says,

"How will you pay the taxes?" Another suddenly takes her attention completely off the hostessing that has been a staple of her husband's success and starts, at forty-eight, to write a novel under her maiden name.

"What do I do now?" an abandoned wife calls at 6 A.M. to demand grimly, hysterically, of me, perhaps unconsciously blaming the women's movement for her plight. What can I say to her? Go back to school, get a job, do something for yourself. You should, you know, whether or not he comes back.

But is that what she and others like her want to do? Should have to do? Will be able to do? As far as I can see, many of their marriages seem to work. There must be trade-offs. Would X be a successful artist, or Y a doctor, without that constant contribution from his wife? What's wrong with doing it that way—if it works, and if neither gives up or risks too much? We used to laugh when she would say, "We wrote five pages today," because, in fact, we knew that *he* wrote those pages.

And yet, I've met younger couples lately who collaborate in that way—as screenwriters, for instance—some married to each other, some not. He might write the first draft, and she edit. They might discuss it, and she do all the writing, or vice versa. They take the byline jointly, share the credit and the proceeds.

I think of scientist couples of my own generation, where she never finished her Ph.D., had tenure nowhere, but silently collaborated in his research, between and after the babies. Belatedly, perhaps, as in the case of Dr. Spock, he might acknowledge they did the work jointly—or, if not going that far, admit that she contributed much more to it than a mere mention in the preface might imply. Only by that time he may have divorced her for a younger woman. Or she may have left in a fury of exploding bitterness, or died prematurely from some strange stress-produced heart condition. (There are other conditions of stress that have led to despair,

debilitating depression or even death in women, besides
superwoman overwork.)

These problems may take a different form in the future,
where couples start out in the same field, collaborating on
professional work and sharing its rewards on a basis of real
equality, pooling separate talents in ways that best use each
partner's abilities and suit the family situation.

But what about the family work? The responsibility that
used to be the woman's, in the home and family, as the man's
duty was earning the money, out in the world? How are we
to put a value on family work? What is it really worth, compared to that other, money-earning kind of work? How long
will she keep doing it, by herself, if it's not valued, or shared?
How will he live without it? Will he say out loud, "I am
afraid she will leave me if she can earn money on her own"?
(And maybe she will.) Does he say out loud, "Why should I
be killing myself to earn twenty thousand dollars a year—or
thirty thousand, forty thousand, fifty thousand—when she
plays golf in the afternoon and looks tan and rested. I'll drop
dead of a heart attack if I go on like this. I need a woman who
can help support us. Like Janey, in my own office—she already earns twenty-five thousand, after taxes." Will his wife
say out loud, "Don't talk to me about ERA, I like being the
lawyer's wife, playing golf in the afternoon. What will happen to me, if he takes a fancy to that Janey who's working on
the case with him? I couldn't care less about torts. It's too late
for me to go to law school. Besides, I don't want to."

None of them will spell out these truths of economic survival. It's easier to rant and rave about "destruction of the
family"—rant and rave all the harder if you suddenly see
through those old masks, and feel the burden, and want the
out that equality could give you before it is too late.

Still, the sophisticates who shrug off all this hysteria about
the family as sentimental cant betray their own blind spot.
We have to break through the cant and the blind spot and
deal with the new problems of the family now, which neither

feminists nor antifeminists can avoid in real life. For the family is the nutrient matrix of our personhood. We all were born and grew up in families; our children, and their children, will grow up in different kinds of families. Even those who live alone, repudiating marriage and motherhood, as "separatist" radical feminists preached, are living a life defined by reaction against the family, whistling a brave tune to hide the loneliness and yearning for some form of family or family substitute. And surely those who live as if the family is and always will be as it always was, sacred forever and protecting them from change, betray by the very shrillness of their protest that they live a fearful lie.

But to confront the American family as it actually is today, instead of hysterically defending or attacking the family that is no more—"the classical family of Western nostalgia," as Stanford sociologist William J. Goode calls it—means shattering an icon that is still sacred to both church and state. And dispelling the mystique of the family seems to be even more threatening to some than unmasking the feminine mystique was for so many a decade ago. But it is that obsolete image of the family that polarizes and paralyzes our power to solve the new problems, politically and personally.

We are now on the cusp of breaking through the obsolete image of the family. That was the real significance of the White House Conference on Families, though it may not have been the intention of those who called it or tried to take it over. Consider, for instance, that the original White House conference on "the family," supposed to have been held in 1979, was suddenly canceled as too "controversial" when the experts assembled to plan it began facing the facts about American families today.

The flak started when participating Catholic priests discovered that the eminent black woman coordinating the conference was herself divorced and raising her family as a single parent. When the Government's own statistics revealed that fewer than 7 percent of Americans are now living in that kind of family to which politicians and churchmen are always paying lip service—Daddy the breadwinner, Mother the housewife, and two children (with background bark of dog and meow of cat, and station wagon parked in the ranch-house driveway)—the White House decided to call the whole thing off. They then started over, with a white Southern churchgoing Protestant safely married male in charge. But they still had to face the same startling, hitherto publicly undiscussed, facts.

According to Government statistics (*Household and Family, by Type:* March, 1980 [Advance Report, Series P20, No. 357, Bureau of the Census], and unpublished data, Bureau of Labor Statistics):

• Only 11 percent of American households include a father who is the sole wage earner, a mother who is a full-time homemaker, and one or more children. (And one study found that one third of all such full-time housewives were planning to look for jobs.)

• 21 percent of American households consist of both a father and a mother who are wage earners, with one or more children living at home.

• 30 percent of American households consist of married couples with no children, or none living at home.

• 6.7 percent of American households are headed by women who are single parents with one or more children at home.

• .7 percent are such single-parent families headed by men.

• 3.1 percent consist of unrelated persons living together.

• 5.3 percent are headed by a single person and include relatives other than spouses and children.

• 22 percent of American households consist of one person living alone (a third of those are women over sixty-five).

Could the White House of Jimmy Carter—who had used the power of the Presidency against measures like child-care subsidies, under the banner of preserving that "family of nostalgia"—ignore these figures? Phyllis Schlafly, the John Birchers and Right-to-Lifers organized a "Pro-Family" coalition to take over the White House Conference, in the name of defending "the family" from the Equal Rights Amendment, abortion and homosexuality.

Meanwhile feminists began moving to confront the family in new terms. A National Assembly on the Future of the Family was convened by the NOW Legal Defense and Education Fund at the New York Hilton on November 19, 1979. Keynoting that assembly, I pointed out, "Despite the rhetoric, the family has never ranked high on the American political and economic agenda, except as a unit to which to sell things. The business of America, as everyone knows, is business, and until recently it's been man's business. Now that women are beginning to have an active voice in the economy and politics, the nation's agenda may begin truly to include the family. Not just because women insist—they don't have that much power yet—but because men have a new stake in the family. The new sharing of parenting and the envy many men are beginning to express now of women's liberation suggest that the family, instead of being enemy territory to feminists, is really the underground through which secretly they reach into every man's life. . . . Women must now confront anew their own needs for love and comfort and caring support, as well as the needs of children and men, for whom, I believe, we cannot escape bedrock human responsibility."

As Muriel Fox, president of the NOW LDEF, put it in her speech to the assembly:

> We will accept—rather than deny—the fact that 93 percent of the American families today fit patterns other than the traditional one of a breadwinning father, a homemaking mother and two or more dependent children. We will accept the inevitability of con-

tinuing future change in the relationships and roles of men, women and children within families.

We do not share the frequently voiced opinion that American families are in a state of hopeless collapse. People are living together in new combinations for the intimacy and support that constituted a family—unmarried adults with or without children, single-parent families, multigenerational communes, various new groupings of the elderly.

The future of the family is an overriding feminist issue.

Not all feminists agreed with that, of course. We were accused of "reactionary family chauvinism." There was that double-edged reaction—shock and relief—that reminded me of what happened when we began the women's movement. We would indeed be turning another corner in history, for feminists to come to new terms with the family. We would be coming to grips, finally, with the problems tormenting our supposed enemies. The energy that the conservatives were expending, hysterically defending "the family" against ERA, abortion, child-care programs, any and every aspect of women's move to equality or the very recognition of new economic realities—and the energy that feminists were therefore forced to spend defending their own increasingly precarious positions against such attack—might be liberated for concrete solutions of the new family problems and needs which we all share.

Why, with the majority of mothers now working, haven't feminists put as much energy into the battle for a multifaceted approach to child care—developing new options, using services and funds from a variety of sources (public and private, companies, unions, churches, city, state, federal agencies, but always parent-controlled), demanding tax incentives and innovations like a voucher system—as they have put into the battles against sex discrimination or for abortion? For the first decade of NOW, it seemed as if there were only two of us really interested in doing anything about child care—Florence Dickler, a young housewife from New Jersey, and I. In the second decade, Adrienne Leaf, the new young woman who single-handedly took on the "Child Care Task Force," would call me for help because she had such trouble getting space on the NOW agenda.

There was, in fact, cold silence, or even open annoyance, in various feminist ranks in response to our appeal, in the fall of '79, that the women's movement come to grips with the practical problems of the family which our move to equality entails.

Many feminists felt the White House Conference on Families was not worth bothering to attend. In many states they did not even try to get elected as delegates. It was simply assumed that the right wing would take over. For the White House even to call a conference on the family was seen as an attempt to appease reaction, giving it a new official forum to wave that "family" flag against the Equal Rights Amendment, abortion, gay rights. Because of my own conviction that the family has to be the new feminist frontier, I asked that I be named a delegate.

To the degree that feminists collude in assuming an inevitable, unbridgeable antagonism between women's equality and the family, they make it a self-fulfilling prophecy. In fact, the media, which take that antagonism for granted now, reported about the White House Conference in those terms, and missed the significance of what really happened. For when we feminists broke out of our own rhetoric and dealt with women's most basic concerns within the larger family context, we were able to bridge that polarization and win overwhelming majority support for second-stage solutions.

Consider that already, by spring of 1980, the experts reassembled to plan the White House Conference under the new leadership of the Southern white Protestant married male— Jim Guy Tucker of Arkansas—were no longer talking about "the family." Their own official documents proclaimed the new diversity of families in America—the statistics which made clear that most Americans were no longer living in that "classical family of Western nostalgia." The official title was now pointedly, "White House Conferences on *Families.*" And the very planning of the workshops and definitions of "problems" dealt with the new reality *that women now work*—outside and inside the home, in single-parent or two-parent families, or living alone—instead of attacking that fact, or pretending it would go away.

Consider that until now, all in the name of "preserving the family," recent Democratic Presidents as well as Republicans have vetoed or ignored the need for child-care programs, despite that exploding majority of American women with children under six who now work. For years now, Government experts, politicians, even eminent academic and medical experts and child-care researchers, have shied away from dealing with the need for new child-care programs and parental leaves and new working arrangements because taking those steps would officially acknowledge the reality that most Americans do not live in that Papa-the-breadwinner, Mama-the-housewife image of "the family." Even the prestigious Carnegie Commission on Children, whose very reason for being was to deal with the new problems of children in families as they now exist, had shied away from the whole question of child-care programs as too controversial.

Churchmen, social workers and public-policy experts whose concern, real and/or politically expedient, for "the family" brought them to the White House Conference had assumed for the most part that women's working and their new aspirations for equality were the real problem. The "problem" could be solved by pretending that women would or could simply go home again.

All the previous year I had sat on a task force of the National Federation of Jewish Philanthropies, dealing with the problems of the new Jewish woman. The women on that task force, from Orthodox rabbis' wives and Hadassah leaders to young feminists studying to be rabbis themselves, knew and were in agreement with what the real problems were. But month after month, rabbis, social workers, psychologists, agency heads, mostly male, would, after the ritual lip service to the new woman's desire for equality, discuss "the problem of getting the Jewish woman to return to her traditional responsibility for the family." It took over a year of monthly meetings for them to get the point that if they really wanted young Jewish women to choose to have more children, as they desperately did, they would have to deal with problems of equal opportunity, maternal and paternal leaves, restructure of jobs and professions, and child-care services.

Now, people from religious groups (Protestant, Catholic, Jewish), as well as child welfare, social service, family service organizations (the Red Cross, Planned Parenthood) and the major establishment women's groups, had organized a coalition to prevent the White House Conference on Families from being polarized between the "pro-family" right-wing forces, led by Phyllis Schlafly, and the feminists. Working with Carter's people, they were so terrified of the right-wing delegates that they wanted to stay away from "controversial," "polarizing" issues such as ERA, abortion, gay rights, or the definition of "the family" altogether. But they were agreed on families' new needs for child care and new job patterns.

When I got to Baltimore, the night before the conference, the few NOW members and other feminists and the abortion rights and gay rights leaders who were there wanted to have a separate caucus, as Phyllis Schlafly and the Right to Life and Moral Majority people were doing, down the hall.

I did not want to have a separate feminist caucus on sexual issues, or even let the Equal Rights Amendment be treated as a separate, sexual issue that would "polarize" the conference. I felt that the new family issues such as child-care programs, parental leaves and restructuring working hours were the new priorities for feminists also, and that this large new coalition of men and women ready to deal with these issues were just the allies we needed. But how could they, or we, hope to get new solutions for these problems if they gave up on the basic rights of equal opportunity in employment and education, and the right to choose in childbirth, which we had already won?

All the night before, I'd lain awake rethinking my own position *in terms of the family*. Forget the feminist rhetoric, I told myself. Still, there was no way, in the face of the economic urgencies facing women and most families today, to gainsay the importance of the Equal Rights Amendment. With men being laid off in both blue-collar and white-collar jobs, with inflation showing no let-up, women's opportunity to earn needed that Constitutional underpinning to insure the survival of the family. And if they could not afford to have a child, women of all income levels needed safe, legal medical access to abortion to insure their future choice to have children.

The economic and educational opportunities insured by the ERA and that entirely separate right to safe, legal medical access to family planning services of all kinds were essential to the choice to have children, as were new options for child care, parental leave and flexible hours of work. And did we not, once and for all, have to acknowledge the diversity of the families people live in now, and get rid of the obsolete definition so it could no longer be a weapon in the hands of those trying to block the new programs today's families really need?

Instead of holding a separate feminist or "sexual" caucus, the others helped me get the floor at the larger church-and-family caucus. Overruling their own leadership, the larger group voted to include the Equal Rights Amendment and abortion in their battle plan. Then we worked together, far into that night—Noreen Connell of NOW, other feminists, caucus chairman Joseph Giordano, Irving Levine of the American Jewish Committee—to separate Equal Rights from the incendiary "sexual" issues, put ERA into the context of economic urgency and family survival, and abortion in terms of "the choice to have children." Instead of trying to get a new, abstract definition of "the family," we would simply insist that all public programs and policies, from housing to welfare, deal with the diversity of families as they actually exist.

The next day, at the official session at Baltimore, a Catholic priest, the Reverend Thomas D. Weise, of Mobile, Alabama, who had spent the past six months organizing Catholic participation in the White House Conference on Families, spoke in support of our resolution on "the choice to have children." He told me that "the bishops" had been trying to come up with something like that. It was clear that the "legal medical help in family planning services" we called for included abortion, but the shift in values was significant.

It has long seemed wrong to me for women, for feminists, to be pushed into a position where they are *for abortion*, and let the right wing preempt the position "for life" or "for family." *I* am for life and for family; those are basic values for me, and they should be for every feminist. I am not *for abortion* —I am for the *choice to have children*. At this stage of medical technological development, when birth-control devices like the pill and the IUD are not completely safe and can, in fact, pose terrible long-term threats to women's health and life, there has to be safe, legal medical access to abortion. It safeguards, among other things, the woman's future choice to have a child. I think it is time for feminists to affirm the value of that choice. To dismiss it or take it lightly is not only to offend the basic values of a great majority of women—and men—but somehow violates something basic in our own roots as women—our reverence for life.

Our resolution on "the choice to have children" passed the White House Conference on Families in Baltimore by a 4 to 1 majority (460 to 114). The resolution on ratification of the ERA, in the context of "families and economic well-being," passed also by a 4 to 1 majority, 471 to 119. (Another resolution, on abortion, in terms of Americans' "deeply held principles of religious freedom, liberty and pluralism," passed by a narrower majority of 383 to 202.)

But at the last minute, a radical feminist lawyer introduced a resolution using the old rhetoric and lumping together ERA, abortion and "sexual preference." This passed the conference by only one vote (292 to 291) and wouldn't have passed at all if fifty Right-to-Lifers hadn't walked out. And *this* was what the media headlined, reporting that the White House Conference on Families was "polarized" on ERA, abortion and homosexual rights.

In fact, the real news was the overwhelming consensus of the White House Conference on Families, not only on ERA and the choice to have children, but on the need for child-care options and restructured jobs, flexible working hours and maternity and paternity leaves—which only a few feminists were seriously demanding before.

The most strongly supported demands of the entire conference, along with action to counter drug and alcohol abuse, were "the development of alternative forms of quality child care, both center and home based" (547 to 44), and "creative development" (by business, labor and Government) of "policies that enable persons to hold jobs while maintaining a strong family life," including "such work arrangements as flextime, flexible leave policies for both sexes, job-sharing programs, dependent-care options and part-time jobs with prorated pay and benefits," which passed 569 to 21.

There was also a very large consensus on asking local, state and federal governments to put an economic value on homemaking in social security and pension funds, recognizing "marriage as an economic partnership" with financial resources earned by the spouses vested equally during a marriage, and distributed fifty-fifty at divorce or retirement. No definition of "the family" was adopted, but housing and other Government programs were now to be geared to the "diversity of families" as they exist, including "single parent," "nuclear" and "extended" families.

A new, broader political family began to emerge. Eric

Rofes, a leader in the movement for gay rights, had been a college friend of my daughter. When he was elected a delegate to the White House Conference, he asked me for advice on "families," advising me that people like him also needed "family." Then, he discovered and enthusiastically pushed the American Home Economic Association's new definition of the family: "Two or more persons who share resources, share responsibility for decisions, share values and goals, and have commitments to one another over time. The family is that climate that one 'comes home to,' and it is this network of sharing and commitments that most accurately describes the family unit, regardless of blood, legal ties, adoption or marriage." Neither this nor the conservative definition of a family as "related by blood, marriage or legal custody" was put forward for official adoption at Baltimore. (Both definitions were adopted at the subsequent White House Conference on Families.)

In this new political coalition "for families," feminists were able to work with such diverse groups as the National Conference of Catholic Bishops, Parents Without Partners, the Red Cross, the National Council of Churches, the American Home Economics Association and the National Gay Task Force—and the feared "polarization" did not take place. Of the more than 670 delegates at Baltimore, only fifty walked out. A great many "conservatives" stayed, and voted with the majority on child care, flextime—and ERA and the "choice to have children."

But evidently some feminists, like the extremist antifeminists, prefer polarization. In their fear of controversial publicity in an election year, the White House had scheduled three separate conferences instead of a single one at the White House. At the second conference, in Minneapolis, which I did not attend, certain feminist and abortion-rights leaders shied away from "the choice to have children" as too conservative an embrace of family values. They stuck to feminist rhetoric and were immediately put on the defensive by a large body of right-wing delegates. The second conference *was* polarized. The energy of the coalition was then defused, defending against resolutions banning abortion, ERA and homosexual rights. Fighting now on terms defined by the reactionary forces, the Catholic priests who had taken criticism from their superiors for supporting the "choice to have children" at Baltimore would have been forced into a position on abortion that went against their own beliefs, and they walked out.

At the same time, representatives of the Carter Administration quietly nixed a bill before Congress on tax incentives for child-care centers. By the third conference in Los Angeles, the polarization on "family values" had become a given of the 1980 election campaign. The Democrats' fearful retreat and the feminists' paralysis in fixed, defensive positions had handed "the family" to the far right—the so-called Moral Majority.

The problem, at and after these conferences, was not figuring out what the solutions should be, but finding or releasing the political power that is locked up in these increasingly dangerous, and basically deceptive, political or sexual power battles with their false polarization over the family. Because that energy is locked in reaction, the new family problems, despite the political rhetoric, are still handled in real life as personal, not political—as all women's problems, including sex discrimination, were before the women's movement.

The solutions are much more difficult as long as they are considered *personal.* But even to deal with the new problems of family and work personally, in real life, as increasing millions of women and men, including feminists and antifeminists, must do now, is to sense the big lie in those hysterical threats and fears about the family, to sense unexpected new strengths emerging, and surprisingly comfortable shifts in the power struggles that used to be played out in the family.

As the family comes into sharp new focus, as more and more women go to work outside the home, we can begin to

separate the true, important questions—answers to which
have still to be worked out, personally and politically—from
the false ones, the leftover shadows from the old sexual
power battles caused by those unequal male and female roles.

The balance of power is undeniably shifting now between
the sexes, everywhere in the world, as women move into
jobs. But the tradeoffs have not been worked out in the family. In fact, for the real tradeoffs to take place, the sharp de-
marcation between family and home as "woman's world,"
and work (and politics and war) as "man's world" will have
to be redrawn. Equality in jobs, without taking into account
family, leaves women doubly burdened. And equality in the
family isn't real for women if it is isolated from economic
measures of worth and survival in the world.

Part of the problem comes from the lack of real economic
measures or political attention to the previously private
woman's work, in home and family, an irreducible minimum
of which is necessary for human and society's survival.
Global statistics record the present imbalance, as the tradeoffs of transition are being worked out, more or less pain-
fully, in isolation, by each family. But the way all this is still
being treated, by society and women themselves, as *woman's
problem*, is in itself the main problem now, the main obstacle
to the restructuring of work and home that is required.

The new imbalance is becoming visible, at least. Equal job
opportunities for women "will turn out to be a recipe for
overwork" unless "the sharing of unpaid household labor between men and women becomes a reality," said a research
report issued by the World Watch Institute in 1980. Although
nearly half of the world's adult women are in the labor force
out of choice or necessity, "they have retained an unwilling
monopoly on unpaid labor at home. The result is a pronounced imbalance between male and female workloads,
with unhappy consequences for women, men and children."

In a certain sense the roles of women and men in the labor
force have virtually come full circle. Historically, both men
and women worked to "support the household in subsistence

production." Then came the split "between women's unpaid work in the household and men's breadwinning." In the current transition, "women increasingly share the breadwinning role with men but retain most of the responsibility for the home." In "the as-yet-unrealized ideal," the family will again become symmetrical, when "both the financial support and the physical maintenance of the family are equally shared between men and women."

Between 1950 and 1975, the number of women considered "economically active" rose from 344 million to 576 million, both because of women's rising demand for equality and inflationary pressures requiring them to seek jobs outside the house. Since this trend was not matched by an increased involvement of men in housework, women are now carrying a double burden.

"If employed women with families also aspire to leadership positions, their extra hours of work, union activism and civic and cultural affairs can amount to working a triple day," the report continues.

When supposed solutions such as part-time work, flextime, and child-care centers are sought as "women's benefits," instead of easing the strain between work and family, they actually do the reverse, merely "reinforcing the idea that home and family belong to women's sphere rather than being a joint responsibility."

The exaggerated power and proliferation of duties built into that housewife role, when it was women's only function and means to identity, get in the way now. Again and again, among women I've interviewed over these years, I've seen these power battles being played out over the housework and the children to seemingly insoluble impasses. But slowly the new sense of self and worth the woman gets from earning, and the actuality of sharing the economic burden, shifts the power balance in the family in surprising ways. We weren't wrong, in the women's movement, to focus that first stage on equal opportunity for jobs and education. Women have to experience at least the beginnings of equality in the world before they can trade off that supreme, excessively burdening power in the family.

The transition isn't easy. There's a chicken-and-egg aspect to it. I've noticed that women who feel least sure of themselves as women—in the shadow of their mothers' self-denigration, those mothers who didn't feel good enough about themselves to love a daughter strongly—are most likely to fall into the superwoman trap, trying to be Perfect Mothers, as their own were not, and also perfect on the job, in ways that men, grounded from boyhood in such games, don't try to be. That female machismo, passed on from mother to daughter, hides the same inadmissible self-hate, weakness, sense of powerlessness as machismo hides in men. The stern demands such a woman placed on herself as mother, and on her children, could never be satisfied in reality. The daughter of such a mother, moving out into the world now, may mask her female machismo in feminist rhetoric, but if she moves from that same core of weakness and self-hate, she will be an easy victim of the double burden, placing insatiable demands on herself in her work, and getting locked into power battles with her husband over insatiable standards of housework. (And if he, too, bears the scars of such a mother, whose female machismo, hiding self-hate, made *his* best never good enough to win her love, how threatened will he be now by women emulating and undermining his own precarious machismo in office and home?)

Exchanging the burdens of the insatiable power battles of male machismo for the insatiable demands of female machismo—or accepting the burdens of one on top of the other —does not add up to liberation for either woman or man. But today, if a woman does not risk herself in the world of work, she suffers from a realistic sense of insecurity, of unvalued self. No matter how often she tells herself, or her husband tells her, that the work she does at home, looking after the children, entertaining his clients, is important, it is not valued, in dollar terms, in social security for old age, or in divorce settlements. And yet it is real work. Shouldn't it be valued somehow? And what about the rest—arranging the flowers, baking the cookies? It makes life more pleasant, surely, even if it's not necessary, or paid for. What would life be like if no one did that work? What if, in reaction, she strips her life clean of all these unmeasured, unvalued feminine tasks and frills—stops baking cookies altogether, cuts her hair like a monk, decides not to have children, installs a computer console in her bedroom? She suffers, finally, a new "crisis of confidence." She does not feel grounded in life. She shivers inside. She is depleted by female machismo. And she does not ask the new questions that have to be asked now to get beyond the no-win power battles in the family, and to change the terms at work.

Here are four women in different stages of transition, working themselves out of the impasse. I interviewed them at a reunion of their consciousness-raising group, which they started in 1970, when they were all about thirty and at home with their children. It broke up two years later, when three of them went to work and the fourth left her marriage.

Tina has just quit her job in a nursery school to work in a garage.

"I was going to be a Good Mother, which my mother wasn't, and which my husband still expects me to be. To be honest, I took it all on my own shoulders, to be the Good Mother, to run it all. Now I'm trying to dump it back on him, and he's running. Ten years ago, I got a job at the nursery school because I had to do something, and I could take my own kids along. I felt I had to clean, take care of the kids twenty-four hours, as well as work. When I asked him to help, he never did it right. He gets home earlier than I do, so when I get home, bone-tired, he gives me the housewife whine—'the dishwasher broke, the dog threw up'—that I long since stopped doing. I tried three Saturdays to have him cook. It never got in the oven. Or it got burned. Not a meal since that I haven't cooked myself. If anything goes wrong with the kids, it's my fault for being gone so much.

"The hard truth is that Ben always relied on me to make every decision—all he did was go to his job. I needed that power, I guess. And then I suddenly fell apart. I'm not a superwoman. I'm not a Good Mother who loves kids all the time. After my own kids were five, I lost interest in teaching nursery school. I always loved machines. I always fixed my own car. So I do that work now, which is dirty but well paid, and I pay to have the windows washed and the floors waxed by someone else.

"For the first time, I feel I could make enough money to support myself, I could get out of my marriage if I want to. I never felt that independent before. It makes a lot of difference. I was much more angry when I felt helplessly dependent on Ben."

Angela, a truly beautiful woman, a cross between Candice Bergen and Farrah Fawcett, is the most troubled. She has been married twice, moving up that traditional way for women. The second time she married her boss and had two babies. Now she has taken off to live with an eminent artist, like a print of *An Unmarried Woman* in reverse.

"The movement's passed me by. It just makes me mad that I'm so dependent on a man, but I'm not going to do anything about it. He's a painter, I'm nobody without him. I feel constricted, I feel that I should go out and earn, but something in me can't do it.

"I'm torn between the effort to make my house and my dinner table look charming and the feeling that none of this has any value. Fred takes no responsibility for anything but painting, all day long, in his studio. I take care of everything in our lives, the house, the garden, his kids and mine, the car, the bookkeeping, the entertaining. Twice, I've made the man utterly reliant on me, and when I take it away, the man collapses. You don't know which one is holding which up.

"But four times the last year, in the middle of fights about his not doing enough, Fred's asked me coldly, What is your contribution? After all, he contributes all the money. How do you answer that question—go into your dreary list, the shopping, the chauffeuring, setting the table for the dinner party, arranging the flowers? The trouble is, I'm not sure what I contribute. Sometimes I have the fantasy I'll end up a waitress at Schrafft's. Fifty years ago, I'd have been just fine, the great beauty, the great hostess. But now it's not enough."

Judy, who had stopped working when she had her first child, started an antique business after her second, and her husband, a photographer, now works at home.

"I was always angry at my husband. Nobody knew who should do what. We were always fighting over that schedule we worked out in our C-R group for equal time on housework. On nights he was on duty, I was off. You weren't supposed to go into the kitchen when you were 'off.' I was so intent on having time to do my own thing, I wouldn't respect his need not to be interrupted when he started working at home. We weren't spending any time together as a family.

"When I opened the shop, those other things stopped being such a chore. We don't decide it with a tape measure any more—the eating hours, bath time, housework time. It's hectic but more fun sharing it. I don't know how women do it all by themselves.

"You have to give up something. Maybe not having the house perfect, not having the dinner party perfect. Like we used to have a seder every year. I can't keep up this life style any more, spend days making the gefilte fish, the chicken soup, the matzo balls yourself. So now we have a cooperative seder. My mother makes the gefilte fish, my mother-in-law the dessert, my sister-in-law the matzo-ball soup, my sister the prune-and-sweet-potato pudding—no, my brother-in-law is doing that this year. And I fix the table and the trimmings and provide the wine. We've done it three years, and everyone loves it, tasting and showing off each other's dishes. I don't need it any more, everybody sitting around saying what a great cook, what a wonderful mother Judy is. It strengthens the family somehow when you stop constantly having to prove yourself the good wife.

"It's a funny thing, the contract, negotiating who does

what, the actual sharing of the chores—because I'm happier, and feeling independent, and not holding on to that importance, it's almost a floating back and forth between Ellis and me, not the hangdog accusatory thing—'Why do I have to do it all? You do it!' Now, it's just a job that has to be done between the two of us; whoever has the time handles it."

Liz, who was forty last week, remembers when she was angry at her husband and all men. At one point she cut her hair short and stopped wearing dresses and makeup altogether. She remembers how isolated she felt as a young suburban housewife and mother, and later in her superwoman years, the first woman ever on her very demanding job at a major news magazine. Then she rebelled at having to be superwoman. Two years ago, she took a leave from her job, and her husband, and spent a year at their vacation cottage, alone with her kids, to get to know them and figure out where she was going herself, before it was too late. She is back at work now on a part-time basis, but she's not sure she wants to be married full time, again.

"It makes such a difference once you make enough money, that you're not dependent. You can choose to be dependent, emotionally, if you want to be. But you don't have to be. If I got married to him again, I'd be afraid I'd fall into the old ways.

"I think we've all gotten so far, so fast, we're still insecure where we are, thinking it could all be taken away. So I fight not to give an inch or I'll lose it all.

"There was a fork in the road for women. It happened in our adult lives. Always before, you did it all through a man. Now, suddenly, you can do it on your own. We were so angry because we were too dependent on men. That's why we hated them.

"The housewife things women can't stand doing anymore, I now love doing. Maybe it's because I do have a choice now. It has struck me the last few years how much I cling to emptying the dishwasher, folding the clean laundry, keeping my car in tune. It grounds me in whatever else I'm doing.

I'm haunted by the women I work with who are thirty and thirty-five and are not having children, or are torn to the core about it. I had them without thinking about it, and I'm so thankful now I did. I am absolutely the richer for it. They ground your life, keep you in touch with the fundamentals."

It should be kept in mind that these women have more "choice" than most women today. Liz was able to take a leave from her job and work out a part-time arrangement because she was at the top of her very competitive profession. Paradoxically, she'd worked out a unique specialty for herself, dealing with domestic "life style" problems (formerly called "the womens' page") that the men and younger women on the news magazine disdained. Fred made enough money to pay all the bills himself—and to hire a housekeeper if Angela wanted to leave, as he occasionally reminded her. Judy's husband could work at home, his schedule, like hers with her own shop, being more flexible than those of most women and men who work today.

But that same shadow of the idealized family of the past— that compulsion to be a Perfect Mother left over from excessive female dependence—keeps many women *and* the experts from coming to grips with the new problems realistically.

It outrages me to find psychologists today still exhorting women to that excessive Perfect Motherhood, still discussing the family as if women could "choose" to stay home and take care of their children all day every day for ten, fifteen years, if they only weren't so selfish and so seduced by those terrible feminists into having ambitions of their own.

In her book *Every Child's Birthright—In Defense of Mothering*, the psychoanalyst Selma Fraiberg tries to make a case that every mother must stay home with her children, full time, for at least ten years, unless she is rich enough to hire a full-time governess for her child. She ignores the fact that the great majority of the more than 58 percent of the mothers of school-age children now working, and the more than 45 percent of working mothers of preschool-age children, cannot quit their jobs and stay home—if the family is to survive financially.

The real questions that the experts need to ask now, and to find answers for, are the how, what and why of structuring parenting time. "Quality, not quantity" is insufficient rhetoric; we must ask now how much parenting, when and how can it be best shared between parents, and with other substitutes for those aunts and grandmothers who no longer live down the block? It is no longer possible to go back to that "ideal" family that maybe never was, and surely never can be again, for solutions. Dr. Fraiberg would not go back herself, from her fine, well-paying professional position as a psychoanalyst who is also a mother. If she is indeed ready to take arms "in defense of mothering" today, let her concern herself with the problems of families where the fact that mother and father share the earning burden is an irreversible, necessary source of *strength* to the family. Or with the supports desperately needed for mothering (or fathering) in single-parent families. Let her concern herself with institutional changes and social innovations which are needed now so men and women can better share the burdens—and joys—of parenting.

For instance, Dr. Sheila Kamerman, professor of social policy and planning at the Columbia University School of Social Work, and author of *Parenting in an Unresponsive Society*, investigated the child-care arrangements of 200 white and black mothers in Westchester County, New York, half of them professional or executive women, the other half low-paid unskilled workers, all of them working full time, with at least one child under the age of five to care for. According to Dr. Kamerman, their children "may experience three, four or even more kinds of care in an average week, as they spend a part of the day in nursery school, another part with a family day-care mother (or two different such women) and are brought to and from these services by a parent, a neighbor, or some other person."

Apart from the difficulty of obtaining good child care, her two-and-one-half-year Working Mothers Research Project concluded that "the greatest difficulty for these women is the rigidity and unresponsiveness of the work place. Employers have made little effort to adapt the demands of the work place to the growing segment of the labor force made up increasingly of women with children—and the husbands of these women. Beginning hours at a job often conflict with conventional school-opening times. The lack of any benefits for maternity leaves, or for sick leaves to care for an ill child, creates financial and emotional stress for families dependent on the income of two wage earners."

"Families manage in a variety of ways," says Kamerman. "In one family, parents work different shifts, thus sharing child care between them. A second uses a complicated amalgam of nursery school, kindergarten, the help of a relative, a family day-care mother, and the mother of one child's schoolmate, to assure adequate care for their two preschoolers while both parents work. A third mother says her problem is what to do when her two-year-old is ill and can't go to his day-care center. A fourth has used a succession of five different family day-care mothers to care for her eleven-month-old baby since she returned to work four weeks after giving birth, unable to stay home longer because she desperately needed the income, and her job provided no maternity benefits. A fifth worries about emergencies when her child-care arrangements break down for some reason. A sixth says the real crisis is when school is closed. And the list of problems— and the complicated solutions—gets longer."

But the most stunning finding of this study was "the increased value these women place on their family," as they juggle the demands of job and home. Further, the husbands of these working mothers are reported to be "sharing home and family responsibilities more when their wives work, especially child care." With less leisure time, they had to eliminate many previous activities and relationships. But "family time" emerged as more important than ever. These harassed working mothers and their husbands place more importance and reliance on family "help, support and companionship" not only with each other and their own children but with their parents and other relatives than do comparable families conforming to the traditional housewife–breadwinner-husband image.

When we look at what is really happening in the family, it becomes clearer now that the women's movement has been merely the beginning of something much more basic than a few women getting good (men's) jobs. Paradoxically, as more women enter the workplace and share the breadwinning, their family bonds and values—human values as opposed to material ones—seem to strengthen.

It also seems clear to me that we will never solve the new problems and bring about the changes in the workplace and child-care options so necessary for the well-being of families if their only supporters and beneficiaries are women. The need for such innovations becomes increasingly urgent as more and more women enter the workplace, harassed by those new problems as mothers, facing these new choices. But the solutions will come about only because more and more *men* demand them, too—not to "help" the women, but because of their own new problems and needs and choices, as fathers and for themselves as men.

But even women who have moved beyond reaction and are seeing the family as a new frontier of women's liberation despair of men joining them there. A somewhat bitter Indiana newscaster put it this way: "Where are the men for women like us, men who can deal with women like us, when they've grown up with mothers and wives who waited on them? What am I going to do, wait forever for my Prince Charming?

"At the moment, I feel like women are ahead of men, and it's a lonely thing. We still have to deal with men who want to control us in the old way. The men are beginning to collapse. If their sense of identity was based on feeling superior to us, they're in trouble.

"Is the new man going to come soon enough for us? Or before women just give up the need for men? It's not women versus men any more—the anger's gone. But there can't be that flow between us until the men stop playing games, too. Women have made the big leap; men are still stuck. Men have to break out of their mold next."

Why were we so angry at the men? Were they truly our enemy, is it they who stand in our way, in the family, in the world? We had to change the conditions that gave them all the power in society, of course, but a lot of our anger came from our very dependence on them. It was sometimes easier to blame them than to risk competing and failing, ourselves. Did we exaggerate their power when we were not in touch with our own? Do we, can we still demand that men be stronger than we are, now that we're affirming our own strength and have stopped playing weak? Are they threatened by our new power—or just afraid that we won't need them?

What surprises are in store for men, and for us, as we give up some of that manipulating control of the family we once used to keep them emotional babies, dependent on us—protecting them from the grounding, warming, human realities of daily life? What will their real strength look like, when men are allowed to take off their own masks and be sensitive and yearning and vulnerable? And even if we no longer need men to take care of us, to define our whole existence as in the past—just *because* we are no longer that dependent, can't we now more freely admit that we still need and want men to love, to have babies with, to share parenting and chores and joys and economic burdens and adventures in new kinds of families and homes? But can women love, and be loved, as truly equal to men? What do men really want?

I believe that a quiet movement has been going on among American men for some years. If I am right, the new questions men are asking about their own lives will converge with women's new questions in the second stage—and provide a new power and energy for solutions that seem impossible today.

4 The Quiet Movement of American Men

 It is nothing like the women's movement, and probably never will be. Each man seems to be struggling with it quietly—at twenty-five or thirty-five, or before it is too late, at forty-five or fifty. It is a change not yet fully visible, not clearly identified or understood by the experts and rarely spoken about by men themselves. Nobody is marching. Most men are turned off by the "men's lib" groups, which try to copy women's. With men there is no explosion of anger, no enemy to rage against, no list of grievances or demands for benefits and opportunities clearly valuable and previously denied, as with women. And yet I believe that American men are at the edge of a momentous change in their very identity as men, going beyond the change catalyzed by the women's movement.

It is a deceptively quiet movement, a shifting in direction, a saying "no" to old patterns, a searching for new values, a struggling with basic questions that each man seems to be dealing with alone. He may be going through the same outward motions that have always defined men's lives—making it, or struggling to make it, in the corporate rat race, the office, the plant, college, the ball park; making it with women; getting married; having children. Or he may be deciding not to get married, or thinking in a new way about

112

having children, or no longer really trying to make it in traditional terms. He is not issuing a public statement. He is just grappling with private questions: success, promotion, senior partner, vice-president, $65,000 a year—is that what he really wants out of life? Will he ever get it? What will it be worth? What kind of a man is he anyhow, asking questions like this? Other men are satisfied with their lives, aren't they? But what does he want out of life for himself? How does he fulfill himself as a man?

Asking these questions about himself, he doesn't feel so angry at women. He feels awkward, isolated, confused. Yet he senses that something is happening with men, something large and historic, and he wants to be part of it. He carries the baby in his backpack, shops at the supermarket on Saturday, bakes his own bread with a certain showing-off quality.

It's happened to some men because of the economy: layoffs from jobs that looked secure, as in the auto industry; company takeovers, budget cuts; a dead end suddenly in a career that he had put his all into for years. Or, after sweating it through to the Ph.D., no jobs in his field. Or making it to the top at forty or forty-five and then having to figure out what to do next—fight off the younger men coming up, or join another company?

Some men just know they don't want to be like their fathers, or like those senior partners, who have heart attacks at fifty—but they don't know what other way there is to be.

It started for many men almost unwillingly, as a response to the women's movement. Women changing their own lives forced men or made it possible for men to change theirs. Some men seem to be making these moves quite independently of women. But they sense, we sense, it's related somehow. The rhetoric of sexual politics that characterized the first stage of the women's movement seemed to demand a hostile stance from the men. But that rhetoric and the response it elicited obscured the real reasons that these changes were threatening to some men, and also obscured the fact that many men supported, and felt a surprising relief about, the women's movement.

At first glance, all it looked like was endless arguments about his doing his share of the housework, the cooking, the cleaning, the dishes, taking out the garbage, scrubbing out the toilet bowl and mopping the kitchen floor without leaving streaks; or about his responsibility for taking care of the children, changing diapers, getting them to bed, into snow-suits, to the park, to the pediatrician. These disputes arose because it was no longer *automatic* that her job was to take care of the house and the kids and all the other details of life, and that his job was to support everyone. Now she was working to support them, too.

But that wasn't the entire issue. Even if she didn't have a job outside the home, she suddenly had to be treated as a person too, as he was. She had a right to her own life and interests. He could help with the kids and the house at night, or on weekends. (The arguments over the housework were worse when she didn't have a job.)

He felt wronged, injured. He had been working so hard to support her and the kids and now he was her "oppressor," a "male chauvinist pig," if he didn't scrub all the pots and pans to boot. "You make dinner," she said. "I'm going to my de-sign class." He felt scared when she walked out like that. If she didn't need him for her identity, her status, her sense of importance, if she was going to get all that for herself, if she could support herself and have a life independent of him, wouldn't she stop loving him? Why would she stay with him? Wouldn't she just leave? So he was supposed to be the big male oppressor, right? How could he admit the big secret— that maybe he needed her more than she needed him? That he felt like a baby when he became afraid she would leave? That he suddenly didn't know what he felt, what he was *supposed* to feel—as a man?

I believe much of the hostility men express toward women comes from their very dependence on our love, from those needy feelings that men aren't supposed to have—just as the excesses of our attacks on our male "oppressors" stemmed from our dependence on men. That old, excessive dependence (which was supposed to be natural in women) made us feel we had to be more independent than any man in order to be able to move at all. Our explosion of rage and our attacks on men, however justified, often masked our own timidity and fear of risking ourselves in a complex, competitive world, in ways never required of us before.

And the more a man pretended to a dominant, cool, masculine superiority he didn't really feel—the more he was forced to carry the burden alone of supporting the whole family against the rough odds of that grim outside economic world—the more threatened and the more hostile he felt.

Sam, an aerospace engineer in Seattle, told me that the period when his wife "tried to be just a housewife" was the worst time in his marriage.

"It was not only her staying home and losing confidence in herself, and the resentment and hostility against me after she joined the consciousness-raising group. It was her loss of confidence in me. If you decide you're going to stay home and be taken care of and you have to depend for everything on this guy, you get afraid—*Can he do it?* It all depended on me, and I was in a constant panic, but I'd say, 'Don't worry.'

"Susie was tired of her job anyhow. It wasn't such a great job—neither is mine if you want to know—but she had an excuse, wanting to stay home with her kids. The pressure was on me, hanging by my fingernails, barely paying the bills each month. But it was crazy. Here I was, not knowing where the next check was coming from after the government contract ran out, suddenly supporting a wife and kids all by myself.

"It's better now that she's working and bringing some money in. But I don't just *help* with the kids now. She has to be at work before I do, so I give them breakfast and get them off to school. The nights she works late, I make dinner, help with the homework, and get everyone to bed. But I don't feel so panicky now—and she isn't attacking me any more."

Phil, a doctor in his thirties who started out to be a surgeon but who now has a small-town family practice in New Jersey, talks to me as he makes pickles, with his kids running around underfoot in the country kitchen that is next to his office.

"I was going to be a surgeon, supercool, in my gleaming white uniform," he says, "the man my mother wanted me to be but I knew I wasn't. So I married a nurse and she stayed home to raise our children, and she was supposed to fulfill herself through my career. It didn't work for either of us. I went through tortures before every operation. I couldn't sleep.

"Then Ellen started turning against me. I always said the children needed her at home, full-time mothering. Maybe because *I* was so scared inside. Maybe she didn't have the nerve to try to do her own thing professionally. All she seemed to want was revenge on me, as if she were locked into some kind of sexual battle against me, playing around, looking elsewhere for true love.

"She got into a women's consciousness-raising group, and I even joined a men's one. At home, I'd grovel, the male chauvinist pig repenting, not letting on how hurt, angry, offended I felt. The worst was when our little girl tried to be as tough as Mummy and went *yuk* at every word I said.

"When Ellen finally got up the nerve to do her own thing —she's a nurse-midwife now—it was a relief. The other stuff stopped. She could come back to being my wife. I'm coming out of this, redefining myself, no longer in terms of success or failure as a doctor (though I still am a doctor) and not as superior or inferior to her. It was a blow to my ego, but what a relief, to take off my surgical mask! I'm discovering my own value in the family.

"Now that I'm not so hurt and angry and afraid that she'll leave me, I can see that it's a hell of a fight for a woman to be seen as a person. I think she's been hiding from herself the fear of accomplishing anything on her own so she made me the villain. Well, I'm happy now to take on the kids while she practices her profession, though every time she goes out of town, I practically wet my pants. I tell my own patients now, the mothers, don't make the kids that dependent on you. That's what my mother did to me. I was so afraid of those messy, needy feelings I couldn't get away from, even as a surgeon. You know, it's as hard for me to feel like a person as it is for her. We couldn't either of us get that from each other."

The change is harder to discern among men because men have a harder time talking about their feelings than women do. They certainly don't talk about their feelings to other men. It's part of the masculine mystique—the definition of man by his "score," competing against other men—that he constantly keep his guard up. And after all, since men have the power and position in society that women are making all the fuss about, why should men want to change unless women make them do so? When men began talking to me about their own new questions (and some refused—which never happened with women—and some just couldn't seem to talk about their feelings, only about abstractions like the economy or the state of the nation), it reminded me of "the problem that has no name" as I heard it from the women I was interviewing for *The Feminine Mystique* twenty years ago, when, each one feeling she was alone, American women were poised unconsciously on the brink of the women's movement.

"Maybe men feel more need to pretend," says a Detroit sales engineer, temporarily laid off, struggling to take "equal responsibility" for the kids and the house, now that his wife has gone to work in a department store. "When I used to see a man on the street with his children on a weekday, I assumed he was unemployed, a loser. Now, it's so common— daddies with their children, at ease. Now, even if a man is unemployed, like I am right now, well, that job is not what makes me a man. I'm not just a breadwinner. I'm a person, I have feelings myself."

With all the attention on the women's movement these past fifteen years, it hasn't been noticed that many of the old bases for men's identity have become shaky. If being a man is defined, for example, as being dominant, superior, as *not-be-ing-a-woman*, that definition becomes an illusion hard to maintain when most of the important work of society no longer requires brute muscular force. The Vietnam war probably was the beginning of the end of the hunter-caveman, gun-toting he-man mystique.

The signs that machismo was dying in the U.S. appeared about the same time as the women's movement emerged in the sixties. The long-haired young men, and their elders imitating them or clubbing them down from repressed envy, began saying they didn't have to be tight-lipped, crewcut or poker-faced like John Wayne to be a man. They didn't have to be all-powerful, superior to everyone in the world, and to napalm all the children in Vietnam and Cambodia and the green leaves off the trees, to prove they were men. They could be sensitive, tender, compassionate, they didn't have to have big muscles, when there were no bears to kill, they could admit they were afraid and they could even cry—and they were still men, their own men.

Books were written such as *The Greening of America*, and hippies played their guitars, chanting "Make love, not war." And the young men said they were not going to live their whole lives for the dollar like their fathers, about the same time as the young women said they were not going to spend their lives as housewife "service stations" like their mothers. How the adventurous good life could be lived on other terms wasn't quite clear. It didn't have to be, while the counterculture was sustained by the allowances from Daddy.

But all that supposedly stopped a while ago, with the end of the Vietnam War, inflation, recession, the job crunch and the energy crisis. Or did it? At the dawn of the eighties, the signs of a quiet, complex, continuing movement among men

emerged not just as counterculture, but as shifting currents
in the mainstream, converging on the women's movement
for the second stage. The men I have been interviewing
around the country these past months are not hippies playing games on those allowances from Daddy. They are members of the college classes in which everyone wanted to be a
lawyer, a doctor, an MBA. They are the men who fought in
Vietnam, or went to graduate school to stay out of the war,
or they are assembly-line workers whose line has stopped.

Vietnam was somehow the watershed. If men stop defining themselves by going to war or getting power from jobs
women can't have, what is left? What does it mean to be a
man, except not-being-a-woman—being physically superior,
able to beat all the other men up? The fact is, when a man
admits those "messy, needy feelings" that men as well as
women have—and which that brutal, brittle machismo is
supposed to hide, but only makes worse—he can't *play* the
same kind of man any more.

Tony, who lives now on the Outer Banks of North Carolina, was a pilot in Vietnam when it started for him.

"I was a captain, coming up for major. I had all the medals, could have gone on for twenty years in the Air Force.
Sitting up there over Nam, the commander, under heavy fire,
the guys screaming into the mikes, the bombers and fighters
moving in, me giving the orders, I was caught up in it, crazy-
wild, excited. And then I woke up one day and found myself
clicking my empty gun at civilians. I knew I had to get out.
The next mission, sitting up there, it felt for real, and for the
first time, I was frightened. It's so heavy, the medals, the
games, and then suddenly realizing that you are dropping
napalm on real people."

He "could fly any piece of machinery," so he took a job
with an airline. "All I wanted was security," he says. "After
one year I was furloughed because the company was having
financial difficulties. There was no security. So I came back
to this town where I grew up and took a job as a school-
teacher, working with seventh and eighth graders who were

reading at the second-grade level. It was the 'reading lab,' the pits, the bottom, and a woman's job. It's the hardest job I've ever done, teaching those kids, and it gets the least respect. Flying a 323,000-pound Lockheed Starlifter can't compare." As a pilot, Tony made $34,000 a year; as a teacher, he makes $12,000.

"But maybe now," he says, "with the ladies moving in and picking up some of the financial slack—my wife works for a florist, and as a waitress, nights—a guy can say 'I'm not going to get much of anywhere, with the money anyhow—how much of it is really going to rub off on me? Why don't I do something really worthwhile from a human point of view?' Now with the ladies out earning, it frees a man from being strapped down to just one job for his whole life. After school, I take out my boat, which I built myself, and if I make some extra money fishing, fine. But there are more important things in life than the dollar bill."

The shakiness of the economy, belying the dream of limitless affluence, is accelerating the change that began with Vietnam. Certain large signs of this movement are reported in the newspapers almost daily now. Corporation heads complain that young executives are refusing to accept transfers because of "the family." Economists and government officials bewail increased absenteeism and declining productivity among workers—blue collar, white collar, executives, even government bureaucrats. In the past ten years, more than half the West Point graduates have resigned as army career officers, as the first women graduated from West Point in 1980, take up careers as army officers. College and graduate-school enrollments are dropping off among men (as they continue to increase among women) and not just because it isn't necessary for men to evade the draft any more.

In many respects it seems as if men and women are moving in exactly opposite directions. Where women seem to be moving out of the home to fulfill themselves in men's world of work, men seem to be disentangling themselves from definition by success in the work world and shifting toward a new definition of themselves in the family and other new dimensions of self-fulfillment.

In surveys before 1968, when public-opinion analyst Daniel Yankelovich asked college students, "Do you believe that hard work will always pay off?" seven out of ten said "Yes." By 1971, some 67 percent said "No." As we go into the 1980s, Yankelovich is finding that a majority of adult American men no longer seek or are satisfied by conventional job success. Only one out of every five men now says that work means more to him than leisure. More than half of American men say that work is no longer their major source of satisfaction.

For men, "self-fulfillment has become severed from success," Yankelovich says. "Men have come to feel that success on the job is not enough to satisfy their yearnings for self-fulfillment, and they are reaching out for something more and for something different. . . . Somehow, the conventional systems no longer satisfy their deepest psychological needs nor nourish their self-esteem, nor fulfill their cravings for the 'full, rich life.' "

In my travels around the country during the past few years, I've begun to notice surprising numbers of men in their twenties, thirties, early forties, and a few in their fifties, leaving or working only part time at conventional jobs and professions, or still climbing the conventional ladder but seeking their personal satisfaction and control over their lives apart from the jobs that used to define them. Their families have become "self-fulfilling" to these men, as they take personal part in the parenting, sometimes even taking most of it over from wives who are newly ambitious in their own careers.

The enormous response to the movie *Kramer vs. Kramer* is a sign of this shift. Meryl Streep, feeling like a nonperson as a housewife and not seen as a person by her husband, leaves her child with him, to find herself. Dustin Hoffman, a hollow, go-getter adman, discovers all kinds of new feelings and strengths as he is forced to take daily responsibility for his little boy. His life with the child becomes more important to him than his life with the corporation. He stops going to the bar with the boys after work, stops toadying up to the boss—and loses his job. He "becomes a man," as one reviewer put it, by doing the daily human chores of life, taking the kind of responsibility for his child that women have taken all along. But she, finding herself in a $30,000 a year (!) job, comes back and wants the child now. She wins him away from poor Dustin Hoffman but voluntarily gives him back to that tender daddy, who, she realizes, is a better parent now than she, the child's mother.

It is remarkable enough that short, sensitive, nervous, loser Dustin Hoffman should replace tall, strong, silent, winner John Wayne as American hero because of his tender prowess as parent! That's a feminist triumph, surely, even if Meryl Streep emerges as a bit of a heavy in contrast. Of course, most American wives don't go from feeling like "nonpersons" to $30,000-a-year jobs. But this movie truly reflects and underscores the malaise of American men whose jobs don't give enough meaning to their lives—don't make them "feel like men." Why do so many men today buy pickup trucks, hardly necessary for their white-collar jobs? Why do so many men jog relentlessly, racing against themselves, before or after work, seeking new marathons to enter? Why do increasing numbers of men seek custody of their children after divorce? Why, in 1981, do three out of every four gourmet dinner parties suddenly seem to be cooked, soup to mousse, by men? (A number of my women colleagues have called this to my attention. Surely the men aren't cooking with such zeal just because women are working now.)

For one thing, explains economist Eli Ginzberg, "good jobs"—jobs offering above-average wages, fringe benefits, regular employment and opportunities for advancement—have become scarce. In the last twenty-five years, more than three out of five new jobs are in retail trade or services where "many jobs are part-time and wages extraordinarily low." These jobs, which are the jobs women are flocking into, don't make men "feel like men." But even policemen now complain about "the ever-growing volume of paper work, about the lack of appreciation for extra effort, about departmental policies which value cost reductions and administrative procedures more than the good job done." Laid off from such jobs now, men who can collect unemployment insurance and/or whose working wives bring in some money from those service jobs (which are not as vulnerable to the ups and downs of the economy as production and executive jobs) seek other ways to "feel like men."

In *Breaktime*, a controversial study of men "living without work in a nine-to-five world," Bernard Lefkowitz reports a 71 percent increase in the number of working-aged men who have left the labor force since 1968 and who are not looking for work. According to Lefkowitz, the "stop-and-go pattern of work" is becoming the predominant pattern, rather than the lifetime jobs and careers men used to pursue both for economic security and for their masculine identity. "In the depression of the 30s," says Lefkowitz, "men were anxious because they were not working. In the 70s, men became anxious because their work was not paying off in the over-all economic security they had expected."

"I thought seriously of killing myself," says a St. Louis man who was forced to resign at the age of fifty when the company he headed was taken over by a large conglomerate. "I saved up the arsenic pills I take for my heart condition. How could I live without that company to run, my office, my staff, six hundred employees, the wheeling and dealing? But then I realized how much of it I'd really hated: the constant worry, getting in at 6 A.M. to read the reports of six vice-presidents, fighting the union to keep wages down, and being hated, knuckling under to people I despised to get accounts. The only good thing was knowing I'd made it to president of a company when my father never got past store clerk. Now I want to work for myself, to live, enjoy the sunsets, and raise begonias. But my kids are gone now, and my wife started her career late, and all she wants is to get ahead in the agency."

It is not only, or even mainly, "losers" making such shifts in values and life style, if not actual jobs. In a *Playboy* survey in 1979, the men from the most oppressed backgrounds were the only group whose main concern was "getting ahead," making more money. The majority of the men polled, age eighteen to forty-nine, valued "personal growth," "self-fulfillment," "love," and "family life" more than making more money and "getting ahead."

But the hold of the old success drive, the competitiveness that always defined men before, hasn't disappeared overnight. It makes for uneasiness, even for men wanting to live by new values.

A young man in Chicago refuses an extra assignment, which would mean working nights and traveling on weekends, on top of his regular job. It doesn't matter that it will probably lead to a big promotion. "We're having another child," he tells his boss, "and I'm committed to sharing the responsibilities at home because my wife's going to law school at night. It hasn't and won't interfere with my job— you were more than satisfied with my last report. But I'm not taking on anything extra. My family is more important to me."

"That man isn't going to get far," his puzzled boss tells a colleague. "Too bad. He was the pick of the litter."

The colleague asks, "What if they all start acting like that? Where are we going to find the men to run the economy, for God's sake, if they all start putting their families first?"

This change among men goes beyond families and is not always triggered by or linked to sharing the child-rearing. Some of my sociologist colleagues at Columbia University who are studying "Sex Roles and Social Change" suspect that the supposed increase in male homosexuality and/or celibacy has less to do with changes in "sexual preference" than this new male focus on "self-fulfillment" and "personal growth." "If he marries and thus entertains the possibility of having children, he will lose the independence he now values for travel and new personal interests, and will have to take on economic burdens that make him dependent on a job and a boss," Cynthia Epstein speculates, after talking with some male students.

"They figure that with a woman, even if she is working, sooner or later she's going to want to have a baby, and there goes the good life they want. They aren't about to risk becoming economic drones." Of course, she points out, there is no data base to confirm the impression that there are increasing numbers of young men moving to homosexuality or celibacy rather than marriage. But that, indeed, is the impression —and the complaint of—the young women in their peer group. Their elders, too, join in, ranting and raving about the "me generation" and the "culture of narcissism."

But the best evidence that something is basically changing among men comes from the business world. Last June a surprising change emerged at the thirtieth reunion of the famous Harvard Business School class of '49—"The Class the Dollars Fell On," *Fortune* called it five years ago, when a quarter of the class were company presidents or board chairmen and 16 percent were millionaires. Now these men who have made it to the top of their corporations and professions were found to be doing more job switching than during the first two decades after graduation. More than a fourth had changed jobs in the last five years, a few to the nonprofit sector, most of them to smaller businesses, and many to starting their own businesses.

One Florida bank president, Simeon Wooten, went back to school so that he could go into teaching—"switching from the sailboat to the library while his wife switched from Junior League to real estate broker." Said Wooten: "Obviously, our living standard is lower in a material way. It doesn't seem to matter much because, in an intellectual way, life is much more stimulating."

At the School of Business Administration of the University of Southern California, James O'Toole, former director of the Presidential Task Force on Working America, was incredulous when a number of his brightest MBAs turned down solid middle-level positions with General Motors, recession notwithstanding. He discovered that only half of his students were looking to climb upward in business in the traditional American way. "The other half hold new values. They could get a job in New York or Detroit, but they won't. And they won't talk about it. They keep it to themselves. Ten years ago, the job was the most important thing. Now, something else. They won't take a job that doesn't give them what they want."

Lately, every few days I've been noticing news items like the following: "Smaller Retailers Luring Big-City Executives" (*New York Times*, Nov. 5, 1979). It seems that executives in their mid-thirties and early forties are leaving big-time department stores in New York, Indianapolis, Kansas City, Cincinnati and Los Angeles to take jobs in smaller towns—Knoxville, Tennessee; Johnstown, Pennsylvania; Wichita, Kansas; and Bloomington, Illinois. They are not getting more money. Most are simply "happy to come live and work in a smaller city." Says a managerial recruiting specialist: "From a personal standpoint, living costs are cheaper and the quality of life is better. From a professional standpoint, there's more room for creativity." (The 1980 census shows that the largest increase in population is now in small towns, not cities and their suburbs.)

Even in the midst of the economic turbulence of 1980, an adamant union demand in contract negotiations with AT&T was, for the first time, a voice for the workers in "quality of work life." As important as increase in pay and pensions, in this time of inflation, was the telephone workers' rebellion at the dehumanizing policing and control of every second of their time on the job.

The men Lefkowitz describes in *Breaktime* talked of their feeling of "renewal" in their sense of themselves as men, living without a nine-to-five job. They even enjoyed what they called "passivity" without shame: they expressed a willingness to "let things happen without planning for them," without measuring each act in terms of what it would get them. "Passivity was not weakness but a state of receptivity, an openness to experience." Above all, they felt a new "wholeness" now that they were experiencing themselves more vividly in relation to children, friends, and open-ended new interests and activities, undertaken for their own pleasure and growth. "They had recovered their capacity for amazement, a quality they said they had lost in the work world." They described their new feeling of "wholeness" as "the pleasure the prisoner takes in walking across an open field after years of being locked up."

The "work protester" in the eighties, like the draft protester in the sixties, is not cynical. The draft resister protested the war in Vietnam because he *cared* about America—and about himself. The work protester, as Lefkowitz puts it, "cares about his work, wants it to make a difference. By pulling out, the work protester stops paying taxes; he has subtracted his labor from the gross national product, and, either by choice or necessity, he will diminish his consumption. Now that's saying: 'Hell, no, I won't go!' "

The bitterness of the man who actually does break out of that binding male corporate role usually passes rather quickly, Lefkowitz says. The anger, in fact, helps the men disengage themselves from the old imprisoning molds, just as woman's rage helped free her from the constriction of her housewife role. For the man, bitterness is replaced by a certain serenity: "Now I can concentrate on myself. Now I get my turn." But if men remain locked in that bitterness—and some do, just as some women have remained locked in reaction—they substitute "fantasies of endless adolescence" as Lefkowitz says, or evasion of adult responsibility, for new moves to wholeness.

The trouble is, once they disengage themselves from the old patterns of American masculinity and success—John Wayne, Lindbergh, John Kennedy—men today are just as lost for lack of role models as women are. This explains the nostalgia for *The Right Stuff* in Tom Wolfe's book about the last daredevil test pilots, the early astronauts, and the desperate gropings of Norman Mailer for a final heroism of man in the death chamber (*The Executioner's Song*), and the appeal of Broadway playwrights or moviemakers who show men incurably diseased, in the iron lung, paralyzed from the neck down, taking control of their own death, at least, as in *Whose Life Is It Anyway?*, or in *All That Jazz*.

The shift that men now secretly long for, and resist, surely explains the surprising appeal of *The Great Santini*, a movie about a Marine colonel, lost without a war to fight, driving his sensitive son to senseless, self-destructive competition on the basketball court, terrified by the soft feelings he does not know how to express, at home, finally, with his family. Some critics felt the movie was flawed by the ending, sending the hero up alone to skydive through the moonlit clouds and stay with the defective machine until it crashes. The real ending was a scene where the son pursues his drunken father through the night, finding him on the ground in tears, and vowing to confront him by saying "I love you, Daddy" night and day, until he drops that machismo mask and lets himself feel.

But confronting feelings is still an unthinkable danger for many American men. Lonely death, fighting phantoms in the sky, staying, in an exhibition of senseless heroics, with a flawed machine, to the end, may seem preferable to some Santinis.

In the movies it begins to seem as if the men have to separate themselves from the women—and even make them into heavies, getting rid of machismo by projecting it onto their wives—in order to affirm their own denied tender, nurturing side. Why, in *Ordinary People*, does Mary Tyler Moore have to be such a monstrous, cold, unloving, rigid, all-controlling bitch-caricature for Donald Sutherland to bring out his sensitive love for his son?

Recently male novelists like John Updike, Saul Bellow, Norman Mailer, Thomas Pynchon and Philip Roth have created "heroes" who go to desperate lengths of violent, or covert, aggression against women because they so fear their own vulnerability and passivity—those "female" qualities men have despised and suppressed in themselves and then feared, and exaggerated into evil powers, as they project them onto women. (Similarly, some women who still are afraid of their own aggression exaggerate the feared-hated power of men. Without denying the progress of the women's movement in enabling women to protect themselves against rape, and to demand police protection without humiliation, I suspect that the current obsession of some feminists with pornography and rape plays into, and is itself an acting out of, such reaction and projection.)

The proliferation of hard and soft porn escalating the depersonalization of human sexuality and the denigration of women in fantasies of brutal, sadistic violence against women, and even the increased incidence of rape itself, is surely the most extreme, last-ditch stand of desperately threatened machismo. For it is becoming almost impossible for men to evade much longer their own "feminine" side. The big muscles in work, the big stick in war, the feigned dominance over women themselves are all threatened now. But the equality and personhood of women must ultimately lead to the liberation of that buried side of men's own personalities. (The sadomasochistic perversion of sexuality was at least in part a byproduct of women's economic subjugation to men. No longer forced to turn their aggressive energy against their own bodies, or eroticize it in sexual masochism, why should feminists now wallow in that last ditch of male reaction, conducting tours of Forty-second Street in the name of "Women Against Pornography"? Is this a last ditch reaction of feminists, secretly yearning for that old masochism beneath their shaky newfound independence, or a new version of female machismo, identifying, in reverse, with the worst, most brutal aspects of male sadism, rather than affirming their own female strength?)

Conversely, in the current fictional "revolt against masculinity," as one critic calls it, male authors project heroes like

Garp, who retreat even further from traditional maleness, questing after a woman in shining armor who will accept, even thrive on, their passivity.

If, indeed, these phenomena of changing sex roles of both men and women are a massive, evolutionary development, as I believe they are, their convergence is almost bound to be marked by contradictory reactions, especially in the transition stage. When women become "liberated" from sexual passivity and masochism, and the complete economic and psychic dependence on men which underlies that, they may, in reaction, or fear that their own soft feelings will make them too "dependent" on men again, start treating *them* as sex objects.

The eminent psychologist Dr. Jane Loevinger, of Washington University in St. Louis, has observed in her test data that young college women now treat sex "objectively," counting up orgasmic scores, whereas young men yearn for more "feelings." On the other hand, wives no longer dependent on husbands for all their identity and economic support begin to demand more "feelings" and sexual satisfaction. Deluged with sexual information from the mass media, they *notice*, and even say so, when their men are not good lovers. Men, who used to be the measure of all things, may indeed shrivel up or flee from the experience of being measured themselves. There is no data base for claims of increased male impotence as a result of women's liberation but it would not be a surprising phenomenon in a period of reaction. As woman's reaction to machismo was frigidity (even when she seemed to submit), so man's reaction to female machismo may be impotence—or flight from submission to that possibly humiliating measure.

Without even resorting to case histories—and the evidence in the exploding sex-therapy industry, where wives are dragging husbands for "help" (not the other way around)— art, both high and popular, records these phenomena. Does the "urban cowboy" negate Dustin Hoffman, or are they merely opposite symptoms of the same phenomenon? As the balance of power shifts, and women demand at least equal *feelings* from men (if not those excessive demands of transitional reaction), men who remain locked in the old narrow masks, or don't dare risk expressing their own feelings, may truly be driven to desperate excesses of machismo. A cartoonist shows an "urban cowboy" at a bar, telling the woman next to him he's going to cuss and spit, and hit her if he feels like it, and she's going to take it and like it—'cause he's a man. She looks at him, more in amusement than outrage, and walks out of the bar. "It worked for John Travolta!" he shrugs, miserably.

In a more elevated vein, the eminent art critic John Russell devotes a full page in *The New York Times* Arts and Leisure Section (February 1981) to "The Retreat of Manhood as Mirrored in the Arts." "Whatever happened to men?" asks Russell, pointing out that the only "compelling male presences" on the current stage are a mass murderer and a freak. In plays, movies, painting, sculpture, even opera, Russell traces the decline of man from powerful hero to whining baby, and the emergence of triumphal, free-standing woman.

"It's a strange business," Russell muses. "Men were big in ancient Egypt, big in Greece and Rome, big in the Middle Ages, big in the Renaissance. You only have to look at the history of art to see that men were once the measure of all things. Their physical proportions were ideal. Our notions of wisdom, justice, regularity and endurance were man-based, man-oriented, man-regulated. Great architecture was predicated on a man's reach, a man's height and a man's stride. 'Man-sized' was a compliment. 'Manliness' was a digest of all virtues. God had made man in his own image, and had done a great job."

Hamlet, Othello and Lear, the heroes of Racine and Corneille, Goethe, Verdi, Tolstoi (Vronsky riding his beloved horse in the steeplechase), Michelangelo's David—"these were centered human beings, one and all. But then, around 100 years ago, man began to run out of manhood." While Nietzsche ranted on about the concept of the superman (reaction, 1880 style), "the news from the front line was that man was in trouble wherever you looked"—from John the Baptist, served up on a platter, like dessert, in Strauss's *Salomé*, or regressing into childhood in Ibsen and O'Neill, to blubbering Willy Loman in *Death of a Salesman*, and Tennessee Williams' pretty, castrated "Sweet Bird of Youth." The most vivid metaphors Russell cites are Henry Moore's narrow, attenuated skeletal statues of men compared to his "doughty and all-enduring" strong women.

Regarding the visual arts especially, Russell repeats what I have heard lately from many art dealers and scholars: the new measures of creative imagination are coming from women. "The creativity of women in the 1980s is one of the great incontrovertible facts of life. . . . [It] operates on terrain, and in terms, that have until now been considered the preserve of men. . . . [It]has nothing to do with what was once called 'feminine sensibility.' It has to do with the drive, the concentration, the power of self-renewal and the gleeful thrust that it was once mandatory to call 'masculine.' . . . There is just no limit to what can be done by gifted and perceptive women who want to treat the current situation of women as the current situation of men has always been treated by gifted and perceptive men."

Until recently, the so-called "men's liberation movement" has seemed a whiny imitation of "women's lib," or a withdrawal into "separatism." But new publications like *M.—gentle men for gender justice* (deliberately lower case) and *American Man* grope for new definitions at national conferences on "Men and Masculinity" that go beyond imitation of or reaction to "women's lib," and that go beyond retreat into sulky separatism.

In real life there's a danger today for men and women who may try to get out of their own binds by reversing roles. Exchanging one obsolete model of a half-life for another, they may copy the worst aspects of the old feminine or masculine mystique instead of building from their own enduring, evolving strengths, and liberating their buried feelings or untried potential in the new experiences now open to them until, sharing parenting and work, they create new role models of wholeness.

I've observed men, suppressing their own disenchantment with sterile corporate jobs or bureaucratic professions, watch bemused as some women jump in, eagerly taking courses in "assertiveness training." I've also seen men shaken, threatened and secretly envious when some women, whose identities, after all, do not depend solely on those jobs, move from strengths that must be rooted in their own female experience and *resist* these same dehumanizing corporate practices men have acquiesced in, too long and to no real advantage.

On the other hand, a woman may become uneasy when a man is so intent on dropping out of the rat race that he clearly yearns for a superwoman to support him as she used to yearn for that strong man to take care of her whole life. "My husband wants me to have another child, and he will quit his job altogether and stay home and take care of the kids," a woman in Vermont told me. "Why should that work for him when it didn't work for me? Maybe I don't want him to take over the family that much. I'd resent it, just working to support him."

Beaten, desperate or self-denigrating "inadequate" men, playing into woman's pent-up hunger for power in the world or simply into her own harassed desperation, toy with fantasies that such reversals would be good. "What I need is a wife," she may joke, trying to be superwoman and doing it all herself, not really able yet to give up or share equally her old power in the home and family. But that half-life which made her insecure can also shake his sense of self.

It didn't really work when Phil, in the first flush of liberation from his surgical mask, reversed roles with Ellen. He stayed home full time after they moved to the country, "mothering" their children, cooking and cleaning, even meekly doing all the dishes "including the pots and pans my daughters were supposed to share," while Ellen went off to work. Is there something suspicious about such an excessively repentant male chauvinist pig? "Let her have the bigtime medical career," he urged, with no trace of outward bitterness, as his wife took on acupuncture on top of her new midwife training. "She shouldn't be a nurse anymore and take orders from men. She's a natural healer; she's the one who should have gone to medical school. I'll grow our own vegetables and heal myself."

But, in the first place, she didn't make nearly as much money as a nurse as he could as a doctor. And when she came home, the house was never clean enough, the meat loaf wasn't seasoned right, he'd forgotten to put the potatoes in, and she would rush around, tired as she was, doing it all over, making him feel just as guilty as she had in the old days.

"Then I began to feel like a martyr," he says. "Nobody appreciated how hard I worked, taking care of the house and kids all day. Anyhow, she missed that security, the money and all the rest of it, of my being a doctor. Working as much as I want to, with my family practice, and bringing money in again, I don't have to feel guilty if the house isn't all that clean on my shift. And now that they're treating her like a professional at the hospital, she doesn't notice the dust on the window sills so much."

It takes trial and error to work out the practicalities and the real tradeoffs, with men and women now sharing work and home responsibilities, instead of replacing the dreary realities of one with fantasies of the other. It's harder for men, because the tradeoffs for them aren't that obvious at first. Women, after all, are fighting for an equal share in the activities and the power games that are rewarded in this society. What are men's rewards for giving up some of that power and getting their own hands wet with the homely chores that used to be done by their wives?

Jimmy, a blue-collar worker in Brooklyn, won't admit there are any rewards for him in the tradeoffs he's been "forced" to work out with his wife. "In our community," says Jimmy, "the men do not freely accept women's equality. It's got to be slowly pushed down their throats. Men are the ones who go to the bar on the corner, drink, come home when the hell they want and expect supper on the table waiting for them. When that starts changing, it scares them to death. It scared me.

"I didn't know what was going on. First thing I know, my wife is going out to a women's organization, the National Congress of Neighborhood Women, and she wants to go do this, do that. She's learning, letting me know that things are wrong with our marriage. What am I supposed to do? It took five years before we got to the point where she went out to work.

"So I was making nine thousand dollars a year, and now she makes nine thousand dollars a year. And when she's out working her shift, I'm home taking care of the baby. It's no picnic. Any man who wants to change places with his wife when his wife stays home and takes care of the house and kids all the time has got to be a maniac. Her job in the house was twice as hard as mine at the plant. I work eight, ten hours. She works from when she gets up in the morning until she goes to bed."

When she started working, Linda says, "There were many battles between Jimmy and me. I wanted equality, which I thought meant that if he put three hours and twenty-two minutes into housework, then I would put in three hours and twenty-two minutes. I wanted a blow-by-blow division on everything, and I was fanatical about it. Jimmy was so happy to be relieved of some of the burden of being the only one with the paycheck that he was willing to do that, although I know he was teased by the guys at the corner bar."

The first payoff for men, obviously, is economic survival: the bottom line. Unfortunately, few of the advantages of equality can be measured as mechanically as making exactly the same amount of money (when women on the average still earn only fifty-nine cents to a man's dollar) or spending exactly the same amount of time on housework.

"What I've gained," says Avery Corman, who wrote the novel *Kramer vs. Kramer* from his own experience of taking over the kids when his wife started a business, "is the joy—and it is a joy—of having my children really rely on me. I've gained this real participation in their upbringing because I've been active in it on a daily basis."

Unlike the Kramers, the Cormans are still solidly married. "What I've given up," he says, "is being waited on myself. There are times when I'd really like to be the prince of potentates in my own home, and sit there with my pipe and slippers with my wife and children tiptoeing around to please me. But it sure isn't like that now, and it never will be again. A secret part of me would sometimes like a less equal marriage, would like to be catered to the way guys used to be.

"But the real payoff is that men can begin to think about who they are *as men*. I could ask myself what I really want in life. With my wife out there earning, I didn't have to be just a breadwinner." (And then, in real life, he found his own creativity, which earned them a lot of "bread." But it didn't have to end that way.)

"Is it true that the momentum's gone?" a cabdriver asked me recently. "It better not be. It's changed my life but I've got some new problems. I'm a *working father*."

This man and his wife each drive the cab three days a week and stay home and take care of the baby three days: "One day a week, we're both off together. It would be fine, except for her parents, who don't think I'm a man. But the emotional part, it's great. I never felt very close to my father. At first, when Tommy was born, I felt left out, I was jealous of the close thing between the baby and my wife. Now, the closeness is all three of us."

Another big change for men is that they find themselves with more independence—more "space"—now that women are becoming more independent. An Atlanta cotton broker, now married at thirty to a woman with her own career, recalls his first marriage to a woman who depended on him for everything.

"She made me feel suffocated," he says. "Living with a completely dependent woman is so draining, debilitating. You don't know why but you just feel awful. She's breathing your air. She's passing her anxiety on to you. She's got no confidence in herself, she's looking to you for everything, but what she does is always put you down, make you feel you won't make it. She may be very sweet, she may be lovely, but all you know is that you don't have room to breathe. I never heard of any ruling class resigning, but as men realize that it's more fun to live with a nondependent woman, the change will come about without bloodshed, because the payoff is real —economic and emotional."

The new emotional and economic cement that holds the marriage together may not feel as rigid as that old double-bind dependence. The new mix is still being worked out, tested, couple by couple. Many men—and women—have told me of no-win dilemmas, when he or she is offered a really good job in another city and the other has to settle for something second best. "If we decide it my way, and she's miserable in the new place, she resents it and I feel guilty," says Tony. "If I turn down the offer, I resent it, and take it out on her." It's especially bad when there is no real opening for her in her own profession and she is once again "treated as a nonperson," just his wife. In her resentment of that, she now refuses to collaborate or help in his work, or even listen, as he's always counted on her to do. And then she begins to nag again that he isn't making enough money.

A North Carolina high-school teacher tries to explain what the boys in the class have to gain from "equal opportunity" for those sweet Southern belles:

"Women can make life unbearable for men by living through them, becoming leeches. Such a woman must express her own ego and identity through the accomplishments of her husband. She may exert enormous pressure on him to pursue goals that do not interest him or that are beyond his abilities. If he succeeds, it may be an empty victory—he has given his life for someone else's ambition. If he fails, she has

no further way to express herself except to slice him up and
let him know in ways subtle and not so subtle that she could
have done it better herself. How much better for him if she
had her own chance to try, or even fail, but get off his back."

But if it wasn't all that good when she depended on him
for her whole life, it's also not good for him when she puts all
her energy and attention into her job or career. Women had
to put up with male workaholics when the main thing they
asked of marriage was a "good breadwinner." Now, men as
well as women are asking for real intimacy, sharing, feelings.

Brad, who would rather be a writer than an adman, says:
"Peggy is less interested now in what I'm doing. Before she
went to work herself, she was so involved in my work, living
through it unconsciously, she was a constant pressure on me.
Everything was riding on me too much. Now it's too little.
Now she's preoccupied with her own career. I miss that constant dependable attention from her. She was pretty good to
bounce things off of.

"But in five years she'll be bringing home enough money
so I can quit the ad business and try my own thing. She feels
like she's doing her own thing now, she got a job in the art
department of my old agency, but all those terrors about the
clients, the accounts, it's a big yawn to me. I call her Samantha Glick—remember *What Makes Sammy Run?* She buys
these suits, a fedora hat, a briefcase from Mark Cross, and
she's going to be successful all right. I miss her full attention
on me but I get a big buzz out of her getting ahead. There's
nothing worse than being around someone who feels they're
not really living their own life. That's the way I feel about
my job."

The problem of men hating their jobs has been swept under the table by women—too uncomfortable for either men
or women to face. But that was the hidden underside of the
feminine mystique, the cult of domesticity which "trapped"
women in the fifties and sixties. Fifteen years ago, anthropologist Jules Henry wrote that men used the home as "a sanctu-
ary where a part of every day they could forget their jobs. In

a society where most people work at what they have to do rather than at what they want to do . . . the function of the American home is to deny the existence of factory and office."

When she installs her own computer console linking her to her office, *in the bedroom*, on the other side of their queen-size platform bed from *his* computer console (see "The Busy Bedroom," *New York Times*, June 1980), is that really an advance toward wholeness for men or women? Compared to that old half-life, which often trapped them both, it probably is. Or it can be. Paradoxically, part of the tradeoff is that when women share the economic burden—and declare themselves equal persons in all other ways—men begin to, are free to, put a new value on the quality of life that used to be considered the exclusive domain of women. (In big-city newspapers, the "life style" section, formerly called "the women's page," is taking up more and more space in the paper and is being increasingly read by men.) And personal qualities, which used to be taken for granted in women, are now consciously valued, in and by men.

A Cleveland hotshot in his late twenties, drawn to independent career women (his first wife used to be his boss), is conscious, in his second marriage (to the assistant treasurer of the company where he is assistant comptroller), of the need for them both to *choose* to make a home and family. He knows that if they don't make that choice, "it won't happen."

"With my first wife, it was like we were just roommates who never saw each other," he said. "We didn't even try to have dinner together during the week. One or the other of us was always working late or traveling weekends. I would have quit my job when she got transferred to Houston, but there just wasn't enough cement to hold the marriage together.

"This time, even if Sue brings her reports home to study while I watch the football game on TV to tranquilize myself after a heavy day, we make dinner together. Whoever gets home first cooks, the other does the cleanup, and our weekends are for us. We built a house in the country, and even if

we don't do anything special, just the two hours alone together in the car on the highway Friday night is something
we both need. She wants to have kids, and she won't quit her
job. Carol didn't want kids. So now I have to figure it out,
because if I want children, I'll have to face the complications
in my career as much as she'll have to in hers."

Coming out of machismo, a man is likely to take a lot of
flak, especially from other men, and from women who are
still locked in half-lives, or who still resist any tradeoff.

At a men's workshop in Minneapolis, Herb Goldberg
said: "Women still want you to be taller, older, or better,
superior—which isn't so easy now. And then they also say
you should have feelings, you should cry. I stand up here in
my coat and tie, a Ph.D. in psychology, giving my lecture,
and any woman I ask will go out with me. But if I go into a
singles bar, a short guy with my shirt collar unbuttoned, and
I go up to a woman, she won't even look at me. It dehumanizes a man, just to see us in terms of how much money we
make, our job status, an economic instrument. It takes our
personhood away, like measuring a woman by her breast
size."

When Brad decided to risk quitting his ad job, and see if
he could make it as a novelist before it was too late, he stayed
out in their cottage in the Hamptons with the kids all summer and took them to meet Samantha Friday night, on the
"daddy" train from the city.

"I'm a big joke for women who are still housewives," he
said. "They'll say things like '*My* husband works for a living'
or 'How's your tennis, playing all day?' They seem to resent
me doing their duty, driving the kids to Carvel for a cone, the
supermarket. The snide remarks of the men bother me more.
'Well, boy, I wish you a lot of luck.' Meaning they think I'm
going to fail. As if I have to prove to them you can quit the
rat race and not perish. Working wives are much more sup-
portive. Women are my best friends now, and painters—people working at home. The things we talk about are exhilarat-

ing compared to the dreariness of office politics, the expense-account lunch with the client. I have such an open way of life now. I stay up all night, putting down ideas; or sometimes go to a movie in the afternoon. I go over to the dock with the kids and their bikes after they get home from day camp. I look forward to putting them to bed every night; they like to talk then. And the exhilaration I feel, doing something of my own, not of the committee. I go to bed tingling all over.

"But you can't keep measuring yourself against the people you used to work with (Jones got the Volkswagen account. I could have done better, even though I can't stand cars any more). I still feel so guilty, not working nine to five, I almost dread the weekend—what have I produced this week to earn it? You can take the man out of the rat race, but it isn't so easy to take the rat race out of the man."

Is it the new American frontier for men, this exploration of inner space, of the "messy feelings" that are the core of personhood for us all but that for too long were awesome, mysterious, forbidden territory for men? When women share the work burden and relieve men of the need to pretend to false strengths, men can open up to feelings that give them a real sense of inner strength, especially when they share the daily chores of living and child-rearing that wives used to shield them from.

"It grounds me—I have to admit it," says Bernie, a divorced accountant, who for the first time, after thirty years of mother and wife doing it for him, is cooking, shopping and washing clothes. "I like the relief from always thinking about money, my job, feeling like a machine or a disembodied head —chained to a calculator."

Or as an Oakland architect named Lars expresses it: "It makes me feel alive. I exist. I don't feel phony any more. I don't have to pretend to be so strong because I feel good. I feel centered. The silence that most men live with isolates us, not only from women but from other men. My wife's assault on my silence was, at first, extremely painful. She made me share my feelings with her. It brought an incredible sense of liberation, and maybe for the first time in my adult life a sense of reality, that I can *feel* my feelings and share them with her.

"But there'll still be a loneliness, for me and other men, until we can share our feelings with each other. That's what I envy most about the women's movement—the way women share their feelings and the support they get from each other. Do you know how isolated and lonely and weak a man really feels in that silence, never really making contact, never really touching another man?"

Some or all of these changes are threatening to men in ways that women find hard to understand. That Marine colonel in *The Great Santini* could deal with his engine's failure alone in the sky and go down with his plane more easily than he could deal with his own feelings of love and envy toward his son. And great numbers of American men clearly identify. The lashing out against women and the backlash against the women's movement are a way for men to avoid confronting these changes in their own lives.

A swarm of books by threatened men (George Gilder's *Sexual Suicide*, Steven Goldberg's *The Inevitability of Patriarchy*, Lionel Tiger's *The Imperial Animal*, etc.) keep up an insistent drone. They say that in demanding equality, women are destroying the natural, inexorable, predestined superiority of the male. These "wicked" women are dooming male sexual potency as well as the reproduction of the human race and the aggressive thrust of civilization itself—all of which rest solely on female submissiveness.

Of course, such books are based on faulty or outright false use of pseudoscientific evidence; their lies can be dismissed simply as "enemy propaganda."

The truth of male reaction is complex. I've suspected that the men who really feel threatened by the women's movement in general or by their own wives' moves toward some independent activity are the ones who are most unsure of their women's love. Such a man often worries that his wife has married him only for economic security or the status and vicarious power he provides. If she can get these things for herself, what does she need him for? Why will she continue to love him? In his anger is also the fear she will surely leave him.

Most men sense they are really dependent on women for security and love and intimacy, just as most women learn, after the old resentment-making imbalances are out of the way, that they are dependent on men for these same qualities. Most husbands will put up with quite a lot to weather their wives' periods of transition as they change their attitudes and redefine their roles (though maybe not quite as much as most wives have always had to put up with from their husbands!).

In a recent lecture on "The Male Sex Role: An Insider's View," sociologist William J. Goode stated that he did not think there was or would be a real masculine backlash to women's demand for equality, though men for a time may both exaggerate and deny the threat to them. Nor did he think that, whatever problems or discomforts might be involved for either sex, women would ever give up the new sense of self-respect and the freedom they now enjoy. "Males will stubbornly resist, but reluctantly adjust: because women will continue to want more equality and will be unhappy if they do not get it; because men on the average will prefer that their women be happy; because neither will find an adequate substitute for the other sex; because neither will be able to find an alternative social system."

Men may feel unjustly threatened by the women's movement because they know they personally didn't create the system or conspire to dominate women. Consciously they aren't even aware of how pervasively the social structure, attitudes and laws give them advantages. Men therefore "assume that their greater accomplishments are actually due to their inborn superiority, so they are more aware of their burdens and responsibilities than their unearned advantages," says Goode. In other words, men notice only the difficulties in their lives. They take the comforts as their due. And because they take their superiority for granted, "men view even small losses of deferences, of advantages or opportunities as large threats."

But the change that disturbs men most, Goode says, "is a loss of centrality, a decline in the extent to which they are the center of attention. Boys and grown men have always taken for granted that what they were doing was more important than what the other sex was doing. Women's attention was focused on them." Far more troubling to men than women's demand for equal opportunity and pay is the simple fact that "the center of attention shifts more to women now."

The threat is also somewhat exaggerated because the women now holding the desirable jobs only men had held before are so visible, so different, that the mass media plays them up. Even so, their numbers are still too small to constitute any real threat to men's dominance.

Yet men are right in sensing inexorable forces that are undermining their previous claim to natural superiority. But these threatening forces are not created by women. As Goode reports, "The conditions we now live in are different from those of any prior civilization, and they give less support to men's claim of superiority than any other historical era." More and more, the work is done by specialists and machines. And there is new awareness that in today's complex society the top posts in government and business are not best filled by the stereotypical male but by people, male or female, sensitive to others' needs, adept at obtaining cooperation—in short, with the intuitions and social skills and nurturing qualities once considered feminine.

So *men* envy *women* the women's movement. They envy women the zest and energy with which we approach jobs that hold no novelty or challenge for *them*. These jobs also seem like exciting new challenges to women because we are not saddled with that burdensome mandate to be superior and dominant. We do not yet have the need to suppress feelings of weakness and vulnerability that men have been locked into for so long. As a young man put it to me, after several years of wandering, dropping out of school and trying to find himself, "Every guy I know is in trouble. They can't seem to get it together. They don't know what they want. Only the women seem to be getting it together now."

Whatever a woman does today, she is somehow ahead of where she used to be, of where her mother or older sisters were.

The practical problems remain, emerging more clearly now from the fog of reaction and backlash. As men seek for themselves the liberation that began with the women's movement, both men and women have to confront the conflict between their human needs—for love, for family, for meaning in work and purpose in life—and the demands of the workplace as it is structured today.

A family therapist from Philadelphia, watching his three-year-old learn to throw a ball, talked of the conflict between his own profession and his personal family needs. "I was working at one of the big family-training centers in the country," he said. "There was constant theoretical discussion about getting the father back into the family. But the way our own jobs were set up, you had to work fifty to sixty hours a week. To really get anywhere you had to put in seventy hours, work nights, weekends. You didn't have time for your own family. You were supposed to make the job Number One in your life, and I wouldn't do that. My life is Number One, and my family—my job is only to be a good therapist. To play the office politics and be one of the big guns you had to devote your whole life to it. I started my own practice where I keep my own hours. Most of the other family therapists at the center are now divorced."

Recent managerial studies have shown that the long working hours and the frequent corporate transfers that kept many men from strong daily involvements with their families or with any other fulfilling commitments or interests besides their jobs were not all that necessary for the work of the company. But the long hours and the transfers do serve to keep a man dependent for his very identity, as well as his livelihood, on the corporation—a "company man."

This process is pinpointed in a depth study of executives in a major Connecticut company by Diana Rothbard Margolis published in 1980, *The Managers—Corporate Life in America*. "Security is not all that binds," this study explains. "Beyond the large paychecks, the benefit plans . . . the corporation controls a trump—the manager's identity. Paradoxically, managers must depend on the corporation for their definition of self precisely because they are moved around so frequently in their jobs. . . . With interests narrowed by the demands of their [corporate] initiation, a manager's thirst for money, status and security grows until other needs are eclipsed. . . . For corporation managers, needs usually fulfilled by human relationships become increasingly difficult to satisfy because almost all relationships outside their nuclear family are distant and fleeting. So like half-starved people who in the absence of proteins will fatten themselves on starches, managers and their families hunger for goods money cannot buy, but reach for those it can."

Is it necessary for a man to leave the corporate mainstream to find himself—and his new identity in the family? Might he not be able to turn that corner for himself by acting, along with women, to change those dehumanizing corporate conditions? With productivity declining and absenteeism increasing, corporations will have to come to terms with men's insistence on human terms and meaning in work—which could conceivably strengthen the system, as women's equality is giving new strength to the family.

It seems strange to suggest that there is a new American frontier, a new adventure for men, in this new struggle for wholeness, for openness to feeling, for living and sharing life on equal terms with women, taking equal responsibility for children—the human liberation that began with the women's movement. Unlike the American hero of the past, the new frontier liberates men from the isolating silence of that lonely cowboy. "I'm not just my work now, not just a bread-winner, I can do something just for myself," says Avery. "But to tell you the truth, my fantasies now tend to be in terms of the family. I'd like to take the kids and Judy on the same trip backpacking to Canada I took at nineteen. It's not my fantasy to go off to the South Seas alone like Gauguin."

Men aren't really going to be able to escape, or want to escape, the work world, any more than most women can or want to escape the family. The men in *Breaktime* had to or wanted to go back to work after their unemployment insurance or savings ran out—but on terms now which left them more room to be human, enabled them to use their own abilities and control their own lives more (if not in the job itself, then by reducing the job's importance and putting their main energies into other pursuits). The new statistics showing how frequently men are changing jobs indicate that somehow, even in this turbulent economy, men are taking more control of their own lives instead of being passive robots of the corporation. And new statistics showing for the first time a decline in the number of hours American women spend on housework suggest that when women no longer need all that power and status from the perfectly clean house because they're getting a little more power in the world—they don't let their houses run them.

Instead of being defined by their jobs or careers, more and more young men—and survivors of the midlife crisis—are holding down one or more part-time jobs, like women (taxi driver, teaching one course, waiter, bartender, apartmenthouse "super" or country caretaker in return for free rent), while "their own thing" may be the cello, ecology, dance, or studying Greek mythology—not for pay at all. Says my young friend David, "I seem to know fewer and fewer men who answer 'What do you do?' in terms of their job. It's 'What is your *shtik?*' "

In the second stage of this struggle that is changing everyone's life, men's and women's needs converge. There are con-

scious choices now, for men as well as women—to set up
their lives in such a way as to achieve a more equitable balance between success in work and gratification in personal
life. And here is the missing link, the power that was lacking
when women tried to solve these problems by taking it all on
themselves as superwomen, the power women did not and
will not have, to change the structure of jobs by and for
themselves alone. But if young men now need and want self-
fulfillment beyond their jobs and the life-grounding women
have always had in the family—as much as women now need
and want some voice and active power in the world—there
will be a new, and sufficient, *combined* force for the second
stage.

So this is the other half of Stage Two of the struggle that
began with women's movement for equality—men's liberation. Men, it seems, are now seeking new life patterns as
much as women are. They envy women's freedom to express
their feelings and their private questions and the support
they got from each other in those years of the women's movement.

After talking to these men, I wonder about women who
struggle so hard to succeed in traditional male roles. A West
Point officer, like a number of executives I've met who are
dealing with women colleagues as equals for the first time,
seemed to have a strange awe, fear, envy almost, of women's
power, a sense that women know some secret men don't. (Or
maybe, now that women are there, in the man's world, the
men are afraid women will discover how hollow men's
power can be.)

This is tricky, because there's been so much hypocrisy
about the power of women. But the West Point man says, "It
always defined women as against men—that we went to war.
'Winners never quit,' 'Quitters never win,' etc. The worst
insult was to be called the four- and five-letter words for
women's sex. Now the women are in the locker room, too.
They have a powerful advantage because they weren't
brought up with the black-and-white view of the world: 'If

he knocks you down, you're a pussy.' 'He has the courage, so you have to knock him down.' Women aren't stuck with the notion that that kind of courage is necessary, or even possible. They just cast about for ways to do what has to be done, push through the phoniness, the lies, to the concrete reality of it. They know it's not black and white, it's gray. It makes men feel guilty for having believed the lie in the first place, and then for having given up so easily. Men are jealous and afraid of women, maybe envious of their power. It may sound corny, but there is power in women's ability to create life, closeness to life, that men don't have, always chasing power, in the company, in the army.

"Speaking for myself, I need reassurance from women. And now there's all this rhetoric that all the things men bragged about are no good. So men are left with gaping holes in their identity, their equation of life. And now that women feel unfettered ambition is absolutely necessary to get ahead in their own careers, they can't turn around and help men. Men don't like to admit their fear of women, and women don't like to be feared, but the hidden secret is coming out now, and it's freaking people. It's scary to have power over people and be able to control them, the way women do with feelings.

"It seems to me, beginning with the Vietnam war, more and more men are reaching a turning point where if they don't turn the corner and get beyond these black-and-white games, they start to die. Women will make a mistake if they reach that turning point and start to imitate men. Will the women move in and take our place? Men can't be role models for women, not even in the army. We badly need some new role models ourselves."

5 Reality Test at West Point

 I was amazed, and a little surprised, when the major called early in the winter of 1980 and asked me to come to West Point. I was invited to participate in three days of lectures, classes and officer-staff seminars—not just for the women cadets, but for the official West Point. It was part of a new program on "American Institutions" started after the Congressional investigations that followed the cheating scandal at West Point in 1976. Certain weaknesses had been revealed, said the major, a possibly dangerous isolation of the military academy from the changing mainstream of American society.

He reminded me that I had been invited to West Point five years earlier, when they were getting ready to admit women under orders from Congress after it had passed the Equal Rights Amendment. Now, though the ERA had not been ratified into the Constitution, those first women were graduating, and women were fully integrated in all classes at West Point, as at the other service academies and in the armed forces generally. "We are interested in what you have been saying lately about the second stage of feminism, the restructuring of the institutions of work and family," said Major William Ritch. "Some of us are thinking along the same lines."

West Point was surely a bastion of the masculine mystique. How would my theoretical optimism about changing
male sex roles stand up against the reality test of West Point?
For that matter, did I really want to face the full implications
of equality for women in the training of those first women
for military command?

Would I find these first women cadets graduating from
West Point grotesque female imitations of the bloodthirsty
jock male military stereotype, the heroes of My Lai—their
"feminine" values (the sensitive, tender, intuitive, life-cher-
ishing values that have always been associated with women)
deadened, drilled away by the brutal cadences of military
command? Had the women, in fact, proved themselves equal
to the opportunity, challenge and ultimate responsibility that
West Point represents? In reality—and as metaphor of a
larger reality—what was West Point doing to women? What
were women doing to West Point?

Confronting the actuality of women training for military
leadership at West Point, one could not avoid certain disturbing implications of women's movement to equality. Was
that really what it was all about, our great revolutionary
women's movement—advancing women to death-dealing
power in the military-industrial complex? In the old rhetoric
of revolution, had feminism simply delivered women into the
militaristic, materialistic bowels of late capitalist American
imperialism? Ever since President Carter had called for draft
registration of young women as well as young men in response to the movement of Soviet troops into Afghanistan,
such questions had been bothering me and other feminist
leaders. Did American women really want to be drafted?
And if not—how could women demand equal rights and opportunities and not accept equal responsibility?

Over the past year, I have been hearing from young
women and seeing in the polls that in the United States today women certainly do not want to be drafted, and Americans do not want their daughters drafted. Phyllis Schlafly
was in ecstasy as she raised a new furor about stopping the

ERA "to save American daughters from the draft." She had virtually stopped talking about bathrooms; war was a more volatile issue. Faced with the actual possibility, how did I myself really feel about women being drafted? Must the women's movement for equality come into ultimate conflict with the profound values of life that, for me as for others, have always been associated with women?

The major takes me into the mess hall for dinner with some of the cadets before my lecture. The two women cadets ("firsties," about to graduate) are roommates. Annie, a sweet, spunky blonde, is an "Army brat"; her father was a West Point man. Marge, black, motherly, struggling to lose weight, was a private in the army when the law admitting women to West Point was passed. She seized on her commanding officer's offer to order her there, to "get the education." They tell me, with good humor and clear satisfaction, how they survived as the first women at West Point. . . .

When the women entered West Point four years ago, there was a sense—among officers, cadets, war-proud veterans of that historic Long Gray Line—of outrage. Whatever the professed commitment to the values of American democracy—and the obedience required now by law to Congress' mandate on equal opportunity—whatever the defense needs that demanded the admission of women to West Point, it was the ultimate threat to male superiority, the breaching of that last sacred fortress of masculinity. There was outrage, fear that women would lower the standards of courage, discipline, physical prowess that were the ethos of West Point—they wouldn't be able to stand up to the rigors, to do what had to be done, to defend the nation. (I remembered also, from the time they had me there as consultant, just before the young women came, there was also a fear that the girls would somehow do better, show the men up.)

From the very beginning, "equality" at West Point was interpreted to mean that the women would, in fact, do everything the men were required to do, on one and the same track, in all phases of cadet life and training—physical, military, academic, social. The law dictated that "only minimum essential adjustments be made in existing standards to integrate women, and that these adjustments be based on physiological differences between the sexes."

Extensive research was done on how best to minimize the physiological differences. West Point's own report of that research, on the 119 women who entered July 7, 1976, for Cadet Basic Training (called "Beast") in the class of 1980, states:

"Although instructors made some adjustment for women to compete with men in physical training, i.e., women carried the lighter (2 1/2 lbs) M-16 rifle in lieu of the M-14 on reveille runs, these changes were minimal and the essentially one track program pushed women (and some men) beyond their limits."

The young women could wear "chest protectors" during pugil stick training and take "self-defense" courses in karate instead of boxing and wrestling, but otherwise they were subjected to the same rigors of drill, bayonet, foot marches, weapons training and bivouacs as the men. The main area where the women could not compete with the men was "pull-ups" (or "chin-ups"). "Few women could perform even one, and less than one tenth of 1% of those women tested could perform the six pull-ups which are considered marginal for a male candidate." So an "equivalent" test was designed for women, "the flexed-arm hang [which] consists of hanging from a bar with both hands, chin over the bar."

Mostly the women couldn't keep pace with the men during the 6 A.M. formation running. The jeers when they fell out were so unendurable that the women started getting up at 4 A.M. to run.

A "voluntary" program was offered to "allow new cadets who could no longer run at the established unit's pace, to run individually at their own pace. . . . Few new cadets participated, choosing to stick it out with their units, rather than face the possible peer sanction against admitting weakness by engaging in a less demanding program."

By the end of "Beast" training, 9 percent of the women had suffered "stress fracture" of bones, ten times as many as the men—and most of the women had stopped menstruating. Many women missed their periods until November—some, like women in concentration camps, missed them for a year.

They also endured another kind of stress—continual mockery of their high, female voices, of their "unmilitary" female walk, of the very fact that they were women.

"Good morning, sir," she would say, with the prescribed deferential salute. "It was a good morning until you got here, bitch," he would mimic, in falsetto. Squad leaders would order the women to "lower" their voices, to stand in front of the mirror and practice "looking mean," to stand in the corner and practice shouting "loud and mean." ("I tried, but I looked so funny, it just made me laugh," said my dinner companion. "I got my voice a little lower," said her friend. "Then I realized if my voice was loud enough to be heard, did I really have to sound like a man?")

Their squad leaders took them into the men's john at night, determined to make them perform those "pull-ups"—hoisting the women on their shoulders till they got their chins over the shower bar, leaving them there to hang until they dropped. "It was good for the pecs," Marge said, grinning, patting her well-developed bosom. They were ordered to sink their chins into their chests, to stand to attention even more ramrod-straight than the men; women would, it seemed, achieve "military" bearing only by hiding the very existence of these unmale protuberances.

The uniforms they were issued included, in addition to pants and shoes identical to the men's, skirts for "dress gray" and other uniforms, and high-heeled pumps. But when one of them would wear the skirt, the cadet officer would order her to go back and change into a "proper" uniform, on the double.

During that first summer training, their fellow male cadets, suffering their own "Beast" wounds, treated them more or less like comrades in misery. But when they marched back

from the encampment, at the end of the summer, the hostility of the upperclassmen became the accepted role model
even for the previously friendly fellow plebes. The men of
the last two classes graduating without women wanted to
design their class ring with omegas—symbolizing the end,
"the last class with balls." The superintendent forbade it.

Pushing away the corn on the cob at the diet table, Marge
recalled how she felt when she would walk under a window
and upperclassmen would lean out, barking at her, and pour
soda or beer on her hair. "I tried barking back," she said,
"and then I thought, why should I let them reduce me to
their level? They were such jackasses."

A diet table had to be instituted because it was found that
the women cadets were putting on weight faster than the
men. (A psychologist could have explained that one.) "Frater-
nizing" (romantic attachment) between the plebe women and
any upperclassmen was absolutely forbidden; even at the Saturday night dances, to which the male cadets brought their
dates from surrounding colleges and girls' schools, the female
cadets were sanctioned by their own officers if they wore
skirts.

Some female officers had been brought in, in an attempt to
provide the women cadets with role models. But those officers, admitted earlier and in even smaller numbers into an
army not yet consciously committed to equality, had suffered
more denigration as women, and self-denigration, than the
cadets themselves; scorned even as they "tried to be like
men"—they were "neither fish, flesh nor fowl," said one of
my cadet informants.

In the neutral tones of "Report on the Admission of
Women to the U.S. Military Academy" (Project Athena, 2
September 1977):

> In some ways, the stress experienced by women was
> of a different nature than that experienced by their
> male peers. Women were made aware of basic sex dif-
> ferences that are difficult to overcome, such as higher

pitched voices, which weren't "commanding," and shorter marching strides, which weren't "military." Some women were made to feel that even if they made it through the first year, male plebes wouldn't take orders from them. Finally, some women felt that to be accepted they had to be "one of the boys," but by so doing felt that they may be sacrificing their femininity and changing their basic self-image.

What the men objected to the most was the greater "protection" shown the women—and the "special attention," by the media, and by upperclassmen, who began to form "special relationships" with women cadets even before the end of that first year, during which no upperclassman is supposed to recognize the existence of a plebe. They also didn't like the invitations the women got to visit for a day with the officers' families.

At first Annie had protested that she wasn't a women's libber, but, as she says, "I realized I was, more so all the time." And then, one night, the women started talking among themselves. And they decided—first two, talking in one room, then going down the hall and enlisting the women there, until eight or nine agreed, scared a bit, hiding behind schedules ("No, not Tuesday, I have guard duty; let's start at lunch on Wednesday")—they would, as one woman, defy their male peers' outrage and wear skirts. "Let them know we are women—why should we hide it?"

Even before they dared to wear skirts, those trouser-wearing female cadets did get asked to dance at the Saturday night hops. Rumor has it that the commandant saw a picture of two trousered cadets dancing with each other and howled, "Order them to wear skirts." The official report says merely:

. . . One additional change was made during the academic year. Women were "required" to wear skirts to hops and dances, where they previously had the option of wearing trousers. This change was made in response to feedback that male cadets were applying sanctions to women wearing dresses to those events.

Now, four years later, of the 61 women cadets who remained out of the 119 who entered originally, almost half were going to marry fellow officers, mostly those excessively hostile upperclassmen who had at first been so outraged by their womanhood. They expected to continue their military careers, and also to have children, without too much concern yet for the practical problems that might be involved. Some of the upperclassmen helped form the "Corbin Seminar," named after a female Revolutionary War hero, to study the new role of women—and men—in army and society. The women's basketball team, nicknamed "the Sugar-smacks," was affectionately supported. When a few women were expelled for being pregnant—and the male cadets responsible went free—there was general outrage. The army began to deal with the facts of life. Now a regulation had just been handed down that a pregnant woman could take leave to have a baby, and come back to West Point—or she could get an honorable discharge—as long as she didn't get married! (After all, male cadets are not allowed to marry.) Now, there were new jokes and rumors—the women would all get pregnant, for an easy way out. "After all the agony of getting here and surviving, do they really think we would have a baby just to get out?" asked Marge, incredulous that men could be such "jackasses."

In my lecture that evening, I was supposed to relate the changes at West Point to the larger changes in society I have participated in through the women's movement. I talked about what I have been addressing in this book. I mentioned that the first stage—the assumption of the personhood of women, the breaking through of the barriers that had kept women from moving as equal persons in the mainstream of society—was almost over. I talked about the anger and frustration that led to a mistaken view of the movement as a sexual war of women against men. I suggested that the next stage would focus in a different way on men—that maybe even here at West Point the hostility against women masked something more fundamental going on among the men themselves. After all, the image of what it is to be a man in America—all-powerful, all-dominant, superior to the whole world, tight-lipped, big-muscled, without fear or feeling, napalming the babies in Vietnam and Cambodia and the green leaves off the trees—had begun to change, after we lost the war in Vietnam. (They stirred in their seats and muttered at that.)

I asked why men are threatened by women's approaching equality. (After all, the women at West Point were not doing better than the men academically, much less physically, when they were measured by the same scales.) Could men, in some strange way, be envious of the women? I asked. There is a certain zest to the women's movement, to the adventure of being a woman today, I suggested. What is old hat for men, at West Point as at other places, is brand-new for women, an adventure. I suggested that men might even be envious that women can have soft feelings and let them show, especially at a male stronghold like West Point. I talked about *Kramer vs. Kramer* and the possibility of a new model of what it is to be a man, a new kind of male hero in America, as men begin to share the care of the children and home with their wives, as women share the burdens and responsibilities of earning—even the hardships and dangers and glories of military careers. I suggested that the entrance of women to the world of work and power, on terms of equality, and the related changes that might be happening among men would lead to even more profound restructuring of all our institutions—and maybe that was already beginning to happen at West Point?

Afterward, an officer stopped me. "It's already happening more than you realize," he said. "The women cadets are only the tip of the iceberg; almost every officer here has a wife working. It's a necessity with the pay we get. That's changed all our lives."

I thought I had been very mild, but the major warned me to expect a lot of hostility from the cadets in the classes the next morning.

The next morning, all the men wanted to talk about was "pull-ups" and "upper body strength." How could they accept the idea of equality of women at West Point when it was a known fact that women couldn't do those six pull-ups, and some couldn't even do one? How could weaklings defend the nation? They insisted that the admission of women was "dangerously" lowering the standards at West Point. And they didn't like it at all that I misinterpreted their reaction as "sexist." They were not threatened, as men, by women at West Point—the *nation* was threatened! And it had nothing to do with machismo.

The big question, of course, was women and the draft. How could I talk about equality for women, if women would not be drafted? I suggested that if a real draft is reinstated—from necessity of national defense and not just as a political gesture to win an election—it is hardly conceivable that women would not be included. Most of the cadets nodded in agreement. But did I believe that women should go into combat?

"If I was going into battle and I had to take someone with me, well, ma'am, personally I wouldn't want a woman anywhere around," said a male cadet.

Another conjured the image of an officer having to order his girlfriend out of the trenches into hand-to-hand combat with a grenade-bearing enemy, breaching the front line. "Even if he pretended he didn't care if she got killed, any more than one of the men, how could he trust her to kill the enemy and defend him?" The major, sitting next to me, muttered something like, "Damn fools, don't they know there won't even be a front line like that in the next war?"

It was as if the whole scene was from some old movie. "They're all scared to death, because they know they don't

know, we don't know, what the next war will be like," one of
the officers told me later.

The male cadet insisted that I answer the questions: Did I
think women really wanted to go into combat, and did I
think women should want to go into combat? The women
cadets had kept quiet during the whole discussion—even during the talk about pull-ups. Now one woman cadet interrupted with a question for the male cadet: "Tell the truth, do
you really want to go into combat? Does anyone really want
to go into combat?" she asked with a quiet passion. "You do
what you have to do. It's your duty, it's miserable and awful
and terrifying and you'd be crazy to want to do it. But you've
had the training, you can be trusted to do what has to be
done. You can trust yourself to do the job."

I meet next with the class studying "Marriage and the
Family." From the Project Athena research I knew that virtually all the male cadets, and most of the women, saw their
future in terms of marriage and children as well as military
careers. (Significantly more women than men saw their permanent future in full-time military careers, but the women
were not so clear as the men about combining those careers
with marriage and children.) The women cadets I had talked
to who were about to marry fellow officers had specific plans
involving missile training in Germany, military intelligence,
ballistic-missile support. They would face unique Stage Two
problems: the practical, concrete questions of what kind of
home, how to raise the children, how to share the domestic
responsibilities and decisions in a two-soldier, two-officer
family. Given the seeming rigidities of military necessity and
tradition, these questions seem unanswerable, difficult even
to think about—the logistics of assigning married officers to
the same or nearby posts; who takes care of the kids when
both parents are ordered to report for battle duty?

In the class, the male cadets do not even want to discuss
the new arrangements that will be needed to accommodate
two-career army families. Ignoring the very presence of the

female cadets, the young uniformed men reiterate the old refrain: Woman's place is in the home; the woman I marry will be happy staying home taking care of her husband and children.

The officer-professors sitting next to me seem embarrassed, even exasperated. *Their* wives work. The major had sent a colleague to pick me up for breakfast at the hotel that morning because he had to feed his kids breakfast and get them off to school—his wife had an early business appointment.

The female cadets simply keep quiet as their fellow cadets mouth the old, stale rhetoric. The Project Athena research revealed that the biggest difference between the male and female cadets was that the males entering West Point were far more traditional and conservative about women's place and sex roles generally than other men of their generation, or than American men as a whole, including older male officers. In fact, the male cadets' attitudes could only be compared to the most "traditional" group in the entire society: very old "ladies." This is a sharp contradiction to the trend in the general population of the U.S.; today people in their twenties and thirties, men as well as women, in far greater numbers than their elders, believe in equality between the sexes, equal opportunity for women in pay and jobs, and sharing of housework and child care. Thus, the young male cadets at West Point deviated from their own generation in their extreme resistance to change, whereas the young women cadets, not surprisingly, scored among the most advanced of their generation in their attitudes on women's place, sex roles, marriage, and the family.

Annie had told me earlier that she might not get married at all—at least not very soon. But she did want to have a child —maybe she should have a child and not get married. There would be fewer problems. . . . Marge, on the other hand, said she would postpone even thinking about that problem. If necessary, after a certain number of years in her ballistic-missile career, she would "retire" and have kids. For army men, careers peak young, and military retirement and pensions do not preclude, and in fact facilitate, great freedom of choice for second careers in industry or academia as they reach their forties and fifties. But in recent years, perhaps because of the low pay, perhaps because of the wives' rebellion, more and more West Point graduates have been resigning their commissions five and ten years after graduation.

The major hands me a news clip about a recent seminar for military wives, held at Fort Myer, Virginia, by the Army Officers' Wives Club of the Greater Washington Area, at which it became clear that "army wives are angry." An estimated 40 percent of wives of army enlisted soldiers work, it was reported. In inflationary Washington, nearly 75 percent of enlisted Air Force men hold second jobs, and 90 percent of Navy wives work. The report went on:

> The growing number of service wives with careers is emerging as a major problem for the Pentagon according to officers and NCO wives at the Fort Myer seminar. Many military wives with good jobs refuse to move when their husbands are transferred. Hundreds, perhaps thousands of servicemen are getting out at the 12-to-20-year point rather than become "geographical bachelors" in Germany, Korea or Stateside posts. . . . No longer are military wives content just to raise children, stay at home and perform volunteer work for the commander's wife, they said. Numerous wives want the challenge and satisfaction of a career. Unless the Pentagon begins to account for this, they said, military divorce rates could skyrocket, morale could plunge, and the whole system could become unhinged.

A Bureau of Labor Statistics report in late 1980 showed an increase in the past ten years from 30 percent to over 50 percent of military wives who work, but their jobless rate was more than double that of civilian wives. Their husbands' frequent transfers keep the wives from accumulating seniority and specialized skills, and make employers reluctant to hire them. As their husbands rise in rank, military wives start over at the lowest-level jobs at each post.

By the time I meet, that afternoon, with the faculty-officer-staff colloquium, I have learned of larger crises at West Point, and in the military services generally, converging coincidentally (or not so coincidentally) on the admission of women. The ten thousand or so West Pointers on active duty in the army have power out of proportion to their number (one out of eight of all army officers, but this proportion in the upper ranks, right up to general, is much higher). The defeat in Vietnam was especially humiliating to such officers, who, in the words of one ex-West Pointer, "provided the ethos for the Vietnam war, led it and were its most devoted and ambitious servants." The demoralization surfaced in 1970 when the then superintendent, General Koster, who had been implicated in the coverup after My Lai, stood on a stone balcony in the mess hall and announced his resignation.

In 1976, the year the women entered, the greatest cheating scandal in West Point history led to widespread Congressional investigations. In violation of the sacred West Point "honor code," 152 cadets were found guilty of collaboration on a take-home problem in electrical engineering and were dismissed. (Ninety-eight were later allowed to return.) In 1977 the resulting investigation led to a highly critical report about West Point's negative attitudes and its resistance to change. General Andrew Goodpaster, a four-star general who had served in Vietnam and for five years as NATO's Supreme Allied Commander, adviser to Eisenhower, Kennedy, Johnson and Nixon on defense and foreign policy, was brought out of retirement to bring West Point into the twentieth century. He let it be known that any officer who couldn't commit himself to treat women and blacks with full equality should resign forthwith—and henceforward all cadets, in their all-important rating for future leadership, would be rated strictly on their performance in accordance with their attitudes on equality—a rating of even a tendency to discriminate would be enough to ruin a future army officer's career.

The year the cheating scandal erupted, the year women were admitted, the mission of West Point was changed from "to instruct and train cadets" to "educate, train and motivate cadets." As a result of the cheating scandal and the experience in Vietnam, traditional West Point leadership techniques, which had relied heavily on "punishment and stress," were changed to "more democratic styles and techniques of training." Outright physical and mental "harassment" of cadets was forbidden now, even in "Beast" training. The "honor court," which had been able to expel a cadet in the middle of the night for alleged violation of the "thou shalt not cheat, steal, or lie" honor code, or even for failing to report a fellow violator ("quibbling"), was forced to observe some semblance of due process.

All this new "softness" was coincidental with the admission of women, and somehow blamed on them, though the causes lay in larger crises concerning the realities of defense of the United States in the post-nuclear world. Exploding nationalist aspirations in the world, a volunteer American army, the increasing complexities of technology and international dealings—these realities called for human skills more "flexible" than "Beast-bred" submission and authoritarian command.

Similarly, the determination of the top brass to make the integration of women work at West Point, as in the army generally, came not from idealistic conversion to the cause of women's equality, but from demographic necessity: because of the falling birthrate, the U.S. no longer has a pool of young "manpower" for volunteer army or draft sufficient to defend the nation—unless women are part of that pool. "The distaff buildup began when . . . Pentagon planners eyed demographic statistics showing that the number of eligible men would drop sharply in coming years—by as much as 25 percent in 1992—and realized they would have to expand the role of women greatly to meet peacetime quotas," *Newsweek* reported (February 18, 1980).

Since 1972, women had been moved from their traditional confinement to health care and clerical jobs into all but sixteen of the Army's 377 military occupations with more and more jobs taken out of the "direct combat" category so women could be used. The fact that the U.S. now has more women and a higher percentage of women in the armed forces than any other nation—and that the Pentagon is moving them into combat roles even without a draft—is not, therefore, a question of ideology but of national survival.

But at the staff colloquium I attended at West Point, officers with raised consciousnesses seemed to be up against a last-ditch stand of "warriors" to deny this reality.

A hefty officer of forty in khaki uniform proclaimed, "The former function of this academy was to train warriors, leaders of warriors. Every man at West Point was groomed for combat arms. Now, with the entrance of women, the men are choosing other options—all hatches are open, the top men go to graduate school. Suddenly, West Point is training managers, democratic leaders, not war-fighting oriented—it scares me to death."

Another officer, a more recent West Point graduate, agrees gloomily. "For the first time, many men in my class are not just bucking for chief of staff; they seem more concerned with their own well-being. The army has to come first, not the individual. It's wrong for men to be concerned with living their own life and not just advancing themselves higher and higher to four-star general."

This is not what seems to worry the officers at my end of the table, who were, I learned, legendary veterans of the Vietnam war. Now, said one major, "Men my age put more value on the family than ever before. It worries me, these cadet couples choosing the same kind of military careers; five

years down the road, will the military be flexible enough so
that the women can have their military careers and a family
at the same time, or will they force the women to choose, and
lose these great women?"

His colleague shrugged: "I wouldn't be so sure these
women will simply throw it all over. I've just finished reading twenty-one career plans, and they're committed, these
women. The real question is, will the army accommodate
itself to the two-career military family?"

Another suggests: "Or will the man's concept of success
change? I can see him saying, 'I'm never going to be a three-
star general; she might. I don't even like the army all that
much. I'll get out and do something else so I can take over
with the kids.' "

The "warrior" is not amused. He conjures the disquieting
image of officer-husband and officer-wife, neither of whom
can be ordered to the front, in the next Vietnam war, because
"the army would have to baby-sit the kids, for God's sake.
This army can't afford that kind of flexibility; it's inefficient."

"Wouldn't it be less efficient to force them to choose and
make them both leave the army?" his much-decorated fellow
officer asked. "I suppose the army could afford that kind of
inefficiency, and just let the women and the men who put
their families first get out—if there were no shortages of
skilled manpower. But where are we going to draw the necessary military power for sixteen divisions if we can't keep
married officers? The army can and will adjust to the practical problems involved. Even if it gets down to the military
providing baby-sitters or child care. Anyhow, what's the difference between a couple where both are in the army and
where one has some other job?"

"Because if he's the one in the army, he can say to his
wife, 'Come with me or else—that's it!' " replies the "warrior."

The others look at him as if he's in some other world.
They evidently know too many army wives who would
choose, or have chosen, that "else." "If the army isn't flexible

enough to deal with the two-career family, you'll just lose more captains and majors," this major says quietly. He reminds them that the army is already dealing with twenty thousand single parents—most of them male—at far-flung posts. "Are you going to force men to sign an oath they won't marry or have a family, or will abandon their kids, to join the army or become an officer?"

A young male cadet, who has evidently been invited to the colloquium because of some leadership position, says, "This problem is going to have to be solved by the army, like any other problem, in peace or war. This institution is going to adapt itself to the two-career officer family, the two-career soldier family, and create the necessary structures as it has for every other major change."

Some of the men were aware that the army is already adapting to the "facts of life" in a two-sex army, perhaps faster than some civilian institutions. "Last year, 14 percent of the women in the Army became pregnant; about half of them were not married. Overall, the Pentagon estimates that 8 percent of U.S. military women are pregnant at any one time," *Newsweek* reported. "The military has adjusted calmly to the phenomenon. No longer grounds for compulsory discharge, pregnancy is a 'temporary physical disability,' and new mothers are eligible for up to six weeks paid postpartum leave. They can also be released from service immediately, if they choose. . . . Many military moms choose to stay, however, so the Pentagon had maternity uniforms designed."

The hefty officer in khaki insists, "The real question is, how are you going to take a young man and turn him into somebody special, with the values of a warrior, when you let women in—and all these other softening, weakening influences? An army of baby-sitters, for God's sake!"

The decorated major says: "Instead of desperately trying to push a new set of circumstances into old niches, we should be asking for what purposes the army will actually need people in the future. Our own research shows the whole process of male identity is changing—male bonding, the question of physical prowess is not so all-important. A lot of this bitching about women lowering the standards at West Point hides the fact that the whole question of standards and goals is being reexamined in the army. The real concern is the number of people they're losing. All that stress and punishment seems to be dysfunctional—the cheating, losing so many officers, what happened in Vietnam—but it's all blamed on the women."

The "warrior" does not give. "You can't prove to me that standards haven't changed here because of the women. I'm sure the enemy will make concessions for the fact that the women were excused from pull-ups."

The other major says, "Can you prove to me these pull-ups will make a man a better fighter when he goes into combat? Those little Vietnamese I was up against, did it affect their ability to lead and fight that they weren't bigger than five feet five, and weighed a hundred and twenty pounds?"

The "warrior" still insists, "A leader who isn't physically able to meet those standards can't be a good leader in the U.S. Army."

The major says, "Maybe such physical standards are not really tied to the kind of leadership an American army needs today. I never did chin-ups or pull-ups in Vietnam." He did not have to mention his decorations.

The other becomes defensive. "Did you ever break down and cry from physical exhaustion in front of your men? If you did, because you let yourself get soft physically, you are not a good leader and should get out of the service."

The older officer at the end of the table speaks up: "It doesn't make sense, this idea that we officers can't ever admit our physical and emotional stress, that we must always wear a facade. Does this really make a good leader? Do we really know the exact nature of the next war? If it doesn't fit the rigid formula we've been teaching, our soldiers will be thrown for a loop. I'd bet a soldier will follow me more readily if I'm honest than if I'm Charles Atlas and lying."

Aren't there equivalents to pull-ups to train the women for whatever "upper body strength" they really need? I ask, noticing that even some of the "warriors" are wearing glasses. Evidently officers are not forced out of the army if their eyesight is less than perfect; they simply wear glasses.

One of the officers explains: "As a matter of fact, for every women who doesn't meet these standards, there are at least three males. We don't continually make people meet those standards to the letter, physically or academically. The standards are arbitrary—three hundred yards, six pull-ups, there's probably zero tie-in with what makes a good combat officer, artillery officer."

The officer at the end of the table had been sent for advanced study in sociology and psychology and had been brought back to West Point to study what actually produces "commitment" in any officer or cadet. He found that the younger men were exhibiting less of "a certain kind of male pride" West Point used to breed. "Maybe if women can get through this, they will think, 'It's not as tough as I thought it was.' They will have blown the myth of that special male toughness. The men will have to wonder, Maybe it takes something else—something that the women have, too."

The major sees more in that preoccupation with pull-ups than I could: "There is nothing else they can point to that the women don't do as well, or sometimes better than, the men. They can't say any more, as they did three or four years ago, that women are too emotionally unstable, that they will crack, that they aren't tough enough to take the rigors of army training or that they won't be able to get the men to follow them to get the job done. The men's own emphasis will have to shift from the purely physical as they realize that it takes some other kind of toughness now—some strengths these young women seem to get more easily than the men."

I met the next morning with the officer in charge of Project Athena and his cadet assistants. Under army orders they have done exhaustive research into the experience of women at West Point—how they met (and changed) its standards, what effect that training previously only offered to males had on women, and what effect the admission of women to West Point on equal terms with men had on that male institution.

There were real differences between the women and men cadets that were more important than the ability to do pull-ups, though the research reports keep reminding that there were "many more similarities between the male and female cadets than differences."

In choosing their service branches for their future military careers, for instance, both the female and male cadets chose on the basis of what they thought would be the most "satisfying" career—and not on how it would fit with family life.

The men chose "combat service" or "combat arms support" primarily in terms of "hero worship," as the officer called it; the women did not. Hero worship did not figure for the women. What was most important for the women was the moral question of "the taking of human life," which did not concern the men. But only 22 percent of the men, compared to 30 percent of the women, would "probably" or "no doubt" stay in the army after five years.

On leadership ratings—perhaps the most crucial element on which future army careers rest—there was no differentiation between women and men in the "ability to get the job done." But women came out much better than men on leadership rating that had to do with their dealings with and motivation of the people they had to lead, "looking out for and being concerned with the welfare of their subordinates."

As for women's effect on West Point, well, there was a certain questioning now of previously taken for granted rigid "standards." Most of the earlier research had been about training women to meet those physical requirements—some of which were now being discarded as unnecessary and "dysfunctional stress," for men as well as women. But the main effect was something harder to measure.

"There's a change in the male identity," the officer said.

"Before women came here, the way they solved this was the stereotype mask—stalwart, strapping, square-jawed John Wayne. Since the women came, the experience of male identity has become more heterogeneous; the men are not all giants roaming the plains any longer. The macho image was so very strong and unchallenged in an all-male environment. There was a disproportionate emphasis on male physical performance. Some hang on to this disproportionately, even now. Others see that relating to people is the key to leadership. Women cadets come out much better than the men on leadership ratings for being concerned with the welfare of their subordinates. This is especially important in dealing with a volunteer army—or for that matter any future draft of American people. It doesn't work here any more, that authoritarian mode—'just because I say so.' But in that other factor critical to army leadership—the ability to get the job done—there was no difference between the women cadets and the men."

The second report of Project Athena, June 1, 1978, showed that women in the next class, 1981, suffered fewer injuries than women in the class of 1980. Among other things, the combat boots, which had caused blisters, were redesigned to fit women's feet. "There has been a marked improvement in the climate surrounding coeducation at West Point," the report said. "Women are becoming more assertive and effective in managing their relationships with other cadets. . . . Men's stereotypic attitudes toward, and expectations of, women's abilities are giving way to a recognition of the talents and abilities of individual women cadets they know."

In the "Yearling" (sophomore) summer field training—where cadets must master firing weapons, throwing grenades, building bridges, adjusting artillery, commanding tanks, and must endure endless runs, obstacle courses, hand-to-hand combat training, survival techniques, patrolling and confidence tests to receive the coveted Redondo Patch—75 percent of the men and 73 percent of the women made it.

I met that night with the Corbin Seminar—the one place where the women cadets and those men cadets who want to support (and know) the women can publicly meet, with defenses down. The women cadets had mostly kept quiet at the lectures and classes, not even answering when the men vented that hostility about women "lowering the standards," the pull-ups, etc. "Let them get it out of their systems," a pretty red-haired cadet said, shrugging it off.

How could the women be so calm and good-natured about it all? Why weren't they more bitter—maimed, scarred, perhaps for life, by such heavy doses of venom and denigration? From history, from my own observation, I would almost expect the first woman in any field to become a bitter, man-hating battle-ax in self-defense—or turn the rage against herself and identify with the master sex, becoming a mousy or a blustering imitation man, hiding the writhing self-denigration behind a female machismo.

"Who says we aren't scarred?" they half-joked, in mock indignation, good-humored, strong and surprisingly serene. Did they find some new core of strength in themselves as women in these four years in which they proved themselves equal to men in their competence as military leaders, in the mastery of the rigorous physical and academic military training previously only available to men? No longer limited by, stunted by, railing against or even denying their difference from men, they seem simply sure of themselves as women. This is what I find most remarkable about these first female graduates of West Point—a sureness of themselves as women quite different from the patronizing, smug superiority of women who have never competed with men, which latter attitude, I suddenly realize, is the real female machismo.

They recall the worst moments of the four years with that surprising good humor—and a kind of gentle forgiveness.

When the men marched behind her in formation, muttering "*Oink, oink,*" Andrea Holden, who became the first female cadet to win a Rhodes scholarship, swore, "I will not cry, I will not cry."

But, of course, some cried. And gradually they lost their awe and fear, and even their bitter rage, at their male tormentors. They understood the danger of being prejudiced against men, in reaction, and becoming "jackasses" like them. "No, I mustn't generalize; not all men are jackasses," they kept reminding themselves.

"It was such a shock, being looked down on because of my sex," said the cadet with red curly hair. "It was the first time I've ever felt like a minority. My parents always told me I could do anything. I wasn't even particularly interested in the women's movement. I just took it for granted. Now I have to watch myself, not to be too defensive about sexist remarks, not to jump every time they say 'girl,' not to generalize about men, not to be bitter against men; it really doesn't help."

They began to sense the envy men felt about the attention being paid to the women. "When *Life* assembled all the graduating female cadets in front of the barracks in full dress for a picture," they tell me, smiling a little, "the men talked about how one bomb, dropped as the flash went off, would get rid of us all. . . . They talked of collecting money for a full-page ad with their picture in it, and the caption 'Men are graduating from West Point, too.' As reporters came around asking the female cadets questions about women and the draft, things like that, they would say, 'Why don't you ask one of the men?'

"They kept asking us why we were here. They never ask the men that. It's like men are put up on a big pedestal, just to be here. But women—they're so surprised if you're not gross, huge, a big-mustached battle-ax—you're not supposed to like getting dressed up, dancing, having fun like other women—you're just a freak cadet who is not a man, you're not supposed to be a real woman. But then you realize this is coming from the men who feel the most insecure. And now it's all behind us, I feel so confident somehow; they don't bother me any more. I feel like it's their problem, not mine. I feel like saying to them, Have fun with your life. I'm going to."

It's as if they gradually realized they were dealing with "little boys" under that ramrod-stiff bluster and as if they understood their rage the way mothers do when their little boys kick at them. They stopped trying to lower their voices and "look mean," and started wearing skirts again. (But not all the women: "Some won't ever wear a skirt, they won't come near the Corbin Seminar, they don't want to think about themselves as women at all.") And they learned how to stand their own ground without being defensive. They even turned away the obnoxious questions with a joke: "Why am I here? To find a husband, of course." The other women laugh. "There must be much easier ways to find a husband. So romantic, coming back from maneuvers, smelly, sweaty, dead beat. 'Can I carry your machine gun?' "

Some say the "hostility just went underground," that because of Goodpaster's edict, it was no longer "acceptable" to make public remarks abusing the women.

But it was more than that. In every company and squad where women cadets actually were present, the hostility declined during the training and barracks life with the men. The reality of women's presence changed things—the hostility, the prejudice, remained only in companies where women were not present, except as abstract threat (or, perhaps, inadmissible longing).

Given the small ratio of women to men—one to twelve—very few men had a chance to "fraternize." But there were at least enough women to give support to each other—against the general backdrop of consciousness of the women's movement—though a few women did not avail themselves of that support. But a growing number of men joined with the women in affirming some of the values that the women seemed to symbolize—and that were so threatening to "the warriors." Three out of four members of the Corbin Seminar are men.

Could it be some hidden undercurrent of sex and mother-

need—and also something *more* than sex and mother-need—
that makes some male cadets so ambivalent, so threatened by
and envious of the women, and of the men who dare to love
and know the women? What makes those others dare to join
the women, in need or love or new questions of their own,
despite the opprobrium of their male peers?

When a woman cadet has a male visitor, according to the
rules, the door has to be left open. "The whole company
parades up and down the hall checking," said a dark-haired
woman cadet. "We used to take turns, socializing with her
company one night and mine the next," said the male cadet,
holding hands with her during the entire seminar. "But her
company couldn't stand the sight of me. After a couple of
times, when I'd get back and find my room trashed, we figured it was better for me not to show my face too much
around her company." The women would have had to be
dumber than they are not to sense the little boys in those
cadets who didn't want to share the attention with—and of—
the women.

And of course, the women also began to acquire a healthy
respect for themselves, and for the men, for the skills and real
confidence they were gaining on that obstacle course. It was
tough, all right—but the mystique was gone. It was not that
tough, after all, if they, the women, could do it. More and
more, they became aware of some other strength that they
could trust in themselves that made them question the model
of those little-boy "warriors."

"The first year you kept asking yourself, Why am I here,
can I possibly make it? Maybe I shouldn't even be here,
maybe it isn't good for West Point, letting women in. The
next year, you felt women had a right to be at West Point,
and maybe you could make it. This last year, you realize that
letting women in was the best thing that could happen to
West Point now," said a female cadet.

"Whether they're conscious of it or not, the men have
begun to change at West Point since the women have come
in," said a male officer. "They had to, whether women came

or not. It used to be if a guy was compassionate, thought of people first and not just the mission, he was looked at like a pansy. I'm not much of a moralist myself, I'm not given to introspection, but I've learned a lot about myself since we let the women in; it's challenged so much we never questioned before. Within this all-male environment, men were punished for being sensitive, flexible—condemned for being weak, cowardly, if they admitted these fears, these very questions. So West Point actually fostered a phony, false strength, covering up unadmitted weaknesses and inability to cope with reality, alienating men from their own real feelings and the realities of leading others."

Said a female cadet: "There are some male cadets in my company who couldn't cry if their life depended on it. That really worries me. I get this feeling that the only reason they're here is that they like war, they like violence, they'll kill, kill, kill. There's something wrong with those men, something missing. It scares me."

As Project Athena revealed, the women cadets did not adopt such male role models. Nor did they resemble the first few women officers who were scarred from the punishment they had taken, lacking the support to affirm themselves and each other in their differences from men. "We got headaches and wondered if we were crazy," a woman officer told me. "We hid our bitterness and tried to fade in amongst the men. We had to apologize for being women."

The female cadets—enough in number to support each other, supported by the new movement-bred consciousness of themselves as women, and by the army's determination to integrate and use women in the armed forces, for its own needs—seem less scarred. They were strong enough to wear skirts, and to speak in their own voices—which were loud enough to be heard over the artillery firing. And they made their crucial decisions as to their own military careers according to values of life that evidently did not concern the male cadets, who still followed the old-style military hero

worship. I find myself smugly congratulating the women
. . . and I stop!

There is a *danger* in this kind of thinking—assuming wom-
en's moral superiority, women's greater sensitivity to the values and needs of human life. That, after all, is the rationale of
those who say women should not be exposed to combat duty,
or even drafted, in the next war. (One thing I learned in West
Point: Women must be drafted if there is another war. And
whatever a Supreme Court backsliding on equality says now,
whether or not they are trained for combat duty, whatever
their technical title or official job, they will all be exposed to
the dangers of being killed in combat.) Well, yes, I am relieved and proud that those first women cadets did not succumb to the machismo role model; they mastered the skills of
military defense, in service still to the values of life.

But why should these values be special to the women? If
women's skills are needed now to get the work done—the
work of military defense as in every other field of society—
then the equality of women, in its first stage at West Point, is
a question of national survival. But the other side of that
question—revealed in the very intensity of the men's reaction to women at West Point, the changes men are resisting
or adopting into their own values and style of leadership—is
even more basic to national, and human survival. Given the
technical possibilities of nuclear warfare, can that sensitivity
to human life be safely restricted to women any longer? Can
this nation survive or defend itself with an army of men—or
men and women—trained to be mechanical robot killers?

The last morning, at the meeting of the second section of
"American Institutions," I said I didn't want to waste their
time and mine talking any more about the women and their
problems and what they were doing to West Point standards.
They must be as sick of that subject as I was. I knew more
than I ever wanted to know about "upper body strength" by
now.

I wanted the men to tell me what they were feeling about

their own problems, as men, training at West Point to lead American armies. I said I was wondering about the excessive hostility and sense of being threatened by the women that I had been hearing from some of them—for it was excessive in the extreme, compared to the basic acceptance by most of their generation of women's equality, and compared to the actuality of the women's performance at West Point. Could they somehow be projecting on the women the fears and anxieties of some identity crisis they themselves were undergoing as men at West Point—a crisis that might have nothing to do with the women? Forget the female cadets—there seemed to me to be much more fuss about pull-ups and measures of physical prowess generally than when I first came to West Point, five years ago, before the women came in. Were the men, in fact, holding on to those pull-ups for dear life because of the fear that they themselves did not have another kind of strength a man might need now for real leadership in the kinds of situations an American army might face in the unpredictable future? Wasn't their real worry that they might not be capable of achieving that unknown kind of strength they'd need as men to survive, or prevent, another Vietnam—a strength that wasn't as simple as doing those six pull-ups, which they could do so much better than the women?

There were mutterings, gasps of outrage, much defensiveness. Who said they were hostile to or threatened by the women cadets? Maybe that was the attitude of the classes of '78 and '79, but *they* weren't sexists! *They* weren't suffering any "identity crisis"; they weren't a bunch of hippies, getting stoned, asking, Who am I? What's it all about? They didn't have time for such nonsense; they had more important things to worry about.

For example, this whole idea of a different kind of leadership than the warrior model—a lot of social scientists telling future officers to worry, Did the soldier boy write home to Mommy today? Does his tummy hurt? Is he scared? Telling us to treat the men like a lot of babies, telling us not to be tough guys. What are these social scientists doing here? Even if that kind of thing might work in training company managers, how would it work in war? What was needed for war, what was needed for America today, *was* John Wayne. They were tense, almost whining, holding on to that image, standing taller and taller, digging in their heels deeper and deeper, leaning over backward to keep their spines rigid. As for all that research that proved women were as good leaders as men, Project Athena was bunk!

One of the majors, in khaki shirtsleeves, his jacket with the Vietnam medals thrown over the seatback, protested mildly that the social scientists and the new approach to leadership training at West Point were brought in by command decision and specific orders, because of expert military analysis of the current crisis, and future needs, for army leadership. The old authoritarian model didn't work. It had covered up real weakness, and worse, in Vietnam. You can't run a peacetime army of American volunteers in the 1980s in the old way, "degrading" men—or women—physically or verbally, and get them to do the job. If the authoritarian system at West Point was aimed at pushing people out that couldn't survive the stress, today it was clear that that kind of "excess stress" was "dysfunctional"—the army was losing too many good people.

There was an unspoken wish behind the macho frenzy: if only that uniform still meant you could just order men to do anything and they would do it; if only you didn't have to have some inner strength; if only you didn't have to face their real feelings, or your own, as men. "Was that really John Wayne?" asked the major from the back of the room. "It sounds more like Mommy or a teacher or a nun, when we were kids, rapping out orders we'd have to obey just because they said so."

Machismo is a mask to demand blind obedience where there is no real strength. The unknown, different situations they, and the nation, might meet in the future could require the real strengths of the John Wayne model at certain times;

and at other times the strengths the women had, and the men might have, or could develop in themselves, that weren't as easy to measure as pull-ups. Pull-ups were not an adequate measure—even as metaphor—for the strengths Americans would need to defend the nation against the real dangers threatening its future now.

The women had been quiet again during this class. At the end, one of the women officers stood up and said with a passionate intensity that she felt sure both the men and the women would meet the situations they might have to face with the strengths that are needed, old strengths and new, similar and different, known and yet to be tried—as Americans always have. There was some quiet applause.

Major Ritch asked if I wanted to see the cadets assemble for parade formation and march into the mess hall, as they do twice every day over the great square parade ground (breakfast was made "optional" as one of the reforms about the time the women entered). Perfunctorily returning the salutes of the cadets as they passed us, lining up, he remarked that mostly now he and his fellow faculty officers took the back way to the mess hall themselves to avoid the chore of all this saluting.

In the arch of the courtyard behind us, he pointed out the top command of the cadet corps, assembling with their "staff." The First Captain this year was black. The third in command was a woman, standing there with her sword dangling and wearing white gloves, at ease with her brother cadets, in the pose of command. A male cadet officer at the head of one of the formations was interrogating a plebe. "He is probably asking him to recite the menu," said the major, "or the baseball score of last night's game." A woman cadet officer was passing between the rows of cadets, inspecting for dirty hair or hands, or shoes in need of a shine.

A small marching band assembled and began the fife-and-drum cadences. The cadets marched by, backs ramrod straight, heads up, chins in, staring straight ahead. They marched with precision, the Long Gray Line, squadron after squadron, behind their commanders. I enjoyed seeing the women, some in pants, but many wearing skirts. One, passing me, looked as though she wanted to cry, obviously upset about something—the women's faces, even with their chins held in, did show feelings more than the men's.

"Do they actually line up and march like this when they have to fight?" I asked the major, and he laughed. "They did line up like that when they went off to fight in the Revolutionary War," he said, "and other battles and skirmishes and training for such, one hundred and fifty years ago." Now, of course, these parade formations that take up so much of their time are mainly for show. To impress who? I wondered— visitors, the enemy, taxpayers, the cadets themselves? There is evidently a growing impatience with such pointless maneuvers among the new warriors and nonwarriors at West Point. It's evidently not so much fun, not so glamorous, "playing soldier" any more.

Does it somehow spoil the glamour of the game that women are in it? Or is there something else? Funny, how the admitting of women to West Point leads to the asking of new questions about survival and, at the same time, provides a simple, practical answer. The question of national survival. Human survival. The survival of women and men.

There is no doubt that the women have what it takes for the new army leadership, which the wisest of those studying "the crisis" sense is needed. They have the strength to survive the rigors, get the job done, and some sensitivity to human complexity; they have the flexibility to adjust to complicated, changing, unpredictable reality—human reality—that is necessary for survival now, even in a military sense, and that goes beyond the warrior model.

I came away from West Point feeling very good about those women cadets. No, they did not turn into imitation jocks, feeble or supertough imitations of machismo—not the ones I met. Those rigorous exercises, the sheer use of all the

aggressive energy they could muster against the physical and
mockup military obstacles, might explain how positive, serene, almost tender they could feel toward their boy-soldier
oppressors. What an advantage for these women, compared
to other women, and to their fellow cadets—the sheer sense
of importance and self-respect, the confidence of having mastered this adventure, these ordeals, acquiring skills not available to women before and discovering not so much that they
were inferior to men in certain things but that new sense of
sureness about themselves as women. What ease, compared
to all the women in all the generations past who have had to
hide and turn their own aggressive energy—and their rage at
putdowns from men—inward against their own bodies, in
sickness and malaise, and self-denigration, and covert revenge against men, and their own children. How healthy to
be trained and rewarded for using their aggressive energy
against outward obstacles, playing soldier like the boys! How
healthy also—perhaps because of the new consciousness that
came with the women's movement, whether or not the
women cadets think of themselves as feminists—that they so
quickly found that core of strength in themselves: the independence to master the male skills and play the male game,
without losing their own identity as women, without trying
to turn themselves into men.

There was a time when such an idea would have made me
cringe. But there is a truth here. Not a new feminine mystique. Not a shying away from the full implications of equality. A sense, from this extreme situation of women at West
Point, the citadel of machismo, that it is necessary now for
society's survival, as well as for women's own survival, that
they take an equal place in these activities which once were
men's domain. In so doing, both the activities and the women
change, evolve. But it doesn't turn women into men; if those
who train the women, or the women themselves, blindly try
to ape the male model of the past, will they not, in fact, miss
the point, forfeit their own evolutionary advantage? For the
stunning revelation is how strangely the qualities women

brought with them to West Point—and the questions the very admission of women led to about male standards and values previously taken for granted—converged on, meshed into, the urgent new questions the wisest of men were being forced to ask themselves, facing new realities and dangers and complexities of national defense and survival.

No, the women don't worry me at all. Of course women will be drafted, if we face again the danger of war—with or without Equal Rights, and whatever the Supreme Court says now. It's reassuring to think that if and when women face necessities of combat and the power of military command, it will be with a sure commitment to the "moral questions," the values and interests of human life—survival, not machismo, not killing for the glory of it.

It's the men I came away from West Point worrying about. I sensed their pain and the panic underneath their hostility, an aching envy for the qualities those women have which the men sense they need. But be careful here: no need for a mystique of women's nature superior to man's, etc. It is much easier for women to acquire the muscular skills and strength to do six pull-ups or play soldier in parades with the men than for the men to break through their armor of masculine strength (which gets more defensive, brittle, unable to brook the slightest new question or challenge, the more vulnerable and inadequate to new situations it truly is) and acquire the flexibility and sensitivity to human needs and the values of life now required of them as men to defend a democratic nation against its own and an ever-changing enemy's capacity for nuclear holocaust.

Of course, it's easier to recognize and admire the new strengths of women, as they acquire confidence and skills always admired in men, and previously available only to men —and even appreciate the different grace and superior effectiveness of these strengths tempered by qualities the women bring with them—than to recognize what those new strengths will even look like in men. Because some of those new capacities needed now for survival—in military as well as ordinary life—have been seen as "weakness" in men. They are qualities devalued as "female."

It is clear from Project Athena that the women who seized the new opportunity to enter West Point were more outstanding than the men—in terms not only of academic and athletic achievement, but openness to change, and self-confidence, with both traditional feminine and feminist strengths —compared to other women their age. (From Project Athena II: "Women cadets rated themselves more than ten points higher than women at four-year colleges on the following six items: (1) do at least 15 push-ups; (2) score a tennis match; (3) swim a mile without stopping; (4) know freedoms in Bill of Rights; (5) referee sporting events; and (6) bake a cake from scratch.")

To go to West Point was a different kind of challenge for the women than for the men. The women who are probably at the front edge of the female evolutionary scale—and the men who cling most desperately to outdated male standards —would be the ones most likely to apply, and to get accepted, according to the standards used. Probably the men who most easily achieve the new strengths and values would not even apply to West Point—they would not be enticed by West Point parades. How infuriating, then, for the men whose very insecurity makes them seek refuge in a monastery of machismo, to have to confront even at West Point those threatening, despised female qualities buried so deep in themselves. (Research done at the Air Force Academy showed that the men, or at least significant numbers of them, became even more macho and denied their feelings even more when women were first admitted than before.)

The young black male cadets at West Point were the only ones who didn't seem defensive. For them, as for the women, there seemed to be a genuine affirmation of themselves in being allowed to develop the old "masculine" strengths previously denied to them. The black cadets also seemed less threatened by the women, and by the new sensitivities now demanded. The ordeal of the White Anglo-Saxon Protestant (or Catholic, or Jewish) American male—facing and resisting the necessity to break through old definitions of masculinity and release these new "feminine" strengths in himself—is described in a dog-eared, unknown tome lent to me by the major, written by a West Point graduate and former ranger-paratrooper army officer. *Tenderness Is Strength: From Machismo to Manhood*, by Harold C. Lyon, Jr., is evidently a kind of primer for the growing underground of military leaders who are breaking out of machismo. Lyon writes:

> Men have become isolated inside the barren barri-cades of machismo, afraid to let anyone in and afraid to let themselves out. They live in constant fear that someone will see, behind the loud posturing, a lonely person locked inside himself. The rage and helpless feelings which result are hard to share. To those who can read it, the language of machismo is a distinct plea for someone to finally break through the rigid postures in which so many men have become trapped. . . . In the last few years, I have begun to discover that the toughness that I developed as a protective shell in order to survive in society's hostile environment is not really my strength as I thought it to be. Rather, it is my ten-derness that leads me to strength—toughness is not strength; tenderness is not weakness.

I leave West Point, as the first female cadets are about to graduate, feeling safer somehow because these powerful nu-clear weapons that can destroy the world and the new human strategies therefore needed to defend this nation will hence-forward be in the hands of women and men who are, with agony, breaking through to a new strength, strong enough to be ensitive and tender to the evolving needs and values of human life—if only the last gasps of threatened machismo do not stop this evolution. As the ex-West Pointer concluded: "We do not need to revolt. We need to evolve."

PART II

The
Second Stage

6 The Limits and True Potential of Women's Power

 As that process which began with the women's movement evolves into the second stage, it is necessary to understand the limits of women's power and the possibilities of transcending those limits and generating a new kind of power.

There *are* limits to women's power, as we discovered this past year. Even on the gut issues of women's rights—the Equal Rights Amendment and the right of choice to have a child or safe, legal access to abortion—on which there is an enormous consensus, as measured in the polls, cutting across lines of race, economic class, generation and political party, women's power, exercised to its fullest, seemed to provoke an equal and opposite reaction in the election results of 1980.

But the question must be asked: Is the new kind of power generated or implicit in the women's movement truly expressed or measured in single-issue, special-interest politics?

There is a discrepancy between the power of the women's movement, as a fundamental change in the consciousness of and about women and their role in society, and the deadlocks and failures of the organized political movement on these single issues. Of course, it could be argued that the Equal Rights Amendment—which would put half the population under the full protection of the Constitution and the Bill of

189

Rights for the first time, guaranteeing inalienable equal opportunity for women in employment, education, and other spheres where laws against sex discrimination are now being gutted, and providing the basis for equality in social security, marriage and divorce law, pensions and military service—is more than a single issue. Surely, half the population is more than a special-interest group. But no matter: as the movement focused its energies on those issues, it took on, at least in part, the dominant, masculine mode of previous political special-interest groups, abstracting one issue from the total context, locking itself into a win-lose, zero-sum, linear, confrontational context that belied the generative power by which women, and men, have transformed themselves and their lives in the women's movement.

On the other hand, in the movement activity of fighting for the Equal Rights Amendment over the past ten years, women have grown, discovered unsuspected strengths and skills, and developed a consensus extending from traditional establishment groups like the Junior League and the YWCA, the Girl Scouts, the League of Women Voters, Catholic nuns, Jewish and Protestant churchwomen, union, business and professional women, to the new women's caucuses in every field, as well as newly organized black and Chicano, student and farm women, and the proliferating mainstream to radical feminist organizations. This consensus is infinitely broader than any special-interest group of men. In fact, the movement for women's equal rights has won the support not only of the majority of men, as reflected in the polls, but specific political support, finally, from labor leaders and civil rights and other special-interest groups. As Eleanor Smeal, the effective president of NOW, has said, "Not a moment of it was wasted, even if we never win."

It was not a "single issue" to fight to get that Constitutional underpinning for the rights won over these years of the modern women's movement. We somehow knew that in periods of economic recession or political reaction, those laws wouldn't be safe—and our worst fears have been realized sooner than we imagined. If only we had won the Equal Rights Amendment in those heady first seven years—as we should and could have, if we hadn't been diverted by sexual politics or co-opted by "masculine" political power—it would not be so easy for right-wing Senators to dismantle affirmative-action programs against sex discrimination in education and employment, as they announced they intended to do, less than a week after the 1980 Reagan landslide election.

The women's movement did not fail in the battle for equality. Our failure was our blind spot about the family. It was our own extreme of reaction against that wife-mother role: that devotional dependence on men and nurture of children and housewife service which has been and still is the source of power and status and identity, purpose and self-worth and economic security for so many women—even if it is not all that secure any more. And not only for the 49 percent who are still housewives. Most of the other 51 percent still don't get as much sense of worth, status, power or economic security from the jobs they now have as they get, or think they could get, or still wish they could get, from being someone's wife or mother. And the more insecure—with inflation, with the increasing divorce rate—the more such a woman is threatened by the very idea that she needs ERA, that she might have to take care of herself, that, God forbid, she might not always have a husband to take care of her and a family to justify her existence.

Something very complex is involved here. Is there a real polarization between the feminist who wants equality and "choice," and the woman for whom "the family" is security? Aren't those feminists who most stridently deny the family trying to deny that woman's vulnerability in themselves? Do women who want equal rights really threaten that clean, pure, sacred family morality that once made her feel secure? Or are ERA advocates threatening because they make her aware of her real insecurity, and her buried wish for independence and autonomy? And if a man stands to lose his job, and the dollars he's worked for all his life are worth pennies now, where can *he* look for security, respect, identity except in the family? All these people who want equal rights for women, abortion rights, homosexual rights—they're destroying the family! (Safer to fight *them* than to understand and fight the powerful economic forces that really threaten family security today.)

It is remarkable, however, that the polls showed an increasing majority of women and men supporting the ERA—and the right to abortion—as inflation forced more and more women to work, their paycheck helping the family to survive even when the husband was laid off.

The Republicans, in fact, probably lost the votes of the single largest voting bloc in the 1980 election as a result of their extreme platform stand, repudiating the Equal Rights Amendment, vowing to amend the Constitution to outlaw abortion, and pledging to appoint judges who concurred with these views. It is noteworthy—though the media and most politicians still have such a blind spot about women that they didn't really note it—that there was a nearly 20 percent difference between the voting of women and men in the 1980 Presidential election. Reagan defeated Carter by an incredible 54 to 37 percent among men, but only 46 to 45 percent among women (New York Times-CBS News Poll). *The majority of women (52 percent) voted against Reagan*— (45 percent for Carter, 7 percent for Anderson). There has never been such a discrepancy between men's and women's voting in all the years since exit polls have been taken. In the previous Presidential election the male and female percentages were identical. Further, women who were for the Equal Rights Amendment voted overwhelmingly against Reagan, 65 to 32 percent, more than two to one. This women's rights bloc constituted 22 percent of the total vote, a far larger bloc than blacks (10 percent), Hispanics (2 percent) and Jews (5 percent) combined, or even than blue-collar workers (17 percent). Women who opposed the ERA constituted only 15 percent of the total vote, and they supported Reagan even more avidly than men—66 percent to 29 percent for Carter.

For women as for men, inflation was an overriding issue. After all, women still do most of the shopping. Nevertheless, for the majority of women to have voted against Reagan, equality had to be an overriding gut issue for a great many of them. The issue of war and peace, supposedly also of greater concern to women, had been largely defused by the debate. Polltakers puzzling this difference between the voting of women and men in the 1980 election could not pin it down to the specific issues of ERA and abortion—only to a general impression that "Carter would be better for women."

After all, Carter had delivered only one state beyond the thirty-four which had ratified ERA before his election—and he had also opposed federal funds for poor women's abortions. ("Life is not fair.") Eleven months before the election, the NOW board had resolved: "Anybody but Carter." But the women's rights groups, in a rare demonstration of united power, had effectively defied Carter's own commandos at the Democratic convention and won a stronger support of ERA and poor women's right to legal medical aid in abortion in the Democratic platform. Would Carter run with this? Well, no, not really. . . . Only at the very end, some of the fine feminists and shrewd female politicians in the Carter Administration—Eleanor Holmes Norton, Anne Wexler—enlisted the help of Eleanor Smeal and myself and other feminist leaders, making a commitment to mobilize the full machinery of the White House for ERA and child care, next time. Too little, too late.

If the Democrats had spent the same amount of energy and serious attention courting women on the issue of equal rights as they spent courting blacks and Jews and other minorities—not only during the campaign, but during the four years in the White House—we might have had the Equal Rights Amendment, and the women's movement might have mobilized in earnest to reelect Carter. As it turned out, we mobilized in belated panic to defeat Reagan and contained our disgust with Carter. But our help was not seriously sought—nor deserved. It is hardly surprising that 43 percent of women in favor of ERA voted against Carter (32 percent for Reagan, 11 percent for Anderson). Women, and some men, told me personally of "walking around the block four times before I decided that if inflation keeps up, ERA will be worthless anyhow. Besides, I wouldn't trust Carter now, on ERA or inflation."

But the polarization that led to the sweep of the Senators on the Moral Majority hit list (Birch Bayh, Frank Church, John Culver, Gaylord Nelson, George McGovern) cannot be attributed solely to the disgust with Carter, or to Reagan's coattails. The women's movement has to assume some responsibility. We underestimated the threat and did not mobilize ourselves in all-out defense of the men who were explicitly fingered by the National Conservative Political Action Committee supposedly because they supported ERA, abortion and homosexual rights.

Is a distorted sexual politics at work if the women's movement did not rise to the support of these men with the same passion as, for instance, it supported Bella Abzug or Liz Holtzman? Is a distorted sexual politics responsible for the lumping of these three issues together in such an inflammable, sexually charged package? It is all very well for leaders of the women's movement today to insist, correctly, that the Equal Rights Amendment has nothing to do with either abortion or homosexuality—in fact, it has nothing to do with sexual behavior at all. But the sexual politics that distorted the sense of priorities of the women's movement during the seventies made it easy for the so-called Moral Majority to lump ERA with homosexual rights and abortion into one explosive package of licentious, family-threatening sex.

There is no doubt that the radical right, with its mysterious sources of endless money behind that pious Moral Majority front, is using abortion and homosexuality as sexual red herrings in its frighteningly successful drive to take over the United States Government and repress dissent, whatever its real aims. It goes beyond the premise of this work—or my own wisdom—to figure out why *sexuality* becomes such a convenient battleground for reactionary political and economic power. Hysteria over sexual license, homosexuality, abortion—and the reduction of women from independent people with rights to passive sexual objects, segregated behind literal or figurative chadors—serves more sinister purposes of reactionary power. For surely homosexuality and abortion are not the main problems in America today (though woman's drive to equality and economic and political independence—for which control of her own reproductive process is, indeed, essential—does pose a real threat to reactionary power). But up through history to Hitler and the Ayatollah Khomeini of Iran—and not exempting Stalinist Russia and most Communist regimes today—control and manipulation of sexuality and the family, and suppression of the rights and personhood of women, have been key elements in authoritarian power.

The manipulation of sexual hysteria and the repression of women are more than diversionary: they build a reservoir of impotent rage and frustrated energies in the family which can be diverted into violence, for one thing. The emotions and repressions linked to sexuality are so powerful that it is relatively easy to divert people's attention from their own basic economic interests and even from asking the tough political questions simply by manipulating sexual hysteria (just as it is easier to sell people things they don't really need with those subliminal sexual messages).

Of course, the more real sexual liberation—and real satisfaction of people's needs for love and intimacy, which may be possible only when women and men can live as relatively secure, self-respecting equals—the less possible for any dictator or demagogue to manipulate people that way, against their own interests.

And, in another sense, our sexuality is a final frontier of privacy and autonomy any woman or man has the right, and need, to defend, according to personal values, in this invasive mass society where so little is left that we can control in our own lives. Beneath the hysteria of the Moral Majority, surely many of the women who respond to its message feel the same sense of basic human value and autonomy imperiled as other women feel when told they can no longer decide when and whether to have a child.

The founding fathers of this republic were not wrong when they wrote into the Bill of Rights the protection of certain basic areas of privacy for the individual conscience, exempt from the state's control, even if, in the beginning, they guaranteed such rights of privacy only for people who were men. Surely it is politically unwise to seem to threaten that area of inviolate sexual privacy now, as part of an effort to secure these basic rights for women. Tactics that smack of sexual exhibitionism, like the lesbians' balloons at the National Women's Conference at Houston proclaiming, "We are everywhere," and even slogans like "sexual preference," distort the basic principle; they seem to invade that very right of privacy for which we fight.

The abortion issue may have further overtones. It is significant that the final straw that reversed the trend in Congress and the courts upholding the right to safe legal medical access to abortion was the use of federal or state funds for abortion. There is a convergence here of sexual and economic threat. To release women from that final sexual control, to free her to move in the world and even to enjoy and control her own sexual behavior without punishment—and then to make the taxpayer pay for it to boot—that's going too far! Of course, it is only a matter of time until Kemp-Roth, *et al.*, figure out that it costs far more to raise an unwanted kid on welfare than to let a woman get an abortion under Medicaid. Then the piousness of Government not sanctioning abortion may become an openly punitive move to forced sterilization. There is an interesting case of a lobbyist even now in Washington who has moved from agitating against abortion rights to lobbying to lower the age of marriage to twelve, and to prohibit girls from going to school or getting any jobs! (*New York Times*, Nov. 12, 1980)

There is also a curious illogic in the fact that the same "Right to Life" crowd, who would sanctify the unborn fetus over the life of woman herself in the so-called Human Life Amendment, also advocates, in the Laxalt Family Protection Act, the right to beat a child in school and the elimination of all sanctions against child-battering and wife-beating.

Still, there was something that went wrong in the terms we used to discuss abortion. Such slogans as "free abortion on demand" had connotations of sexual licentiousness, not only affronting the moral values of conservatives but implying a certain lack of reverence for life and the mysteries of conception and birth which have been women's agony and ecstasy and defining value down through the ages. There is a mystique of motherhood; but the conception and bearing of children—the ongoing generation of human life—is surrounded, in all religions, by an awe and mystery that is more than a mystique. Being "for abortion" is like being "for mastectomy." It completely overlooks the life-enhancing value for women and families of the choice to have children.

Yet an evolution is taking place here. Younger feminists, now aware of the possible consequences of the Pill and the IUD to women's future health and future ability to bear children are promoting, in the women's health network, the diaphragm and even the new natural method, based on the mucous and temperature changes that signify the ovulation period. The Catholic priests at the White House Conference on Families were ready to join us on "the choice to have children." More importantly, the official American body of Catholic bishops, at the recent Synod on the Family at the Vatican, objected to the definition of birth control as "sin," noting that 85 percent of American Catholics use birth control, motivated by human responsibility and moral conscience, not "sin."

It was a second-stage approach, when NOW president Eleanor Smeal invited leaders of the Right to Life movement to meet with feminists in Washington in 1980 to discuss how we might jointly work to further research that would enable women to transcend the divisive issue of abortion and be able to choose to bear children responsibly and joyously and with full respect for all of our values and rights to life.

The limits of women's power, and its true potential, were masked by the first-stage preoccupation with sexual issues. The power of issues like abortion in countries like Italy and France as well as America to ignite women into united action, across lines of class and race and political difference, was deceptive. Focusing on such single issues, no matter how basic, blinds one to the totality of women's movement to personhood in society, which is what the women's movement was all about. Preoccupation with sexual issues can blind us to the larger economic and political situation which affects both women and men, and which women now as persons can actively affect. On the issues of war or peace, or inflation in the United States, or revolution in Iran, or national survival in Afghanistan, or Israel, or Cambodia, I do not think that women have a different stake than men, nor a need to organize in a separate women's movement (except to protect or advance their own rights which the revolution itself may threaten or ignore). I do not believe that sexual issues, where women may indeed have a separate stake, or even women's rights, take precedence, even for women, over larger issues such as war and peace, or economic survival, or revolt against tyranny, or threats to basic human freedom, in any nation or system. But women's own freedom is one basic human right that women themselves can never ignore.

At the United Nations' Mid-Decade World Conference on Women in Copenhagen last summer American feminists, including myself, were shocked when Third World women hung a huge portrait of the Ayatollah in the conference hall, and defended the chador ("it gives us more freedom really; we don't have to take so much time to dress up when we go out"), which to us seemed the very symbol of the denial of the personhood of women. (The forced shrouding of Iranian women, in fact, accompanied the repression of many rights of women, in the name of the Ayatollah's Moslem revolution.)

That Third World women would try to defend clitoridectomy seemed even more outrageous. But certain American and British feminists, pursuing more exotic sexual issues now that abortion and homosexuality were becoming banal, were launching a veritable crusade on clitoridectomy, still evidently practiced in some African countries. Some Third World women rose up and told the American feminists to please lay off; clitoridectomy was their problem, they would deal with it in their own way. But they had more pressing problems to worry about right now, such as the fact that technological "development," now coming to their countries, was taking away from women the chores in the field that used to give them some economic function and power. But the literacy necessary to use the new technology, or to leave the farm for new jobs in the cities, was going only to the men.

At an Iranian press conference, the Iranian women in their chadors took their signals from a man. Bella Abzug took them to task for this. An Iranian woman came up to her afterward and said, "At our stage of development, it is all right for us to take leadership from a man if we want to."

The American delegation, which included many good feminists, charged that the UN Conference was being "politicized" when PLO resolutions condemning Israel, bewailing the "special oppression" of female Palestinian refugees, and seeking UN funds for PLO were pushed. More sophisticated, or more cynical, women delegates and reporters from other countries were incredulous at this charge. Of course the conference was "politicized"; women were and should be "political."

It came as a shock to American feminists that for many women delegates at the conference the enemy was not "man" but our own country, America, "the imperialist aggressor"; or it was Israel, the scapegoat.

I began to sense, in those frustrating days at Copenhagen, the limits of women's power, organized as a separate interest group along sexual lines. Five years earlier, at the first UN Women's Conference at Mexico City, the modern women's movement, then at its peak in America, was spreading through the advanced nations—at least the democracies, where women were free to organize for their own rights. Many American feminists, and new feminists from other lands—Egypt, Australia, Japan, India, Nigeria, Ghana, France, England, Holland, New Zealand, Sweden—went to Mexico eager to compare notes, learn from each other, agree on a common world feminist agenda and set up some UN machinery to help implement it.

But the official delegates at that Mexico conference, if not men, were, for the most part, officials' wives or other passive, nonfeminist women, not really interested in women's rights at all. And in the parallel, nongovernmental conference, the men running the show used every possible means to keep the women from really getting together, finally breaking up our meeting with disruption from anonymous armed men. I was warned to get out of Mexico for fear of my life. The day after I left Mexico, the official World Women's Conference became the first UN body to launch an attack on Israel. It seemed clear that an alliance of Communist, Moslem and Latin despots, now in control of the UN, was threatened by the world spread of feminism and was using the UN to co-opt it and manipulate women for their own political purposes. But in Mexico, feminists from all parts of the world at least got together and fought to move women's rights ahead.

At Copenhagen, it began to seem that feminism would never be allowed to function as a world political force. On the one hand, a great many of the official delegates now were women who had risen to some political power in their own countries, as a result of the women's movement. But the official agenda, set by the UN before the conference began, offered nothing that would materially improve the status of women worldwide except a "World Covenant Against Sex

Discrimination," written by Koryne Horbal, then U.S. Representative to the UN Commission on Women's Rights, which would mean nothing unless machinery was set up to monitor it. The real priority at this conference seemed to be not women's rights but UN sanctions against Israel.

And at the nongovernmental forum at Copenhagen, steps had clearly been taken to keep the women from getting together and proposing anything on our own, as we had succeeded in doing in Mexico City. Feminists from Denmark itself, evidently aware of this, boycotted the whole conference. The workshop on clitoridectomy created a press sensation, as did the swaggering PLO woman terrorist who had hijacked a plane and was treated as the conference's heroine. I was allowed to speak at a panel on "The Future of the Family," one of the few where women from Communist, European and African nations and American feminists managed to have a dialogue without disruption. But every attempt at a larger plenary session in which a world feminist agenda might have emerged was disrupted by supporters of the PLO, breaking up discussion of feminist issues to denounce Israel, "the Zionist entity," or American imperialism.

In desperation, I got together with Bella Abzug, Jan Peterson of the National Congress of Neighborhood Women, and some of the feminists in the United States delegation—Sarah Power, Virginia Allen, Dorothy Height, Ruth Hinerfeld, Esther Landa, Odessa Komer of the United Auto Workers, Alexis Herman, Congresswomen Barbara Mikulski and Rose Okar—in an attempt to salvage something for *women* out of the UN Women's Conference, or at least to keep it from being used only as another weapon against Israel.

Since every plenary meeting at the forum was disrupted by the PLO, we set ourselves up at an old Danish church for a meeting of delegates and other women at the UN Conference to discuss feminism. Over five hundred came, having heard about the meeting by word of mouth and hastily hand-passed invitations. It was probably the only *feminist* discussion the official delegates heard. Speaking in that church, I said maybe it was not possible to advance women's rights through the UN, but this conference was, at least, supposedly called for that purpose. Despite the political differences that divided our nations—and, of course, women *were* political, and they shared these differences—was it possible to get together as women and create some machinery in the UN that would help us all advance to equality? Was it possible that this UN Women's Conference was being directed into divisive issues it had no real power to resolve, such as the Palestinian matter, because in fact the men that run the UN did not want anyone looking over their shoulders with regard to women's rights in their own countries?

Was it possible to refer those other issues to the World Court of Justice and at least come out of Copenhagen with some UN machinery to monitor the World Covenant Against Sex Discrimination? And perhaps set up a UN tribunal to monitor "development" and the introduction of technology into Third World countries so that technology did not displace women? And what about organizing a UN commission to look into ways to ameliorate the double burden of work and home that was oppressing women in advanced nations?

Many of the women delegates had expressed private disgust at the travesty of this supposed UN Mid-Decade World Conference on Women (the official UN report revealed that women the world over had fallen behind, not advanced, since the decade began). But with the exception of a few bold women from New Zealand and Canada who made passionate speeches denouncing the insult to women's rights, there was virtually complete public acquiescence by the women in their own political manipulation. I doubt they even argued with the men who gave them orders. They seemed too clearly to be enjoying the heady new perquisites of pomp and illusion of power a woman might feel in being for the first time an official delegate to even a minor international conference.

Nevertheless, the foreign ministers back in their capitals

must have feared the women might rebel and demand that some action on women's rights come out of this UN Women's Conference—because in its last two days, when the crucial votes were cast, many countries flew in male diplomats to replace the women delegates to do the actual voting.

Co-option, or the lure of being "inside," part of the political establishment—the illusion, if not the reality, of participating actively in political decision-making instead of being its passive pawn—can keep the most ardent feminist quiet on women's rights once she gets elected or appointed to office. There were many feminists in the Carter Administration, and some good Republican feminists, as well. That they tried as seriously as many of them did to get action out of Carter on ERA or abortion—and to keep the Republican convention from declaring war against women's rights—is remarkable enough.

Effective women politicians do not campaign on women's rights alone. On the other hand, both the women and the men who fought for ERA at the Democratic and the Republican conventions in 1980 did so not only on principle but from real knowledge of the political stakes involved. And, I suppose, based on political realism most of the Republican women politicians on the fringes of power supported Reagan after they lost their battle for women's rights, just as Democratic women, including NOW leaders, swallowed their bile over Carter's insults and ineffectiveness, and supported him in the end out of realistic fear of the political alternatives.

But the woman Senator from Kansas stopped supporting the right to abortion after she was in office. The new woman Senator from Florida campaigned as an antifeminist. All four new women elected to Congress in 1980 told a *New York Times* reporter (January 11, 1981) they weren't "interested" in women's issues—"both sides" should please leave them alone! Evidently trying to clear their skirts of any suspect feminist smear, they disavowed concern for women and children altogether, not only ERA and abortion, but also "housing for

single parents" and child-care programs. Representative
Lynn Martin, who took Anderson's Congressional seat in Illinois, when asked how she rated women's issues on her
agenda, answered, "Zip. . . . There isn't any politician,
male or female, who likes these issues, because they're such
trouble. You think anyone who got far enough to be elected
to Congress is going to bring up these issues on her own?"

Why should we expect women to be any better or worse
than men when they get some power? And yet, as Hannah
Arendt wrote of the American Revolution (in *On Revolution*),
the women's movement did not seem like other revolutions.
Overthrowing power, polarized against the group in power,
revolutionaries usually take on the tyrannical attributes of
the oppressors once they achieve power themselves.
Robespierre and Napoleon became as bloody, fanatical, dicta-
torial, imperial as the Kings of France, or more so. Stalin's
oppression in the name of the working class and the Communist party outreached the Czar's. The Ayatollah's revolution
may impose more torture than the regime of the Shah.

The glory of the American Revolution, in contrast, was
the democratic process, the heady individual participation as
equals in the decisions of their own destiny by the men who
made that Declaration of Independence, and the embodying
of guarantees that that process would continue, in the Constitution. The women's movement was, in a certain sense, the
beginning of the second stage of that American Revolution.

Today, even in America, old political modes no longer
give people that sense of their own democratic power. In the
face of dwindling economic growth, political apathy, corrup-
tion, cynicism and disillusionment with gigantic national
public programs and bureaucracies, people feel increasingly
helpless and impotent in their efforts to meet their real needs
for housing, education, health, security in old age, a clean
environment and protection from nuclear war.

The true political potential of the women's movement
will be realized in the second stage if the process that made it
the most vital movement of this decade is used, in or outside

the mainstream political parties, or in other new alliances of life-affirming, life-tuned men and women, to give people a new sense of control over their own destiny.

Should we then ignore, or can we transcend, the political polarization of women against women on the basic issues of ERA and abortion in the face of deepening economic crisis and reactionary tensions?

An extremist scenario—fantasy wish of the Radical Right or apocalyptic nightmare of the Left—would have all the rights women have won in this era raped during the eighties by Neanderthal Senators, with President Reagan's approval and abject appeasement by the remaining liberal Democrats and Republicans. Without the government programs and laws to protect women against sex discrimination, employers and universities would start to fire women from their jobs, remove them from professorships, executive offices and church pulpits. Younger women coming up would be told, as before, not to bother to apply for a job in this company or a seat in that law school. And husbands and fathers would have permission to stop their pretense of sharing more and more of the responsibility for the housework and the care of the children. The husband would be free again to put his feet up and watch television while the wife cleaned the toilet bowl, or even, after pocketing her miserable paycheck, to kick her newly meek and defenseless rear if his supper wasn't warm when he got home from the corner bar.

Then, the women's movement would be forced to disband, with new laws decreeing it a "subversive" plot to undermine the family. And it would go underground, like a real revolution, with women daring jail and blacklist to meet in secret cells, or forming their own vigilante squads to take revenge on those born-again male brutes who had the Government behind them now, forcing women back into their place, barefoot and pregnant, even getting them convicted of murder if they refused to bear a child.

That is not the second stage I envision. It would be a

serious misreading of the election results and even of the appeal of the Moral Majority if responsible conservative leaders tried to take away women's basic rights. It would be a serious misreading of the election results and ignoring of danger signs, including the appeal of the Moral Majority, if responsible women's movement leaders stayed fixed in the win-lose positions of first-stage feminism, inviting a fight-to-the-death confrontation between the false poles of equality and the family. No matter how feisty we were when the going was easy, or what reservoirs of real courage we might tap, if our lives or our families were in danger (or our own personhood, which has become a conscious, concrete value to many women in this time), if abstract rights are seen to be in conflict with the priorities of life, our own or our families' survival, will women keep fighting?

The limits to women's power as a separate sexual force, in terms of abstract sexual politics, will be sharper as recession-inflation-unemployment and reaction increase. Women married to successful men will hold desperately to that security, as will women with a tenuous hold on jobs and professions. Will either identify with the women who are "out"—of husbands, jobs, any security at all? And if jobs become harder to get, how much easier to persuade younger women they wouldn't even have ambitions if not for the nasty women's movement witches? As the security of their jobs is threatened, women whose own professional advancement has taken the place of women's movement goals may become newly disillusioned. For without the women's movement to bring new social solutions to the family-career conflict, the deepening pressures of the superwoman syndrome will bring new allure to that old kind of security—a man to take care of you, the home and family that feminism seemed to deride. Even if new economic reality removes the very possibility that most women can ever go back to reliance on that kind of feminine mystique security "to take care of my whole life," that won't keep fundamentalist preachers and demagogic politicians, male and female, from manipulating that dream for their own profit or power, or wishful, tired women from buying it.

The true potential of women's power can be realized only by transcending the false polarization between equality and the family. It is an abstract polarization that does not exist in real life. The political dilemmas it creates over ERA and abortion are insoluble—in the abstract. But the circumstances that forced women to move to equality in the first place and to seek control of their lives—the economic changes and the increased life span—are confronting more and more women with the concrete problems of the second stage, which transcend that polarization. Those problems are not going to go away. As inflation gets worse, and we all live longer, and jobs get scarcer, and more and more women have to work, and the very choice to have a child becomes more and more agonizing—the problems of living and working, on old or new terms of equality and family, individuality and intimacy, fulfillment and responsibility, will become more and more urgent, cutting across lines of generation, class or previous political differences.

As we come to the dead end of the first stage of feminism, that abstract polarization on ERA and abortion makes it seem as if there are two kinds of women in America (or the world). But that sharp polarization, manipulated by demogogues and unfortunately accepted by too many feminists, hides the underlying reality: an evolving continuum of American women defining their own personhood today both within and beyond the context of the family, in varying and ever changing proportions for each woman. Instead of the polarization of two kinds of women—or feminism versus the family—which has plagued the women's movement in the last years, and prevented the very possibility of political solutions, new research shows that *virtually all women today share a basic core of commitment to the family and to their own equality within and beyond it, as long as family and equality are not seen to be in conflict.*

Given the political polarization among women on ERA and abortion that is taken for granted by media, politicians, feminists and antifeminists, a number of social scientists in recent years have undertaken in-depth research studies to pin down and analyze the root differences between women subscribing to ideas of equality, on the one hand, and values of the traditional family, on the other. But when they interviewed cross-sections of women nationally and regionally about their lives and their views, they were not able to find such a polarization. Instead of finding two kinds of women—those who believe in the traditional family, and those who believe in equality—a number of different research studies found that women, *in their actual lives*, succeed in transcending abstract, political polarization.

One such study, "Juggling Contradictions: Women's Ideas about Families," was conducted by Nancy Bennett, Susan Harding, *et al.*, of the Social Science Research Community of the University of Michigan in 1979. The women in this study were between the ages of twenty-eight and forty-five, white, with children, living within a radius of small and medium-size Michigan cities, neither poverty-level nor upper-income, a third with some college, most with family income between fifteen thousand and thirty thousand dollars, and over half the women employed, most of them part time, at jobs ranging from nursing and selling real estate to hairdressing and cleaning houses.

The researchers admitted that their "preconceptions and virtually everything we read" had prepared them to put the women they interviewed into two categories—feminists versus upholders of the family. But the researchers found that while some women were more, and others less, sympathetic to reforms associated with the women's movement, they could not, in fact, categorize women along these lines, without obscuring "the extent to which women combine and reconcile positions and ideas that in the political arena are diametrically opposed."

They reported: "Instead of finding categories of women,

we found categories of ideas . . . bits and pieces of two distinct belief systems—familial and individualistic ideologies. None of the women we spoke with subscribes completely to one ideology or the other; they all expressed some combination of the two, in their words and in their lives. The ideologies are opposed in the political arena. . . . The women we spoke with, however, did not present these ideas as contradictory."

The "familial ideology" places a tremendous value on the family and on motherhood, both as an activity and as a source of identity. It holds that family—husband and children—should be the primary focus of a woman's life, and that the needs of the family should be placed above all else. In contrast, the "individualistic ideology" places the individual on an equal level with the family—mothers have needs and goals to meet as persons apart from the family.

The researchers stressed: "We were not surprised to find conflicting ideas or ideologies expressed by the women we interviewed, but to find them combined in the views and behavior of each woman."

All the women assumed primary responsibility for homemaking in their own families, although they accepted "alternative arrangements" for others. "In general, when women spoke about their obligations as mothers of small children and their ultimate responsibility for homemaking, they expressed ideas and assumptions associated with the familial ideology." They all also believed in women's equality, and specifically in equal rights of women to jobs, education, etc. They did not experience these beliefs as conflicting. For instance, while they thought "children need full-time mothers" until they go to school, they would or did work themselves if it was "financially necessary."

Within the familial ideology, the role of wife not only embodies a distinct set of tasks and responsibilities, but also becomes a source of identity. Children are essential to this ideology—they "virtually define the woman's role, and the household cannot be considered a complete family without them." Reforms affecting women are approved or disapproved on the basis of how they will affect the "family as a whole." The individualistic ideology embraces the belief that men and women are all unique human beings, neither having any natural predilection for household maintenance, nurturing or wage working. Tasks of family life are divided according to the special needs and preferences of each individual. Couples desire children for the experience of parenting, and family reforms which "increase people's options" are welcomed. But all the women in these Michigan towns "articulated and acted upon both ideologies."

The sense of the identity and the power women get and hold on to, in their home and family—whether or not they also work and have "individualistic" ambitions—comes through strongly in the words of these women. "My domain is here. And my word is law here, I feel. And you know, I don't want him infringing on that area. I don't think anybody can mother like a mother can."

For the women to whom "each family member is an individual person first, separate from his or her familial role," marriage is an even more important decision, an ability to share and communicate is more essential, and "happiness and fulfillment, for both the man and the woman, means equal participation in decision-making and in taking responsibility for the marriage."

For all the women, "marriage offered a kind of secure independence—independence from parents, and the security of love and livelihood. The women could have no guarantee that their marriages would be good ones, but alternative routes to these gains were even riskier and more remote."

And all these women were for equal pay and for equal rights, as long as it didn't imply opposition to the family, or to men, or restrictions on their own choice to be housewives. "But for a while there, it seemed like the women's movement was pushing that unless you were out there working, and making the bucks—you were nothing, right? And you were downtrodden, because man has jumped on you and forced you into his will. . . . And, you know, they [feminists] made the housewife feel pretty bad, and that her job wasn't worthwhile. But the thing of it is, a lot are there by choice. And then they started saying about maybe they [housewives] should get equal pay—and I thought this is great. . . ."

Such a woman is satisfied with her marriage and with her children but "really not so much with myself." She also wants to make and reach her own goals, which she has sacrificed for marriage and raising children. "I just don't want to get into that kind of situation where I'm always in the house and no one sees me. I need to *do* things again. Instead of feeling that I just don't have it in me, I'm starting to look at barriers and saying that I can think of a solution."

Even for the most family-oriented women, there was a sense of new options and choices for women which almost all of them were very conscious of, and accepted, even welcomed "for other women," though they might admit not having enough "confidence" to take advantage of such options themselves. In many instances, their husbands had encouraged them to finish school, to plan a career. One such woman feels "very inadequate because I don't have a career now" but she couldn't find a job, in her town, in her field. She carries more of the household load than her husband, though "the minute he walks in the door he takes over with the kids." They have friends who divide up the tasks fifty-fifty but "I never thought of it [child care—housework] as diminishing me as a woman. I always thought of it enhancing me—but diminishing him as a man. The more choices you have, the more alternatives you have—you're just going to have a lot of change. Change is healthy in one respect, but it's not very neat. It messes things up."

None of these women wanted "out" from the family, but even those who "subscribed to traditional values" already perceived "different ways of living within the family structure."

In half the families, the wives did all the housework and child care; in the other half, the husbands shared or assumed part of it, but the wives remained primarily responsible. "However, there was a real acceptance of others' negotiating arrangements in which familial roles were restructured or reversed, even among women who felt the conventional arrangement was the more natural one."

All the women were working or had worked at some point in their marriages, had relatives, friends and neighbors who worked, and felt that if both husband and wife worked full time, they should share homemaking responsibilities equally—in *other* families; not their own. The resistance to sharing fifty-fifty came not from the husbands but from the wives' consistent and more or less conscious "conservation" of their family roles.

The husbands of four women who worked full time had taken over or shared at least one major task, such as cooking, or they "pitch in and help out" with a number of tasks. But the only wives who approached doing just half the housework or child care were those whose older children, as well as their husbands, picked up some of the chores. For example, one woman's husband cooked two nights a week, each of her two children cooked one night, she cooked three dinners herself. The wives retained primary responsibility by doing more of the tasks than their husbands did—and by their assumption that "wives ultimately 'own' homemaking and husbands 'help out.' "

Even arrangements in which husbands took over or shared some homemaking tasks were often arrived at without any discussion. Wives clearly preferred that their husbands help out without having to be asked, told or reminded what to do. Often, however, when a wife asked her husband to do something, he ignored, resisted or refused her. Many concluded that when husbands resisted it was easier to do the chores themselves.

The researchers concluded that the accepted division of roles in the home "can be fallen into but not out of without conscious effort and the kind of total discussion that reformulating the roles would require." Even women who wished their husbands would share more tasks resisted the idea of planning the division of labor between them in the home. "That's too structured for me. And that's not family life either . . . every day you check off what you will do—well, that's more hassle than it's worth."

And yet, despite or even because of this lack of equal sharing of housework (or refusal to give up that control), these women spoke of themselves as equals to their husbands, especially when they described how they and their husbands made major decisions and how they shared responsibility for making theirs a successful marriage.

The political impasse, when ERA and abortion are put in terms of woman's "choice" to have a career or an abortion rather than have a child, begins to make more sense. For instance, if women's core identity is still seen primarily in terms of the family—even if she herself needs and wants the job and gets satisfaction from it, and would, if necessary, have an abortion rather than another child—it threatens that core of her identity to put this in terms of her own "choice." Economic necessity requires and permits her to make that choice in real life today, and reconciles any conflict between her individual goals and family values. The other children would suffer, her husband would be doubly burdened, the twins might not be able to go to college if they had another baby, given the economic pinch they're in already: it's not from her own selfish choice she'd have an abortion, but for the whole family.

The Michigan study found that preservation of that familial identity dictated the ways that women juggle employment and mothering. Being employed part time, or at work that can be done at home, is "less quickly construed as a competitor for a woman's identity and commitment." Part-time employment can be arranged around the children's schedule, and thus does not detract from the familial concept of a mother whose first and foremost consideration is her children. When a mother "chooses" to work outside the home full time, she comes too close to adopting an individualistic family arrangement which considers her needs as important as those of her children. ("We feel it's important to be there to send them off and I'm usually home by one thirty or two in the afternoon. So I don't want to be a women's libber and go out and work full time or have a career.")

But, reflecting the reality that 52 percent of women with children ages three to five and 41 percent of those with children under three now work (Bureau of Labor Statistics), these women, while stressing the early years as the time when mothering is most important to the child's security— and thus mothers should be home nurturing their children— in the same breath supported mothers working outside the home "depending on the circumstances." Financial "necessity" resolved the conflict. "If a woman has to work outside the home, she is not choosing to do so," the Michigan researchers pointed out. "Choosing to have a job would mean choosing motherhood as a secondary role. Some women stretch their definition of necessity to include a strong personal need for employment—especially if a woman needs her job in order to feel better about being with the children when she is at home. She may derive fulfillment from employment, but she retains her identity as a mother and is employed because it helps her to better care for her family."

They accept, and try to reconcile, both beliefs: that women have a right to employment, and that children need a full-time mother. Whether these women are themselves employed or not, and no matter what solution they themselves use or approve to reconcile the needs of women as individuals and of their children, for all the women in the Michigan study "the perceived needs of children emerge as the central consideration."

And they were concerned not only with the mother-child relationship itself, but with "preserving its centrality in their families." Thus, they accepted the reality of mothers' employment, but wished to retain their role and identity as mothers, having no desire to become "career women."

These women resisted, in the abstract, federally regulated

day-care programs. That idea that "no one can mother like a mother," that child care is the mother's responsibility and the core of her identity, permits, at most, a temporary mother substitute. When it was necessary to work outside the home many women preferred to have a relative, neighbor or regular baby-sitter care for their children.

But many women who said they would not use day care themselves thought there should be more facilities for mothers who needed them. "I would never, never, put them in a day-care center. But, see, mothers have to work nowadays. That's the problem. So I think they should perfect the day-care centers. Maybe get someone who really knows what they're doing. And they'll take care of these children. It's not going to hurt them that bad."

Similarly, whereas "family planning" and "the right to choose" abortion, in the abstract, conflicted with the familial ideology of motherhood as "natural" and the core of women's identity, birth control was not only approved of, but it was widely practiced (by all the women but one, including the Catholics) "as a practical necessity, particularly given the current economic situation; more children require both more parental care and more income, and it would be difficult to provide both at once."

The tension between the two ideologies—woman as individual and woman serving her family—looked insoluble, in the abstract, but was, in fact, reconciled in the women's lives. Even two women who felt that mothers of small children had an "absolute obligation" to take full-time care of their own children were now working, one full time while her mother took care of the children, another part time, leaving her child with her husband.

Other studies have found this same juggling of traditional and feminist ideas of family and homemaking among professional women: doctors, lawyers, college professors. (See "The Myth of the Egalitarian Family," in *The Professional Women*, edited by Athena Theodore.)

Even those who themselves symbolize or preach one or

the other ideology can be seen combining both in their own lives. When Rosebeth Moss Kanter, the eminent sociologist and author of *Men and Women in the Corporation*, brings her two-year-old son to a corporate or academic or NOW-LDEF board meeting, and her partner-husband, Barry, takes over with the kid while she makes her presentation, they describe their arrangement in feminist terms (see *Notes From the Front Line*, by Barry Stein). But when Marabel Morgan "saves" her marriage, not be decking her body in ostrich feathers but by enlisting her husband as partner-manager to keep track of and invest the money she earns lecturing on "The Total Woman," she describes this arrangement as "feminine," not feminist.

There are *not* two kinds of women in America. The political polarization between feminism and the family was preached and manipulated by extremists on the right—and colluded in, perhaps unconsciously, by feminist and liberal or radical leaders—to extend or defend their own political power. Now, as that ideological split is continually being resolved in real life by juggling and rationalizing of new necessities in traditional terms, and old necessities in feminist terms, women's strength can strengthen the family in evolving ways. But as political and economic tensions increase, if women continue colluding in this false polarization, then they will only weaken the family, as well as women's equality, by playing into reaction and preventing the new social solutions real families now need.

Politically, for the women's movement to continue to promote issues like ERA, abortion or child care solely in individualistic terms, abandoning the family to the Right, aborts our own moral majority. The previous limits of women's political power in terms of that first-stage feminism (women versus family) can be transcended by a second-stage focus on women *and* family. Issues like ERA, abortion, child care become urgent not just for the individual woman but for the very survival of the family. And women who merely tolerated or even disapproved of these concerns in the abstract, or assumed they applied only to other women, will now face them as matters of concrete personal urgency in their own families.

Until now, women's political power—which only became visible as such in the years of the modern women's movement—has been limited, and virtually defined, by this polarization. The women's movement has appealed to women as individualists; the Moral Majority has played to, and elicited an explosive, defensive reaction on behalf of, women as upholders of the family. But if, in fact, the great majority of women—who in real life do marry and have children, even in these crucial years of the women's movement, as they also move increasingly into paid jobs—reconcile these seemingly opposite directions in their own behavior and belief, this polarization itself is what limits the true potential of women's political power. Perhaps the reactionary preachers of the Moral Majority who decry women's moves to equality as threats to the family are merely using "the family" to limit women's real political power. In a similar vein, feminists intent on mobilizing women's political power are, in fact, defeating their own purpose by denying the importance of the family.

That Michigan study showed something very important. All the women believed in equality and all of them believed in the family—from the same or converging needs for security, identity, and some control over their lives. Whether or not they supported a particular issue—like ERA, abortion or child care—depended on how they perceived it as affecting them. No appeal to their own personhood would be acceptable, even to the most individualistic, if it denied or conflicted with their commitment to the family, which they all shared.

In the wake of the 1980 elections, paternalistic pollsters and political scientists were gratuitously advising women's movement leaders to push on with ERA and abortion, leaving "the family" to the right wing. "The 'family,'" we were

told, "has simply become a buzz word for reaction." I believe
we should take our cue, instead, from these women in Michigan. They were moving, with varying degrees of conscious
feminism or individualism, into their own personhood with
utmost concern for, and no conflict over, its foundation in
the family. It is the same kind of political mistake for feminists to abandon the family to reaction as it was for liberals
and radicals to abandon individualism to the right.

"Family" is not just a buzz word for reaction; for women,
as for men, it is the symbol of that last area where one has
any hope of individual control over one's destiny, of meeting
one's most basic human needs, of nourishing that core of
personhood threatened now by vast impersonal institutions
and uncontrollable corporate and government bureaucracies
and the bewildering, accelerating pace of change. Against
these menaces, the family may be as crucial for survival as it
used to be against the untamed wilderness and the raging
elements, and the old, simple kinds of despotism.

For the family, all psychological science tells us, is the
nutrient of our humanness, of all our individuality: our personhood. The Michigan women, and all the others they exemplify, may show great political wisdom as well as personal
survival skills in holding on to the family as the base of their
identity and human control.

That beleaguered demand for some personal control of
one's life is basic, I believe, to the strong appeal of both feminism and "pro-life," "pro-family" groups. The realization
that inflation and other forces seemingly beyond our control
truly threaten our families and our own autonomy (our human survival), channeled into revulsion against big-government bureaucracy, was surely basic to the overwhelming Republican sweep in the last election. But this was not
necessarily that absolute "swing to the right" that reactionary extremists are trying to make into a self-fulfilling prophecy—unless our own paralysis, and/or collusion, in that false
polarization makes it so.

At this writing, most Democratic, liberal, radical, labor

and civil-rights leaders are either wringing their hands in impotent acquiescence to the gutting of fifty years of social programs or are parroting old rhetoric in their impotent defense without recognizing that something new has to happen. Feminists, reacting in outrage, or retreating in terror, in the face of the extremist assault on abortion and equal rights, are accepting as given a polarization that may already be unraveling at the other end.

Consider, for instance, the sharp public warnings, after the 1980 election, by sober conservative spokesmen (like Republican National Committee Chairman Bill Brock, Vice-President Bush, columnist William Safire) that "no one group"—such as the Moral Majority or Phyllis Schlafly's Eagle Forum—could take credit for the Republican landslide in 1980, as they were all doing, claiming a mandate for extreme actions against abortion, civil rights, women's rights.

Consider that by 1981 such a former extremist as Anita Bryant had divorced her fundamentalist husband and confessed to years of smoldering resentment against the antiwoman dictates of the fundamentalist preachers whose hysterical crusade against homosexual rights she had fronted for in Florida, demagogically linking homosexuality to ERA. Repudiating that crusade, she is quoted in the *Ladies Home Journal* (January 1981) as saying: "When I was growing up in the Bible Belt, the kind of sermon I always heard was, '*Wife, submit to your husband even if he is wrong.*' . . . I often have had to stay in pastors' homes, and their wives talk to me. Some pastors are so hard-nosed about submission and insensitive to their wives' needs that they don't recognize the frustration—even hatred—in their own households. . . . I guess I can understand the gays' and feminists' anger and frustration."

Consider the anger of Phyllis Schlafly when that Moral Majority preacher refused to continue a debate with her on television, when she, a woman, dared to uphold her Catholic view of the Scriptures against his absolute, my-word-is-law fundamentalism. Consider the frustration of Phyllis Schlafly when the Reagan command did not give her the Cabinet or sub-Cabinet post she evidently expected.

The limits, and potential, of women's power can be seen on both sides of this divide. Here is what Phyllis Schlafly wrote to subscribers of her Eagle Forum ("the alternative to women's lib") in December 1980:

It is clear from our victories in the November election that the subscribers to the Phyllis Schlafly report have become the most powerful and effective movement in America today.

We are the movement that has achieved the most amazing David-and-Goliath victory of the 20th century —the defeat of ERA over the combined opposition of the White House, the Congress, the Governors, television, radio, most newspapers, the universities, the schools, the unions, the NEA, the "good"-sounding semantics of "equal rights," the tremendous head start ERA had before we got started, and the ERA'ers psychology of "inevitable" victory. It took a hard 8 1/2 years, but now all the momentum is going our way— against the ERA and the feminist movement.

It is clear that, if our movement can defeat ERA, it can achieve *any* goal we seek. . . .

Do we let our leaders disappear into the bureaucracy of the Reagan Administration? Or, do we use our movement and its weapons—sharpened and polished through 8 1/2 years of battle—to achieve other goals for God, Family, and Country?

Instead of seeking a position in the Reagan Administration—in Defense, Education or the Justice Department—Ms. Schlafly said she has decided, "after much prayerful consideration," to "build Eagle Forum into a mighty force which can affect federal policies in Washington just as we have been determining policies in the State Capitols."

She revealed that her total membership is fifty thousand,

reached in 1975. (It is unclear whether those "members" are invited to meetings to vote on officers and policies, or are simply the "subscribers to the Phyllis Schlafly report.") After 1975, she says, "we were too busy defeating ERA and winning other battles to sign up new members." In contrast, she laments, NOW "has just certified a paid membership of 108,000" (it increased to 135,000 in the two months after Reagan took office).

So she proposes opening a Washington office, creating a "Pro-Family Court Review Panel" to investigate judicial appointees to insure that future Reagan judges are *not* for ERA or abortion rights, and *not* opposed to "sexism." She proposes a campaign to counter school programs and textbooks that have advanced ideas of equal opportunity and to bring back "traditional stereotypes." She even proposes to redefine as "discrimination" any policies on jobs, promotions, taxes and inflation which do not favor "the traditional family, the one-paycheck family, where the father is the primary provider and the mother the primary homemaker." She proposes fighting the very reforms in social security which would right current inequities that deny housewives their own protection in old age, in the event of divorce, as well as those penalizing working wives. And she wants to set up committees in every religious denomination to preserve "the image of God as our Father."

The short-range decision for feminists is whether to let this paper tigress trap us in these battles on her terms or to project the real battle for equality in larger terms, in terms of the family's economic survival, and the new options needed, in job and home, for younger women to be able to choose to have children, and older women not to live out their lives in lonely poverty. And go on ourselves to forge those new alliances with men. Then we can carry the passions, the outrage, and the hopes focused on the battle for ERA these many years past that first-stage deadline with a new vision and new energy for the second stage. And when its larger human politics emerges, as it must, transcending those old conservative-liberal poles, women will be in the mainstream of it, and the Equal Rights Amendment will fall in place, the Phyllis Schlaflys a quaint memory buried by history or changing their own minds, as Anita Bryant already has. On the other hand, if we continue in the narrow terms of first-stage feminism, and abdicate the family and the new problems and fears of the young and old to the Far Right, feminism could suffer another fifty-year sleep, as it did after 1920.

What we are facing now is not an absolute division between women, but an evolving continuum—an evolution from those age-old roots of female identity in the family, in the biological necessity of childbearing, to the new necessities of selfhood, personhood, economically rewarding work and the new possibilities of choice, personal control, personal growth. The either/or swings of the pendulum, the excesses of reaction on either side of this critical leap in women's identity, can be seen as a stage in that evolution.

From these recent studies, from the women I have interviewed myself in this and other nations through these crucial twenty years of breaking through the feminine mystique to our new personhood, and from all that is known about the workings of human personality, it is clear that women cannot tolerate experiencing basic aspects of their selfhood in conflict. An either/or approach might seem simpler, easier than struggling with and resolving that conflict, if women are basically moving in the dark, feeling that they are alone, without role models or social supports, dealing with ambiguous, continually changing pressures, signals, rewards, responsibilities and the constant burden of choice, decision, new freedom.

Under the challenge and the lure of the new, we can forget for a while, personally or politically, how deep are the roots of women's identity in the family—even as we ourselves are living them, taking them for granted, or denying, defying our own yearnings. They go so deep into the dimensions of our memory, our feelings, tradition, biology, wherever our needs and heart and soul reside—we do not feel truly alive if we deny those roots for very long. As the Michigan study showed, those roots of female identity in family are there, and basic for every woman, even those most consciously striving for new personhood. But that mysterious spark that now drives women to new possibilities of growth is also not easily denied. They are not unrelated. Generation, evolving life which women have always served, now demands that we give birth not only to the young, as before, but to our own new selves. It is all mysterious. It is all part of our personhood as women. That new spark of selfhood is also rooted in necessity—the changed realities of economic necessity, the new possibilities and necessities of our biology; for women as for men, the old and new necessities of evolving human life: to survive, to grow.

When the reaction is most extreme—on either side of the either/or polarization—look for the buried roots, or new shoots, of the other side, held down and choking, grasping for life. That necessity, of *life*, is not easy to hold down. Reaction can seem most extreme just before the breakthrough. It was that way with the determinedly "happy happy housewives" in 1950s America just before they broke through the feminine mystique. It was evidently that way with Anita Bryant. It is that way with some of the new career women, I suspect, defiantly disclaiming any wish to have children, just before they get pregnant.

But in these twenty years, an evolution surely, unmistakably, has taken place in women. The women who experienced this movement—"It changed my whole life"—in full consciousness, struggling through the conflicts, knowing in the dailiness of their lives that they *had* to move, risking, even fighting for their personhood, juggling the daily realities and choices, somehow putting it all together and feeling finally the *difference*— the new strengths and options and the painful, surprising elation of their own aliveness—have come out the other end of women's liberation with a sureness different from that of those younger women who take the new rights for granted. The ambiguities and complexities, the very diffi-

culties of juggling unfamiliar new choices and putting together new roles and old, demand and create a strength, a
maturity. The last Virginia Slims poll showed women in
their fifties and sixties today more committed to equality
than women in their twenties and thirties fifteen years ago.

Another study, over an eighteen-year span, of American
families by University of Michigan researchers found that
only 28 percent of mature women today feel that major family decisions should be made by the man of the house, compared to 66 percent who felt that way in 1962. Today these
women's eighteen-year-old daughters—and sons—are more
likely to hold such sexist or "traditional" views than their
mothers, but in the case of daughters not much more (32
percent of daughters compared to 28 percent of mothers—
but 50 percent of sons!).

The evolution continues, however, for the daughters and
the sons are less likely to experience these two strands of
women's identity as in conflict. They have experienced from
these mothers, in their own families, a new role model and a
new balance between the sexes. As studies have shown (see
The Employed Mother in America, by F. Ivan Nye and Lois
Hoffman), daughters who experienced their mothers' selfhood in professional work or in serious political or volunteer
activity, as well as in the family, have a different, more positive and more complex image of woman's role, and unlike
American daughters for many generations previously, *they
want to grow up to be like their mothers.*

They have experienced those two strands reconciled in
their mothers. They can move on from that either/or conflict
and the excesses of reaction. That same University of Michigan study of American families that followed one thousand
women from the Detroit area during the past eighteen years
found that by 1980 64 percent of the women—and 73 percent
of their children—agreed that it is all right for women to be
very active in clubs, politics and other outside work before
the children are grown. In 1962, only 44 percent of the
women felt this way.

By the year 2000, I doubt there will be any need for the likes of Phyllis Schlafly, or, for that matter, Gloria Steinem or Betty Friedan. The arguments about equal rights for women will be nostalgic history.

But the problems of living equality cannot await another generation. They are the new necessity, political and personal, which neither women nor men, conservative or liberal, can avoid in the 1980s. Facing those new problems on a day-to-day, personal basis as we share the burdens and choices and rewards of earning and parenting, pay-work and housework, and as we seek new forms of intimacy and family, we are, in fact, already entering the second stage.

7 The
New Mode

When I began writing this book, my intuition that the women's movement was coming to an end in its present stage was based on the new personal questions and problems I was hearing from women and men around this country. My urgent sense that we had to move into the second stage if we were to keep, and to live, the equality we fought for was borne out more quickly and drastically by massive political reaction than I could have guessed.

Even as the new problems emerge and enter into our personal consciousness, they seem to have been rendered politically insoluble. For Republican 1980 platform declarations of war against the Equal Rights Amendment and legalized abortion were followed by legislation and new Constitutional amendments proposed by the radical Right outlawing any and all government programs against sex and race discrimination and empowering states to prosecute those practicing abortion—and some forms of birth control—as murder, even in cases of rape, incest or threats to a woman's life or health. Not waiting for such changes to become law, the Reagan Administration in its first year in office began using executive powers to dismantle the government machinery protecting women against sex discrimination in employment and education. Budget cuts slashed long-standing government services vital to women and families, from food stamps to school lunches, and shut down traditional as well as new opportunities for women with funds cut for nurses' training as well as women in science and small business loans for women. Men and women opposed not only to medical abortion but to birth control and sex education for teenagers were put in charge of government health agencies.

The overwhelming Congressional approval of these budget cuts and appointments in 1981 testified to such a general political acquiescence—or political paralysis—in the repudiation and dismantling of government social programs as to prohibit the very consideration of government solutions for new social problems. While the outrage and anxiety of women over these developments increased the membership of NOW by ten thousand a month—threefold the previous rate—the energies of the women's movement were necessarily consumed in a last-ditch defense of what could still be saved of rights and opportunities previously won.

Yet can even the present massive wave of political reaction kill the dream and the heady experience of equality and independence and the new sense of possibility that has changed women's lives in these years, or make the new problems disappear? Reaction cannot erase the basic needs, and the irreversible economic, technological and structural changes in work, and the longer life span, that forced women to break through their obsolete sex role and move to participation in society as persons in their own right, and that are now forcing men to break through *their* obsolete sex role and move to new values in the family and in work.

More or less consciously, millions of women and men in America today are already living on the frontier of the second stage, working out the solutions to the new problems, personally and privately, on a concrete, practical, seat-of-the-pants, no-time-to-think-about-it, day-to-day basis. Yet, in the abstract, in all known political terms, the women's movement as we knew it has come to a dead end; the problems are insoluble.

I suspect that not only the women's movement, but American democracy itself, has come to the end of a stage—the last stage for a certain political mode, a style of political leadership that has been defined as "masculine." Even the ideology of the women's movement has been defined in that mode.

What is necessary now is to get beyond ideology, old modes of political thinking, and to move into the second stage—for women, and for American democracy. Does that sound too grandiose? The tipoff is simple: as harassing, or exhilarating, as it has been to live with these seemingly insoluble problems in the current flux of the movement to equality, such problems are evidently easier for women and men *to live* than to think about, at least in the old political terms.

The first stage of the women's movement did not involve a new mode of thought. Once we broke through the feminine mystique and said that women were people, we merely applied the abstract values of all previous liberal movements and radical revolutions, as defined by men, to protest our oppression, exploitation and exclusion from man's world, and to demand an equal share of its rewards and powers as previously wielded and enjoyed by men.

In fact, we got into ideological trouble when we tried to apply too literal an analogy from old revolutions of class or color to women's situation in life. The newness, and the power, of the women's movement was the style and strategy and substance that came from women's experience itself; the movement brought that experience for the first time into political consciousness. "The personal as political" was indeed a new frontier. But not, I think, as it was often used in the first stage, in which some women distorted the actuality of their concrete experience in the family, with children, with men, to fit old modes of male political revolution—seeing women as an oppressed class, rising up against men, the oppressors. That borrowed rhetoric often blinded us to the complex, changing reality of our own experience.

The *experience* of the women's movement, as opposed to the rhetoric of "women's lib"—the experience of women fighting for, winning, and beginning to live some measure of equality—seems to involve a *new kind of political thinking*. The personal pitfalls and paradoxes that face women and men who are trying to live equality expose the blind spots of old liberals and radicals, including some feminists, still espousing obsolete big-daddy government programs (for *others),* and the simplistic reactions of old conservatives and new fundamentalists, still trying to deny the complex changes they themselves are beginning to live. The new problems defy solution by the old models of liberal or conservative, radical or reactionary ideology, and demand transcending the obsolete boundaries of that liberal-conservative, radical-reactionary war map.

The implacable passions, the sullenness and apathy and confusion that seemed to mark that 1980 Götterdämmerung can be explained, at least in part, as death throes of first-stage thinking—liberals as well as reactionaries blindly, stubbornly holding on to old models that won't float, defending against phantom enemies and fake dangers, rather than facing the concrete realities of unprecedented change.

The second stage is hard to think about, or conceptualize politically, in old masculine terms because its mode is defined by experience that up until now was considered women's domain, or known mainly by women, and thus not conceptualized at all.

The problems seem insoluble because of "either/or" thinking. The solutions are inherent in the paradoxes, which imply "both/and" thinking. It seems too simplistic to talk about this as "male" and "female" modes of thought. But talking about the new bridging of those "male" and "female" spheres brings us within grasp of the second stage.

For instance, as working wives for the first time in history outnumber housewives, problems of the family, child care and home, which used to be considered women's problems, emerge now into the public political sphere. But the first stage focused on equal opportunity and equal pay for women doing work that *men* did before. Today not only that shrinking percentage of women who are housewives but a growing proportion of women, and men, who hold jobs are doing the kind of "service" work that has not been valued in the gross national product (GNP) or covered by social security or seen in terms of "productivity," because it used to be done almost completely by women in the private sphere of the home.

The second stage must establish the real value of "woman's work" to life and to society, whether it is done by women or men, inside the home or out. Shared now, by women and men, it must be included in new measures of productivity, social security, GNP. But at the moment, reactionaries, liberals and even feminists are locked into the first stage, either blindly defending that "classical family of Western nostalgia," or refusing to think in concrete terms about the family at all, or proposing first-stage solutions like "wages for housework" or massive, federally financed childcare programs that imply more bureaucracies taking more money out of everyone's pocket and invading the final sphere of privacy, where women, and men, don't want to lose a sense of personal value, meaning and control.

The public programs, which once seemed the solution if women and men are to share the joys and responsibilities of parenting, as they must now by necessity share the burdens of earning, are hardly conceivable in the face of political reaction, economic recession, inflation, unemployment and the energy crunch. The last national child-care law to pass Congress—a comprehensive $15 billion child-development program making "quality child care," preschool and after-school, available to all according to "ability to pay"—was vetoed by President Nixon in 1971 as a "threat to the family." Though many times more children's mothers are working today, that kind of massive federal program no longer seems a politically viable solution to the child-care problem.

Why should companies bother with flextime or child-care

programs to lure women workers when so many are unemployed, desperate for any job? How can the women's movement honestly talk of wages and social security for housewives or a housewives' Bill of Rights to education or retraining, or "equal pay for work of comparable value," when the minimum wage itself is under attack? Who is going to pay for social security or pensions or reeducation for housewives, much less "wages," when the systems for those already covered are being gutted?

And yet, without any hope of such solutions, isn't the very notion of real equality of women with men a bitter dream, which tired, lonely or disillusioned daughters will repudiate completely within a few years—dreams become too painful when they cannot possibly be lived—just as women turned their backs on the first feminists' dreams a half-century ago? Is it not an irrelevant luxury now, this dream of equality between women and men, with political reaction and economic chaos threatening our most basic rights and freedoms as Americans and our very survival?

There are no separate, single-issue solutions for women now, not the kinds of solutions that have characterized radical, liberal and reactionary ideologies, and the first stage of women's movement for equality.

The urgencies of the second stage will, I believe, force women into new alliances with life-affirming men. These may or may not arise out of the special-interest, single-issue groups in which women are currently organized. But I believe that the mode of political thinking that can get us all through this crisis of reaction into the second stage—the mode for the new kind of political leadership and new kind of public policy, as well as private strategy, that has to replace obsolete liberalism and simplistic conservatism in order to solve our real problems—has to come much more clearly and explicitly from a kind of experience and according to a style that up until now has not characterized public policy or leadership because it has been largely associated with women.

The women's movement to equality has given an active voice and an explicit value to this mode. Because it can now be recognized and conceptualized and is being used in the public activities of society, people can be made conscious of it in terms valued by men. Because men are now sharing experiences which had previously been defined and devalued as female—and women's qualities nourished by such experience are becoming visible in activities previously reserved for men —those qualities acquire new value. The evolutionary processes at work in society in recent times (which caused the women's movement in the first place) have pushed activities and experiences previously thought of as female increasingly to the fore, bypassing earlier male activities and the qualities of leadership they developed in survival value. And this mode of leadership is now being discovered and conceptualized by male social scientists—and taught to corporate executives and even future military leaders at places like Harvard and Stanford Business School, West Point and the Air Force Academy. (They do not call it "female"—nor do feminists.)

It is ironic that men who "discover" this "feminine" mode —in part through their new immersion in such day-to-day details of life as caring for those complex, ever-changing children from whom women used to shield them—are confident enough to conceptualize it as the most effective style for new corporate, political, environmental and military problems, even as some women now shun that soft style, and shudder at its "female" label. Overawed, at least at first, by man's world, some women are not confident enough to trust the sense and skills they learned as women.

Women have used this mode a long time, without putting a name to it or being able to measure its value on scales set by men. Now some male social scientists who have stumbled on it as the possible answer to new world problems intractable to old methods prefer to give it a nonfeminine, abstract name, simply assigning it a Greek letter so they can more comfortably adopt it themselves.

A week before the election, on October 29, 1980, a Stanford Research Institute scientist told an unusual meeting of women and men from industry, government, labor and the public sector that the "crisis of leadership in the U.S. may be less in the particular leaders we have than in the style of leadership we have come to expect. To resolve our problems, we may need to balance the dominant Alpha, or masculine leadership, style with the Beta, a more feminine leadership style."

Alpha-style leadership "in our society considered more masculine" (as described by Peter Schwartz of Stanford Research Institute International) is based on analytical, rational, quantitative thinking. It relies on hierarchical relationships of authority and looks for "deterministic engineered solutions to specific problems." According to actual data collected by social scientists from Harvard and elsewhere on differences in male and female power styles and negotiation behavior, the Alpha, or male, power style is more "direct" and "aggressive," is based on the experience of "abstracting one particular task or demand from its surroundings at a given time," strives competitively for an all-or-nothing solution, expecting "a clear win or lose"—a "zero-sum solution" —with "any non-win conclusion resulting in a loss of face."

The Beta style, "generally perceived as feminine," is based on synthesizing, intuitive, qualitative thinking and a "contextual," "relational" power style. It is tuned to more complex, more open and less defined aspects of reality. Its concern is the whole picture being presented rather than concentrating on a given task; growth and the quality of life, rather than fixed quantities and the status quo; the sharing of internal resources and the establishment of interdependent adaptive relationships of support. It is more tuned to "the subtleties of human interaction" than the direct style. The Beta style is able to deal with change, while the Alpha style focuses on the short range, perceiving change as chaotic and disruptive and relying on "order" to control it.

The man from Stanford Research made it perfectly clear

that "no studies indicate that these behavioral tendencies are innate to one sex or another." Men and women, in fact, exhibit the characteristics of both styles to various degrees when acting in leadership positions. "However, sex role expectations have been found to polarize these behaviors."

His major thesis was that "past reticence to use the feminine style must be overcome so that our major national problems can be addressed by leadership appropriately balanced to take advantage of both masculine and feminine styles." For, as he pointed out, the most urgent problems of society today involve value choices and new perceptions of reality: the Beta style of leadership is needed to inspire the consensus that can resolve the dilemmas deadlocking every issue with "the tolerance for diversity that will permit freedom."

Strangely enough, most of the women leaders present felt impelled to object to characterizing the new style needed as either "feminine" or "Beta," which implies that it is "secondary" and "not as good as the masculine." And yet, as the discussion proceeded, Eleanor Holmes Norton, Joyce Miller, Rosebeth Kanter, Muriel Fox, Joan Ganz Cooney, Eleanor Smeal and I easily related to this style. It was, of course, the style we ourselves had used, and observed, in effective leadership of the women's movement, or in our own professional or political or labor leadership. (We had also seen women who were as rigidly bound in an authoritative, win-lose Alpha mode as any man. And we had seen feminist projects fail because of rigid refusal to adopt any leadership, any hierarchical structure, any decision-making powers or rigor of execution—fail, in other words, because of too much Beta and no Alpha at all.)

The men present, heads of Bell Telephone Company, the Diebold Corporation J.C. Penney, the Yale School of Management, were spending good money trying to develop more Beta thinking in executives because, as the research showed, it gets the job done more effectively and quickly, and is, in fact, increasingly necessary for business survival in such a time of massive change. But they also seemed bemused at the labeling of this style as "female," or abashed at discussing it with newstyle female leaders.

It also emerged from the research that younger women moving up in the traditionally male-dominated fields of engineering and business now test higher than the males in the dominant male Alpha mode. "Could this reversal indicate that females felt they had to assume male-associated attributes, and embrace them strongly, to assure success?" the scientist asked. "This would be dangerous to society," he felt, for "the current paralysis is in part a function of the dominance of the masculine style of leadership. If it continues to be the sole model of leadership available, [it] is likely to lead us increasingly in the direction of an authoritarian and homogeneous society. Balancing Alpha with Beta leadership, the masculine with the feminine—in both men and women—is necessary to break the deadlock and to preserve a free and diverse society."

Seen in this light, the leadership style of the Reagan Administration and other aspects of the American political scene in the early 1980s signal a resurgence (last gasp?) or counterrevolution of harsh, Alpha-style masculine dominance under the veneer of Reagan's soft-spoken cowboy charm. Consider the virtual absence of women in the Reagan Administration, reversing the progress of two decades. Consider the reassertion of punitive, "law-and-order" measures in the courts, including the death penalty, in reaction against the "soft," "liberal," "permissiveness" of the courts in the previous era. Consider the repudiation of concern for human rights, women's rights, the poor and the weak, or for conservation of natural and human resources and ecological balance. Consider the disclaimer of any Government responsibility for people's lives. Consider the renewed emphasis on fixed, quantitative costs and budgets, belying complexity and changes in the real world, as opposed to sliding scales and sensitive measures of environmental and family impact. Consider the attempt to impose a fundamentalist religious doctrine of absolute "creationism" in the schools, to counter the study of the natural evolution of life.

Evolution itself, however, seems to be moving in what might be called a "feminine" direction. According to this analysis, Alpha, the masculine style, evolved into a dominant position out of the countless survival crises confronting our primitive ancestors. A harsh style, intent on controlling and manipulating the environment to reduce known threats, it viewed the world as a place where "mastery is essential to the attainment of one's niche."

The scientific method, evolving from interactions with the physical world to discover "the one 'truth' or reality," is a product of Alpha, masculine-style reasoning. It is effective in mastering the physical world and in implementing short-range tasks, specific objectives and lower-level goals, where speed is required. But it has serious drawbacks and limitations for today's most urgent problems, which increasingly involve people, not things, and where events are in flux and there is no single answer or fixed hierarchy; rather, fluid shifts of power are needed to meet each situation.

Beta, feminine style also evolved out of the resolution of countless day-to-day crises. But in contrast to the masculine style, which developed from confrontation with the physical environment, the Beta style developed in dealing with small groups of human beings—that is, the family.

The Beta style is nonlinear. Rather than focusing on a fixed, single goal, it has to embrace and integrate differences and a range of values, goals, perceptions, hopes and methods. The Beta style is needed to cope with problems that require a long-range perspective. Instead of seeking absolute control, it views change as a process of incremental adaptation by steps or stages, in which form, or order, evolves out of apparent disorder. This requires a tolerance for ambiguity and a certain trust, during the period of confusion, that the order will eventually develop.

The woman's movement was perhaps the first large-scale political application of the Beta style. I remember realizing, and telling myself and the others, that it is not possible to predict our future now, extrapolating from the present in a straight line. We could no longer live our lives as women according to the pattern of the past. Anatomy was no longer destiny—not completely. We had to conceive and create new possibilities for women's lives. Events set in motion by men or women—like the women's movement itself—keep impinging on history's line now, belying ideologies of strict biological or material determination. Beta style also means our knowing now that women's strategy or goals cannot be seen in isolation from other developments in society.

It is impossible to solve the dilemmas of living equality according to Alpha thinking. The very gains of the women's movement to equality will be wiped out by reaction under Reagan, and we will have to start over again, according to Alpha thinking. According to Alpha thinking, the enemy has finally won.

Or is it that we ourselves now must consciously transcend our own tendency to Alpha, masculine, win-lose, zero-sum, linear thinking—even as that thinking seems to prevail in the present reactionary political climate—and explicitly use and share our Beta intuitions to evolve fluid solutions to the problems of living equality, embracing the diversity in values, perceptions, hopes and methods that has been women's—and America's—strength?

In the second stage, we must resolve the apparent dilemma between women's passionate drive for that equality and personhood from which we will not retreat and the values of the family which we can now embrace anew, out of that same concern for growth and the quality of human life whose roots in female experience we share with the most threatened Moral Majority housewife. The women's movement is over, in terms of the dominant Alpha, masculine mode that polarized women against men in the sexual politics of the first stage, and also polarized women against women—even as the basic evolutionary thrust of women's movement to equality was bringing us inexorably, but in

varying routes and rates of speed, to the verge of transcending that polarization.

The true potential of the women's movement may be seen
in the second stage, as its generative mode—and the new political force of women it has generated—is applied and sub-
sumed in a larger movement that confronts problems of national and social survival going beyond the special interests
of women. The seeming death of liberalism may be due to
Alpha dominance in conventional liberal thinking that ren-
ders it obsolete. Yet the escalating new problems of inflation,
productivity, pollution of the environment, nuclear war are
not likely to be solved by the resurgence of Alpha dominance
in the monolithic rhetoric and fixed positions of the radical
Right (or their mirror-image counterparts in the hawk-ex-
tremists of the Communist world).

At this advanced industrial stage of modern society, our
main problems of economic and even physical survival have
to do with the complex relationships, behavior and values of
people, not things—and the people who control critical things,
as, for instance, oil, are themselves controlled by diverse and
changing values, in different stages of development. The old
political polarizations are themselves obsolete.

One can hardly suggest that the style women developed in
the past as they dealt on a day-to-day basis with small problems and relationships in the family, mostly without thinking about it in the abstract, could be more appropriate than
the win-or-lose, dog-eat-dog, do-or-die methods of the hunter
or the warrior in dealing with such large-scale new problems. But the concrete tradeoffs and the shifting, fluid balance of power between women and men as they transcend
the age-old sex-role polarization in work and love may be
more than just a political metaphor for the second stage.

Without resorting to a crystal ball, it's important to distinguish right now the features of the women's movement that
were unique and that gave it vitality and strength, in a time
of increasing political apathy in the nation as a whole. For in

a certain sense, the style, or process, or mode of the women's movement could be seen as a preview of that new political mode for the nation. On the other hand, the organized women's movement itself is in some danger of aping the accepted dominant Alpha mode of established movements and organizations in its zeal for acceptance and respectability, and its own acceptance of polarization.

The current political threat to women's rights has already given new urgency to the movement as a special-interest group. It will surely go on fighting for the Equal Rights Amendment and the right of abortion, though I hope that fight will evolve into a larger battle for the choice to have children. But, more important, will women, in the second stage, take the lead, or follow, or help to organize a new movement or coalition, with men, confronting the problems of saving and living equality, and the dilemmas of survival and the increasing dangers to freedom in our nation as a whole, with the same concrete, life-oriented energy with which we confronted our own oppression a generation ago?

I was bemused recently as I heard a report on "The Professionalism of Feminism" at the Seminar on Sex Roles and Social Change in which I participate at the Center for the Social Sciences at Columbia University. The political scientist who delivered the talk had embarked on her study to find out why and how the women's movement could have accomplished as much as it has in less than twenty years—in the sense of changing lives and consciousness and laws, opening new opportunities, etc. —without money or any of the other appurtenances of, or access to, power.

But what she found, in 1980, was a "professionalization" of feminism very different from the women's movement as it began (or as I experienced its actual history). She found that "the movement" was now a set of professional feminist groups organized around single issues, operating from headquarters in Washington, like all the other lobbying groups, its activities consisting of the professional efforts of a relatively few well-trained women graduates of the best law schools.

They were well respected and accepted by other professionals in Washington—the staffers of Congressional offices with whom they mainly dealt and the lobbyists for other groups. In the political scientist's view, the professional feminists were pragmatic and their approach concrete, compared to other pressure groups. They did not get into unnecessary confrontations but managed to steal small advantages where total victory was impossible (hints of Beta style?). What worried her was their lack of "ideology," lack of funds, lack of "charismatic leaders," and lack of "members" in a grass-roots sense.

If her report is accurate, then the women's movement may be supplanted in the second stage by some new center or coalition that will use the mode of the women's movement before its "professionalization" (and the mode that is still its hope of vitality) to mobilize women and men to take actions in their own communities on their new problems, with a new vision that inspires them to grow and transcend their previous limits.

For the women's movement, in the beginning, was a movement of *voluntary* political responsibility, a matter of individuals who had never participated in political power taking responsibility to mobilize women to change the conditions of their own and other women's lives. A new kind of political power was generated, a generative power, in and by women, making a politics of dealing with life as it is lived, in the way women do deal concretely with life, in the kitchen and living room and supermarket and playground, bedroom, laundry. There was an ideology, of course, though not what people used to mean by ideology. The values of "equality" and "freedom" and "personhood" are abstract, but in this instance, they were interpreted and applied to the concrete reality of daily life as it has always been lived by women.

And because we were sick of being treated like children as women were in other volunteer organizations—given busy work to do by male social worker "executive directors," or lesson plans to follow as Cub Scout leaders, or not allowed to make our own decisions locally by the timid bylaws of the League of Women Voters, or given the zip codes to look up in the Democratic or Republican parties, or told to run the mimeograph machine or cook the spaghetti in the radical student movement—we organized our own movement with as little structure as possible. Agreeing on the general values of equality as our long-range agenda—the Equal Rights Amendment, an end to sex discrimination in every field, child-care programs no one else was even proposing at that time, abortion, which was not even discussed yet in the newspapers—we would get together nationally once a year to decide on goals and priorities. By telephone mostly, we would keep in loose communication, nationally, so we could act together, when necessary.

But we would mainly deal with these problems in our own communities, in the style most suitable, with whatever means at hand. And because we had no money, we had to improvise and do it all ourselves, learning on the job, developing strengths and skills we never knew we were capable of. At least that's the way it was in NOW in the beginning—and when I look around the country, younger women are coming up in that same concrete, responsible, individual, unflagging, improvisational, growth-promoting, life-affirming style. There was no power we conceived of overthrowing, exactly. (Some of the radical feminists did go on about "patriarchy," but their rhetoric got boring even if it did contain titillating half-truths.) We didn't get into too many win-lose deadlocks, because almost anything we did was an improvement—just doing something about conditions that we had always submitted to passively gave us, and other women, new strength to take on problems and possibilities we hadn't dared before: that new sense of our own power.

Because we had no money or fixed organizational structure behind us—and because we knew how weak we had been, each woman alone, bearing all our burdens as our solitary cross and guilt—we knew it was important to resolve our differences as they came up, so we could move ahead together. We *listened* to each other with care and respect, at least at first. We took ourselves and each other seriously, as people—which was new for women. We didn't go for hierarchical relationships; we were sick of being secretaries and service stations for others. We all wanted to be political operators—that was what it was all about. And we were.

It was not the cause, or its rhetoric, or any single issue that emboldened and exhilarated us—though we only acted on what we seriously believed in, and all our issues were *real*, from life. It was the movement itself, the process, the activity of taking control of one's destiny, and helping to shape the future. John F. Kennedy once called it "the political passion." The Greeks said it was what distinguished free men from slaves, the human condition from animals. Women never had a chance to exercise that political passion before (at least women who weren't empresses or queens or Joan of Arc). And it was more compelling, for many of us, than any sexual passion.

Without thinking about it, we used politically the intuitions and the skills that were familiar to us as women, and in so doing created a new political agenda much closer to life than the agendas of the political parties, Right or Left. Without realizing it, we improvised as we went along a new political mode and style, adopting and borrowing bits and pieces of all kinds of laws and techniques to solve problems that had never been considered political by men. It always puzzled the experts that there were no charismatic leaders, male political style—and no blind followers either. Everyone was potentially a leader, no one a passive follower. Everyone was a self-determining professional volunteer, as former housewives became politically professional in the movement, and formerly undervalued or invisible female executives or lawyers volunteered professional services no such movement could have paid for. In NOW, until recently, there were no paid officers or professional "career" feminists, and a continual flow and interchange between members and leaders—Washington lobbyist this month, housewife or teacher or secretary back in Pittsburgh or Peoria, next.

We took on impossible political battles men knew better than to try—like the extension of the deadline for ratification of ERA. We defied conventional wisdom, conservative and liberal, with a growing confidence that did not come from fixed ideological positions, but from being always rooted in the concrete daily life we shared with other women, sensing new political possibilities as we moved. It was always surprising to the experts and political scientists to see how many women and men seemed to identify and move with us—from that first nationwide strike for equality on August 26, 1970, to women's victory over the Carter forces on ERA on the Democratic Convention floor in August 1980.

Politicians of both major parties are strangely blind to this new political force. Because it was a different style of power, and because it was *women*, it was not even taken seriously enough at first to be threatening to traditional political bosses of the Right or the Left. That's why our early battles were won so easily. That's why we ourselves were taken by surprise by the reaction and the polarization that stalemated ERA, after thirty-five states had already ratified it, when with only three states still needed to get it into the Constitution, it suddenly was locked in seemingly impassable deadlocks.

In that first stage, our own explicit political programs and rhetoric were concentrated on breaking down the barriers that kept us out of men's world, and achieving equality in it, in the dominant Alpha "masculine" style of all previous liberal and radical movements of "outs" wanting to get "in." We now seem to have come to a dead end on that route. The counterrevolution endemic to that kind of movement, threatening old power, has materialized to a degree that may wipe out all we have won. Women do not have enough of the old kind of political power to possibly overcome the forces pitted against us in a win-lose battle: the limits of women's power, in those terms, are already visible.

But the forces that made it necessary, and possible, for American women to move to equality and our own personhood at this time in history are not going to disappear. The millions of women who take themselves seriously as people now and take for granted their entitlement to equal rights —even if they say they are not feminists, disapprove of feminists, feel threatened by feminists, are closet feminists, or are still unconscious of their own feminist fire—are not going to turn into bland plastic robots, à la Stepford Wives, or Doris Day simpering housewives, overnight. Besides, the economy and their own need to survive—and grow—won't let them.

The problems of women and men, trying to, forced to, live on new terms, remain. Confronting those problems, personally and politically, women and men even now are transcending sex-role polarization. Confronting the new problems in family and work, we can emerge from our own blind spot and transcend that false antagonism between feminism and family. The true potential of that new mode, which gave the women's movement its real power, may be realized in the second stage—not in further permutations of the in-out, win-lose power battles, based on old revolutionary models—but as women and men, in shifting, fluid new political coalitions, begin using this power to solve the problems they can't evade, living that precarious equality . . . and move beyond sexual politics.

8 Take Back the Day

 In the first stage, the women's movement directed too much of its energy into sexual politics, from personal bedroom wars against men to mass marches against rape or pornography to "take back the night." Sexual war against men is an irrelevant, self-defeating acting out of rage. It does not change the conditions of our lives. Obsession with rape, even offering Band-Aids to its victims, is a kind of wallowing in that victim-state, that impotent rage, that sterile polarization. Like the aping of machismo or obsessive careerism, it dissipates our own wellsprings of generative power.

In the second stage, women, with men, have to take back the *day*— take a stand on regaining human control over what was once called women's sphere (family, children, home), and join men in jobs, unions, companies, professions, asserting new human control over work. Focusing our new political mode on what once were ignored as women's issues and are now being exploited by male demagogues, we could perhaps transcend some either/or dilemmas that currently seem intractable, and take back from the Right the offensive "for family" and "for life."

For instance, in the first stage, childbearing and child-rearing, in the abstract, became the insuperable, insoluble problems that seemed to set feminists demanding "equal rights" (to jobs) and "the right to choose" (abortion) against women defending their own stake in "the family" (mother-hood, bearing and caring for children). In the second stage, with inflation and unemployment among husbands forcing most women, even young mothers, to take what jobs they can get, and with the escalating costs of feeding, housing, cloth-ing and educating children forcing the most devout Catholic parents, with the sympathy of their priests, to agonize over the choice to have children—why should we let the radical Right mau-mau us into a costly, diversionary battle to the death over abortion *on their terms?*

Do they really want to force women to have more chil-dren? Do they really want to outlaw abortion? Or do they want to keep pushing it as a diversionary issue, twisting and manipulating the agonizing conflicts people can't help facing now, about the costs and problems of having children, and their own values of life—diverting the rage away from those who profiteer from inflation, with sexual, "moral" red her-rings? But the power of their campaign, and the rage they are able to divert against those who speak openly and honestly about the choices all must make now, comes, at least in part, from the pain and the deep insult to their human core that people may be truly experiencing as they are manipulated deeper and deeper into the depersonalizing material rat race, losing control of their lives. The very rhetoric of the first stage "pro-abortion" campaign exacerbated or played into that rage.

Do we really fight for abortion—or do we fight for a diver-sity of pluralistic means whereby women, according to their own consciences and values, can choose to have children, or to be generative in other ways? Do we really mean ourselves to push abortion, except as last resort—not as lightly used birth control, and surely not as fad or substitute thrill for those who want to prove their fertility without having a baby (as the *Village Voice* reported as the new "abortion chic" in their February 4, 1981, issue)? In the second stage, feminists would *not* consider abortion preferable to the Catholics' new method of precise, "natural" birth control—for women and men mature enough to take responsibility for it. Responsible Catholics, including priests and bishops, are in honest turmoil today in their family ministries in dealing with teenage pregnancy. We can respect the values and conscience—and agonies—of those who truly regard abortion as sin. They are not the real enemy.

If the radical Right ever got the so-called Human Life Amendment passed, they would lose the abortion issue as a scapegoat for diverting the rage and many poor women would die or be mutilated from unsafe, illegal abortions. Why do we let them draw us into battle against the "right to life"? Why don't we join forces with all who have true reverence for life, including Catholics who oppose abortion, and fight for the choice to have children?

It is no secret that childbearing has dropped drastically in the United States since the end of the baby boom in the late 1950s. Today, the only child is becoming the norm; the national average is down to 1.8. In a 1979 study, the U.S. Department of Agriculture put the cost of raising a child up to age eighteen in a moderate-income family—assuming 10 percent inflation—at $165,300, compared to $34,300 in 1960. In a recent article in *Parents* magazine, Thomas Telling, adding an average of $61,000 in salary that a mother would give up by staying home during the first five years, estimated the cost of raising a child born in 1980 to age eighteen at a quarter of a million dollars.

In the face of these economic facts of life, the choice to have a child becomes for many women and men a profound statement of human values, an assertion of human priorities in defiance of pressures to material and career success.

In the end, a great many Catholic and Orthodox Jewish women, men, priests and rabbis, might join us in the battle we must wage against that cynical Human Rights Amendment—which denies pluralistic freedom of religious belief and privacy of conscience as well as the personhood of women—if we would assert our own value for generating life.

At the NOW-LDEF National Assembly on the Future of the Family, that prophetic science-fiction writer Isaac Asimov said that the choice to have children will soon be so cherished, and rare, that every child will be regarded as a national treasure.

The second-stage problem is for women and men to be able to choose to have children responsibly, which means not only safe legal medical access to birth control and abortion but maternity and paternity leaves and benefits. Above all, it means really coming to grips with the question of who is going to take care of the child when both mother and father have to share parenting on top of necessary jobs or professional training or commitments.

Recent studies indicate that worry over child care and its real difficulties—with the economic or professional impossibility of taking leave from jobs, the inflexibility of professional training or working hours and the lack of sufficient child-care options of any kind—is seriously threatening the choice to have children. Owlish economists, who foresee a nation of old people, with too few young to do the work, are beginning to worry about this, too.

Survey after survey shows that mothers of young children prefer part-time work, if they can find it. Or, if they must work full time, they do not want impersonal "government day care," but good, reliable, personally caring substitutes for themselves. Their own identity as mothers—and men's new identity as fathers—means they want personal choice and control of their child's care.

It would seem to me that in the second stage we should move for some very simple aids that make it possible for mothers (or fathers) who want to stay home and take care of their own children to do so, with some economic compensation that might make the difference. Some form of "child allowance"—which is taken as a matter of course in virtually every advanced nation but ours—could also be used to help pay for child care within a range of possibilities from which parents could personally choose when they returned to work.

For the second stage involves not a retreat to the family, but embracing the family in new terms of equality and diversity. The choice to have children—and the joys and burdens of raising them—have become so costly and precious that child-rearing will have to be shared more equally by mother, father, and others from, or in place of, the larger family. It will probably not be possible economically for most women to have a real choice to be just a housewife, full time, lifelong. But men as well as women will be demanding parental leave or reduced schedules for those few years—or in early, middle or later life for their own rebirth. A voucher system, such as Milton Friedman and other conservatives have already proposed for different purposes, could be used to provide a "child allowance," payable perhaps as a tax rebate, to every man or woman who takes primary responsibility for care of a child or dependent parent at home. She or he would get equal credit in the wage-earning spouse's pension and old age social security vestment; this credit would not be lost in case of divorce. If both parents returned to work and shared child care responsibilities, they could use those vouchers to help pay for child care or other services from any number of possible sources—local school board, company, union, church, private for-profit, or not-for-profit company.

Stripped of polarizing rhetoric, the practical problems of restructuring home and work may not be as difficult as they now seem. For instance, for economic reasons—and in consonance with the new emphasis on "quality of life"—more and more young couples choose to have only one child, or, at most, two, especially if they postpone childbearing until age thirty or so, when both parents have established themselves professionally. A combination of parental leaves—full-time for a year or two, on the part of one or both parents, and/or part-time or other reduction of schedule flexibly arranged between the two—would cover the three, five, or seven years that childbearing or early child-rearing encompasses for this generation of parents.

Such combinations of leaves and flexible scheduling would fit into other new developments in the workplace—including the alternative of shortening hours and rotating layoffs, spreading jobs rather than creating massive permanent unemployment, that may appeal to both unions and companies, liberals and conservatives, if the current economic dislocations continue. (The structure of the economy, even now, and the nature of the service jobs most women hold, means that it will not be possible to solve a 1980s recession or depression simply by sending the women home again —as much as simplistic politicians of the so-called radical Right might favor such a solution. On the other hand, the increased pressure of many jobs—such as intensive-care nursing, or the maintaining of the robots and computers that are replacing assembly-line workers—are already causing companies to face the alternatives of reducing work shifts, making them more flexible, and introducing job sharing, if they are not to lose the trained nurse, monitor or manager because of "burnout," health problems or simply quitting in favor of work with less tension!)

Then let the communities or states, or the private sector—yes, even profit-oriented companies, developers, shopping centers, as well as unions, churches and voluntary agencies—be encouraged, with tax incentives, to develop good child-care programs, which parents could choose and actively control. They could utilize empty or underused church facilities, school buildings, parks, playgrounds or other public spaces for the preschool and after-school programs that are now needed. And offer the job rehabilitation and retraining that is needed for good child-care careers to men as well as women in places like Detroit and Pittsburgh, where they have been laid off from auto and steel plants or replaced by computers. If only one mother out of four is going to be able to stay home full time and take care of her own children by 1990—maybe she or a second woman, or even all four, in different shifts, could use those vouchers or tax credits to pool and share the care for each other's children.

The real extended family for my children's childhood, with their grandparents at opposite ends of the continent, was the other parents and the teachers at the cooperative nursery school which was the main attraction when we moved into the Parkway Village garden apartments in Queens, New York. Other parents found that same family-type support in neighborhood day-care centers run, for instance, by the city of New York, before budgets for such services began to be cut. Of course, children would have to be protected by standards of quality child care, safety and health, and competency through training or its equivalent of these parent-substitutes. But instead of a vast federal bureaucracy, a second-stage approach might have community and parent boards overseeing such standards—with parents themselves having the final control in the option to use or not to use a given program or switch to a better one.

Then parents would not feel they were turning their children over to the impersonal state. No serious child psychologist ever denied that Head Start or a good nursery school—or the children's house in the kibbutz—was anything but good for the child. The real problem is whether such child care enhances or takes away real value, worth and function for the parent.

So labor unions and Beta-type company management—newly concerned, for reasons of productivity, profit and competitiveness, with the human needs of workers, managers and professionals alike—might find it conducive to both productivity and profit to set up such child-care programs in or near the workplace, as hospitals have had to do to lure badly needed nurses to stay on their increasingly demanding shifts.

For while it is true that there has been no advance in the kind of massive federal day-care programs feminists used to talk about—twenty-four-hour, quality child care free for parents of all income levels, like parks, libraries and public schools—there are, increasingly, in small communities, big cities and suburbs, South and West and Northeast, nursery schools and child-care centers run by churches, community agencies or companies both for profit and nonprofit, with fixed or sliding-scale fees. There are child-care centers demanded and won by the students in universities, or in the union contract by the Amalgamated Clothing Workers, or at Stride-Rite Shoe Company, or started cooperatively by parents themselves. And even those mothers (or fathers) who choose to stay home and take care of their own children want their children in such programs part of the day, if they can afford it or can work it out cooperatively with other such parents—for the children's, and their own, better growth.

An example of Beta-mode evolution: the American Jewish Committee, appalled by the prospect of the surviving remnant of the Jewish people dying out if young Jewish women continue to seek careers instead of having children, set up a Center on the Family in 1980. Its logo was so clearly traditional—Mama, Papa, the two kids—that feminists bristled. Would they *never* learn that if they want Jewish women to have more children, they would have to deal with the real problems of families now, when mothers need to and want to work and where sometimes there's only one parent, etc.?

But because Jewish feminists, men and women, stayed in there and kept their attention on the concrete problems that must be solved if the real, evolving new Jewish families are in fact going to be able to choose to have children, and to continue to participate in Jewish religious and communal life— and because the Jewish establishment's concern for the survival of the Jewish family was real, and not just a buzz word for reaction, and the Jewish feminists clearly shared that concern—within one year the Jewish Family Center newsletter was reporting the following:

• A study of how ninety-seven Jewish working mothers with three or more children in the Washington area have "met the challenge of career and motherhood."

• The finding that Jewish beliefs, attitudes and values have helped those women cope with problems and crises "but they got little aid and encouragement from Jewish community agencies."

• The urgent recommendation that such agencies begin forthwith to "provide good Jewish day-care programs at affordable prices."

The Center also recommended that Jewish communities provide:

• Baby-sitter pools of teenagers and old people.

• Car pools to help transport parents to work and children to school or after-school activities.

• Time-sharing and child-care arrangements for staff members (male and female) of Jewish organizations, to enable them to be home with small children part of the day.

• Revised Jewish texts presenting a *positive image* of career-oriented wives and mothers.

• Credit for responsible volunteer work in the Jewish community that women can point to when they are trying to pick up professional careers after a hiatus as homemakers.

Thus, with the cooperation of the National Council of Jewish Women and neighborhood residents, the Hebrew Union College in Cincinnati initiated a cooperative day-care program for children of rabbinical students, providing space, legal advice, bookkeeping lessons and money for one full-time staff person; furniture was supplied by the neighbors, and other staff functions rotated by the young rabbi-parents themselves. It "opened just in time to accommodate the baby of Gila Coleman Russell, the first Cincinnati rabbinical student to give birth."

Also reported were:

• An after-school program for five-year-olds in the Jewish Community Center of Marblehead, Massachusetts, with transportation to and from the public kindergarten.

• An "extended day" with flexible hours as well as a full weekly day-care program for children two and one-half to five, in Denver.

• A Single Parent Family Center at the Flushing, Queens, YM-YWHA (offering a legal clinic, child care, a library, a clothing swap shop, as well as job and housing information and social activities).

• An active single fathers' group and joint rap session with single mothers in Scarsdale, New York.

• Widow-widower outreach in Philadelphia and an after-school program for children rotated in supervised private homes.

And the artist was sent back to the drawing board to dream up a new logo reflecting the true strength of family diversity!

For in the second stage, when we talk about family, we will no longer mean just Mom and Dad and the kids. We are fast becoming aware of the new shapes a family can take over a lifetime. For instance, the Catholic Conference of Bishops has set up its new Ministries on the Family, concretely serving the needs of singles and single parents, separated and divorced Catholics, and recognizing the needs of working parents. The pastoral letter in the *Long Island Catholic* from Bishop John McGann proclaiming 1980 as the Year of the Family states that "Family life has become more truly human and consistent with its Scriptural meaning by its liberation . . . from various restrictions."

"Softening the rigidity of role assignments within the family," the Bishop says, "has made possible the development of each person, which is a condition for true family unity."

As Joseph Giordano put it, in a column on "Families" in the Italian-American magazine *Attenzione* (March 1981): "When an Italian-American priest in Staten Island conducts weekly counseling groups for Catholics who are divorced and separated, he is not only preaching Christian love, he is providing real help and effecting changes in attitude. Five years ago, a divorced Catholic was regarded as being 'outside the Church.' "

The Catholic religious stand on abortion as sin remains. Increasingly, however, concerned priests as well as Catholic lay leaders and nuns (who have been courageously feminist and in the vanguard of the women's movement for fifteen years) are divorcing themselves from the extremism of the so-called Right to Life movement and the fundamentalist Moral Majority. "There is something wrong in a movement," the *National Catholic Reporter* editorializes, "which can value life in just one stage of human development."

Also in similar vein, at a conference of Southern Baptists in Dallas, Texas, in March 1981, a protest was voiced against the "evangelical political action" whereby groups like the Moral Majority "judge a political candidate's Christianity on the basis of his agreement or disagreement with the conservatives on a narrow list of moral issues." They questioned the "Christianity" of any such list that excluded women's rights specifically. A leading Southern Baptist theologian, Professor William Hendricks of California, said that "religious politics" was "self-serving" and jeopardized the Baptist principle of toleration for differing points of view. Those who "speak as God instead of for God may be idolatrous at best and blasphemous at worst," he warned.

And again in similar vein, the National Urban League has called legislators on the carpet for treating the black family as though it were weak and pathological because it is often "matriarchal" and for failing to recognize that extended family structures, active church affiliations, and the strengths of women have traditionally kept black households strong.

In the second stage, the solutions may come not neces-

sarily because of or for women—or, at least, not in the first-
stage feminist sense of "for women only," dragged under du-
ress or from altruistic good will out of reluctant men—but
from converging causes, related or unrelated technological
changes, that add up to profits or other benefits for the men
and institutions involved. The women's movement itself may
have been a key factor in this evolution, but converging
changes in the economy and society give it momentum beyond ideology.

For instance, in the middle-class suburban development of
East Meadow in Nassau County, New York, where sixty
thousand conventional church- and temple-going souls live
in twenty thousand single-family houses, split-level or ranch-
style, high school guidance counselors report a marked
change in the career choices of both boys and girls, increasingly free from sexual stereotyping. Boys routinely take
home economics classes now. "Young men and women are
going into areas they would not have dared a decade ago,"
says Dr. Judith Healy, counseling director for the school district. "Boys moving into what were traditional female job
situations, studying practical nursing and cosmetology and
dress design, and girls studying math and science in increasingly large numbers and also taking auto shop."

A ten-year follow-up study of these suburban high school
students showed that girls had raised their level of career
choices, as from "nurse" to "doctor," or "secretary" to "accountant" or "business management," whereas boys tended
to lower their levels or to branch out more. Dr. Healy concluded that this was a result of both sexes being freed from
the past sex stereotyping which had led girls to think only in
terms of stopgap jobs until marriage, and which expected
boys to achieve "success" in a few prestigious conventional
male careers, whatever their actual abilities and interests. In
this same period, in this community, most mothers had to go
to work to maintain the family's living standards, and so both
the boys and the girls saw in their mothers new role models
as wage earners, and saw their fathers doing work previously

seen as feminine at home. Yet for the first time in eleven years, a poll of United States teenage leaders listed in the 1979–80 "Who's Who Among American High School Students" showed a majority (52.9 percent) against the Equal Rights Amendment. (Some 87 percent favor a traditional marriage for themselves, 61 percent believing a woman can be fulfilled by working in the home full time and raising a family, 39 percent thinking women should have marriage and a career to be fulfilled.)

The economic realities—hard-to-find jobs and ceilings on hiring—take some of the false glamour out of the feminist mystique of "careers." Yet these same economic realities, while giving haunting power to the fantasy of "a man to take care of you the rest of your life," force such young women to train themselves to work and earn—in order, perhaps, to marry now and have that home and family—if not for their own independence and growth. (It's instructive, listening to young men, and men not so young, once they've been out in the world, discuss the respective charms of young women in terms not only of breast and hip size, but of jobs and earning ability!)

It is not hard to understand the need that makes those young high school leaders—and even sophisticated, mature, successful feminist or antifeminist movement leaders—yearn for a return to the old, simple family where just finding that man will "take care of your whole life." Even if it means denying one's own hard-won strength to take care of oneself, and the reality facing women approaching their sixties, like me, that we will have to create new forms of family or live alone. Even if it means denying, for those sixteen-year-old girls, the reality that they will have to work most of their lives to support themselves and their families, or even to have a home. For these daughters and sons above all, the battle for equality has to go on, and change direction now—embracing the imperiled dream of family.

When these boys and girls start their own families, the women may or may not earn less than the men, and may or

may not feel the need to keep an edge of "control" over home
and children. The "flow" may be closer to fifty-fifty in both
spheres, or eighty-twenty in one, forty-sixty in the other. But
in the second stage I doubt that women or men will be measuring these matters on a zero-sum, win-lose scale.

As a matter of fact, given certain directions in the economy as a whole, the liberation of new skills and interests in
men that were previously seen as "feminine" may be their
own best protection against layoffs and long-term unemployment.

In January 1981, for instance, on the heels of several reports that too many doctors were being turned out by U.S.
medical schools, it was revealed that many hospitals were
having to shut down or turn away patients for lack of sufficient nurses, especially for the intensive-care units, where
the complicated new medical technology can save previously
doomed heart and accident patients only with constant moni-
toring of subtle signs in the patients' condition. Of 1.4 million registered nurses in this country, 300,000 no longer practice (*New York Times,* November 24, 1980). Many are refusing
to work long hours for the relatively low pay and slim
chances of promotion. Younger women are seeking more
"prestigious careers."

To induce nurses to stay, despite the stress, and to get
more nurses with the requisite human skills, the hospitals
were warned by their own doctors that they must not only
give nurses better pay and more status, but also more flexible
hours to reduce the stress, child-care centers for the nurses'
children in or near the hospital, and "alternative training"
for persons who want to become nurses but do not have or
want a degree.

In this same period, not only were auto workers and steel
workers and aerospace workers being laid off, but also executives in significant numbers. It was also reported that those
eager, ambitious law school graduates were not finding jobs
in law firms. Widespread disillusionment with the MBA's

coming out of the nation's business schools, from Harvard down, was being voiced by company owners and managers fighting desperately to compete with the Japanese or Germans and to stem the seeming decline in American productivity. When they called in Harvard psychologist David McClelland to investigate what distinguished good executives—from aerospace and the navy to sales and civil service—who could actually deliver (produce, sell, raise productivity and morale, change methods that weren't working), they found out that too many of the MBA's had been trained in terms of the old Alpha style of "masculine" aggressiveness, linear-mathematical certainty, computer models, etc. But the most effective executives or human-service administrators weren't the ones who did best on those numerical tests or who were the most aggressive; they were those "competent" and "sensitive" in dealing with people, able to sense their special needs and interests.

These and other signs of second-stage movement in industry seem to be happening for reasons that have nothing to do with women—but they facilitate, even demand, that new flexible mode and the transcending of sex roles. For instance, with inflation and other economic factors reducing the value and possibility of wage increases—and with men as well as women wanting more control of their lives—unions are showing more interest in "quality of work life" issues, such as flextime and flexible benefits geared to individual and family needs. And for bottom-line economic reasons—increased productivity, better employee morale and simple cost efficiency—companies are agreeing to, or even themselves introducing, flexible job benefits as well as flextime. The American Can Company, Educational Testing Service, Pepsico, Northern State Power of Minneapolis, and TRW Inc. of Cleveland have adopted "cafeteria style benefits" in place of the increasingly expensive standard benefit programs geared to the needs of traditional families—working men with dependent wives and children.

Instead of a standard program of vacations, retirement

plan, disability pay and medical insurance, a woman or man who works at American Can is able to choose the benefits that suit his or her own family needs, and get compensation in other forms for those they don't take. A woman systems programmer, already covered by her husband's medical insurance, takes an extra week's vacation every year instead of health insurance. A single secretary with no dependents saves money for her own future in a capital accumulation fund instead of the life insurance she would have automatically received. Only 10 percent of the employees stick with the standard-benefits plan instead of a flexible plan in which they choose their own.

In 1980 over 10 million workers, or 12 percent of those holding full-time jobs, were on flextime schedules permitting them to vary the beginning and ending hours of their workday, or were working their full week in three to four-and-a-half days. Ironically, these flexible schedules were used more by men than women, according to the U.S. Department of Labor; among working parents, the option was more common for fathers than mothers. Local public administrations led in using these flexible or compressed work schedules, especially for police and fire persons. Some flextime schedules permit variations of a half hour to two hours or more in starting or leaving times, some permit a mix of shorter and longer days. The flexible schedules were found to reduce absence and tardiness, as well as commuter peak loads and traffic stoppages and crowded buses and subways. Of course, such flextime work schedules make it easier for young parents to live that dream of equality. And people in the child-rearing years used flextime more than those in later middle age. But most of those who seized the opportunity for flexible schedules were men and women of sixty-five and older. As more and more older people are forced by inflation to keep working they will make powerful allies, in unions and companies, for the new young men and women who want more control of their days.

       •   •   •

Education in Stage Two will transcend its age-old sex-role polarization—and masculine definition—in ways that go far beyond women's studies, or homemaking for men.

In the second stage, women's studies themselves may evolve into, or be replaced by, more basic studies of the changing sex roles of both women and men in all their social, political, economic and sexual implications, but such studies will be integrated into and transform the study and the practice of the whole discipline.

Twenty years ago feminists like myself were concerned with the great need among those women who had stopped their education to have children to get back into the educational mainstream for serious professional training. Establishment educators then—even advanced foundation types and women deans—would not consider the possibility that women be allowed to do graduate work at top schools like the Harvard School of Education on less than a full-time basis, or that they be given "equivalency" credit for serious volunteer or political work or jobs, much less "life experience." And educators frowned on admitting women over thirty to professional programs. "Continuing education" started as a contemptuous device to keep those aging housewives out of educators' hair.

Today top universities and graduate schools are competing to woo "midlife" students for part-time, evening, split-shift, "weekend college," falling over themselves to certify "equivalency" credits for "life experience" for entrance even into serious professional programs. The first beneficiaries of this change are, of course, women who need to resume or retrain for work careers after full-time housewife-motherhood.

But the change did not come about in a sudden outpouring of altruistic goodwill toward women, or even as a result of women's movement militancy or affirmative-action lawsuits. It happened primarily because colleges, losing students as the postwar baby boom came to an end and as boys no longer had to go to graduate school to evade the draft, had to find a new source of tuition fees and student bodies to stay in the black. . . . And there were all these aging housewives they had previously sneered at, very eager indeed to come back to school—if only arrangements could be made more flexible. Suddenly that wasn't difficult; it didn't alter the basic content of the education, after all.

And then, of course, they discovered how very good these women were. With whatever they had learned in their "equivalent" life experience, or volunteer work, or jobs, they sometimes seemed better prepared than students who had gone straight through the educational lockstep. And the more educators learned from these women, the more they were able to gear education to the changing lifetime needs of men as well as women. And now more and more men are coming back to school, after some years out working, motivated by a midlife change in personal direction, or a change forced by technological obsolescence of their jobs or simply the need for growth. So, more and more, on the great campuses of the United States today, the average student is not that stereotypical carefree eighteen-to-twenty-one-year-old college Joe or Jane, but a twenty-six- or thirty-six- or over-fifty-year-old man or woman.

Such is the pace of change in every profession—medicine, dentistry, law—that states and professional bodies increasingly require in their very licensing regulations that everyone, man or woman, go back for refresher education every five or ten years.

Because of these converging changes, the rigid educational lockstep that women once found so difficult to combine with child-rearing has already become a much more flexible, lifetime, drop-in-and-out process, more nearly suitable to the flexible needs of women and men in the parenting years.

As more and more public high schools and elementary schools built for the postwar baby boom are being closed, farsighted educators, school boards and local officials are themselves suggesting that these facilities could be used for the daycare, preschool and after-school programs now so badly needed for the children of working parents. Instead of being laid off, excess school teachers and administrators could be reoriented, with some retraining, for work with younger children. As a matter of fact, the excess school space might be used at the same time as community centers for senior citizens, some of whom might welcome the chance to be volunteer teachers and assistants with the little ones. It makes better business sense than wasting or razing that costly educational plant and then having to rebuild it when the babies of those grown-up baby-boomers reach school age.

For their own reasons I can even see business managers, in the second stage, having figured out the kinds of training that give young executives the skills to deal with people and continual change, waiting impatiently for eager Joe Beaver to take his year's paternity leave to counteract that rigid, number-bound computeritis he got along with his MBA.

How ironic, then, if Jane Beaver, with excess reverence for that Alpha-style male lockstep as the one and only road to success in her new corporate world, should, in the interests of superwoman efficiency, give up that period of human-learning time which motherhood meant for women of my generation, even if we paid a price of postponed advancement in career, or permanently lowered sights, or barriers getting back in, when we took, not one-year or two-year, but eight- or ten-year leaves from the wage-work world.

The broader question, in the second stage, is this: Will women, in a new assertion of the priority of human values, which goes back to their traditional feminine roots, join men in resisting dehumanizing and, in the end, counterproductive corporate pressures to "produce," or will they become even more slavish robots to the obsolete workaholic time clock than men?

There is evidence of real danger—and a tenuous, desperate hope—if we look at women alone. It's only if we look beyond women to the family again, with both women and men playing new roles, that the hope becomes substantial.

For instance, *Savvy*, the magazine of "superwomen" executives and aspirants to that exalted state, carried a report on
"The Time Pressured Life" (December 1980), in which a
number of women (age thirty-two to fifty-seven, married and
single, with and without children) were asked to keep logs of
their daily schedules, hour by hour, around the clock. *Savvy*
wondered: "As women live lives more like those of men, are
they adopting the very values of male society they formerly
criticized, ignoring their traditional concerns?"

The logs gave a general impression of constant activity, of
"virtual enslavement to schedule." Every woman reported
"happiness and satisfaction with her personal and professional lot," but they led days (which began at 5:30 or 6 A.M.)
of "austere, machine-like productivity." These logs offered
evidence that such superwomen had gone beyond even the
male workaholic treadmill. The average high-level male executive works a sixty-hour week. One married childless female
executive reported "100 hours of work out of 122 logged."
Another, a financial consultant, whose work involves "doing
the same thing for hours and hours on end," didn't realize,
until she looked at her "boring log," that the only hours she
wasn't spending on work were from 2:30 to 6:30 A.M., when
she slept. The logs barely mentioned sex; one woman "reserved" Friday night for her husband. Some of the married
women had decided that the demands of their careers ruled
out children; two felt "panic" at even thinking about having
children. Asked to report not only what they did, but their
feelings, some women were "not sure what you mean by
emotions."

Strangely enough, the logs revealed that these women, despite their relative youth and good health, thought quite a lot
about death. I remembered noticing the same thing twenty
years ago, when I was interviewing those frenetically busy
feminine-mystique housewives with their incessant routine
of chauffeuring - cleaning - cooking - shopping - dishwashing
- laundering. Does such a woman's worry about death come

from some existential sense that she is not really *living* her own life?

Perhaps the only hopeful thing about the article was *Savvy's* own horror at what it revealed—and the enormous response they got from their readers.

A few years ago, when I was teaching a course I called "The Sex Role Revolution—Stage II" at Yale, I asked my students to write term papers examining changing sex roles in some institution they were close to and to look for evidence of second-stage solutions. One student selected the Yale psychology department, which, in the fashion of a major Ivy League university, exerted great pressure on faculty to "publish or perish." It was only recently that women had been hired. My student found that the women psychologists were putting in more hours of work than the men. Men and women spent the same amount of time in teaching; the men seemed to spend slightly more on their own research, but the women spent more hours than the men on "Brownie point" committee duties. And the men spent as many hours as the women on housework and child care. But almost all the men were married and living with their wives, and they had children. A number of the women were either not married or were divorced, or not living with their husbands, and most did not have children.

Of course, only the most assiduous superwomen might have gotten into the Yale psychology department at that time, and many of the men still had wives who took over the care of the home and children, freeing the men to "publish or perish" in the traditional manner. But my student found that the only evidence of new patterns, second-stage solutions, came not from the women psychologists' life styles but from some of the younger men who shared the child-care and household responsibilities with their working wives.

"I carry a full teaching load," said one of the men, "and I'm available to my students, but I won't take on a lot of the other things any more. And if it takes me six years instead of three to publish this research, so be it. I won't work evenings and weekends. I do my share with the children and I'm committed to it. But it's hard, here, where the whole pattern is that pressure—publish or perish. Where my wife works, the whole place is younger, no one makes enough money for wives not to work, so everyone is sharing these responsibilities for children and home. They don't expect you to work nights and weekends, and I'm not sure their morale isn't better. They may not publish as much, but they do good work. Everyone is more relaxed."

Those superwomen who made the logs for *Savvy* had even resorted to consulting experts on "time management" and using "flow charts" at home to juggle the demands of their various roles more efficiently. But business itself is finding that these mathematical flow charts and old-style "efficiency" or "time management" programs don't necessarily produce the innovations, the mobilization of creative energy and human motivation needed to meet the demands of change in these times.

There is reason to believe that, in the second stage, women and men will move on to new attempts to control their own time. Recent interviews with young women in college now indicate that they intend to have children, and even take eight years off to do so, if they can.

"Many Young Women Now Say They'd Pick Family Over Career," *The New York Times* reported deceptively, in a front-page story on December 28, 1980. A Princeton senior, winner of a Rotary fellowship, expects to attend business school and work in international finance. But "she plans to quit whatever job she has for eight years to become a full-time mother.

"She is not alone. At a time when young women have more job opportunities and chances for advancement than ever, many of them now in college . . . are questioning whether a career is more important than having children and caring for them personally."

The report cited a recent study of three thousand students at six Ivy League colleges, where 77 percent of the women and 84 percent of the men said that mothers either should not work at all or work only part time until their children were five years old.

Many of the women interviewed by *The Times* said they felt threatened by the high divorce rate and the large number of professionally successful women who did not marry. "Even some of the most career-oriented women said they planned to take time off from their professions to raise their children even if it meant jeopardizing advancement."

These women, unlike women twenty-five years ago, "want and expect to work." Still, said *The Times*, "it appears clear that much of the feminist ferment at institutions of higher learning a decade ago has dwindled. Job opportunities are now taken for granted. Rather than carry on the struggle for equality, many college women are now grappling with other concerns. ('I'm not interested in being a bachelorette.' 'I've had enough of the superwomen with their top-executive jobs.')"

They expected that the men they eventually married would share the child-rearing. They hoped their employers would allow them to take maternity leaves of as long as seven years, if they waited until they were thirty to have babies, so they could "watch over their first steps" themselves, and then return to their professions, say by age forty. "But when told that most employers did not have such policies today, they replied that they would then be prepared to sacrifice their own advancement."

The Times reported that many of those interviewed did not "identify with the women's movement." Indeed, some said they resented what they characterized as "pressures imposed by feminism: to work, to marry, to raise families without providing the answers to how all of this should be done. At the same time, they said they had become alienated from women's centers on campus because those concerns were not addressed."

But a closer look at those same figures does not justify that headline—"Many Young Women Now Say They'd Pick Family Over Career." For it seemed that only 27 percent of the women in that study thought mothers shouldn't be working at all when children were between two and five years old. Fifty percent thought mothers should work part time, and 16 percent full time. As Ellen Goodman warned, such headlines make a "self-fulfilling prophecy of the retreat to traditionalism." As a matter of fact, you could read these figures at least three ways: (1) 77 percent think women shouldn't work full time when children are little; (2) 66 percent think women shouldn't be at home full time, even when children are little; and (3) 50 percent prefer part-time jobs.

I don't think this means that these young women are turning their backs on equal opportunity or that they lack ambition and goals of their own. They are reasserting certain values, repudiating the either/or. When I lectured at Harvard Law School not long ago, young men as well as women were asking the Wall Street recruiters about their policies on maternity and paternity leave.

With new awareness of the limits of their own most basic resource—time—women and men in the second stage will demand, through unions and from companies, more control of their days. Flextime, part time, job sharing—not for women only—will also converge on energy and technological changes. More and more, the kind of work that will be required of people will involve creative, innovative, and decision-making responsibility. (The rest will be done by computers or machines.) This kind of work can often be done as well at home or under a tree as in an office—and done better sometimes by the individual alone than by "committee." And yet, the new kind of work will require at other times the catalyst of all the people meeting together, coming up with solutions together—deciding how they will execute and control a new process or problem. Advanced technological processes and problems can't be managed any more by workers, male or female, taking rote orders, down the hierarchy from the boss on top, or following a rigid Alpha manual. Alvin Toffler's *The Third Wave* predicts that flextime and a shifting

flexible *adhoc* racy must replace rigid, centralized massive bureaucracies in the next stage of advanced industrial civilization.

But the image of Mr. and Mrs. Future spending all their
days working and living by themselves in their own isolated
electronic cottage is not the real spatial implication. Toffler
himself predicts that socializing will increasingly be shifted
from office to community. The second stage, above all, requires a different kind of house. Or rather, a new concept of
home.

9 The House and the Dream

We come full circle here. Listening to young men and women, and those not so young, living these new problems, I keep having the feeling that in *the house*—the space-time, physical, concrete dimensions of what we call home—is somehow the basic clue to where we have come, and where we have to go, in the second stage. It is that physical, literal house—or its lack—that somehow points to the heart of our problems, that keeps us from transcending those old sex roles that too often have locked us in mutual misery in the family.

Consider: The house, the very shape of the house all Americans are supposed to dream of—and must now pay not 25 percent but nearly 50 percent of their joint or single earnings to support—was based on the continuous, full-time, unpaid services of the woman whose place was in the home. It physically held in place that family mystique—Daddy the breadwinner, Mama the housewife, the two children, the station wagon, the second car, the appliances, the dog and cat. And this family remained unchanged over time—static as the frieze of shepherds and shepherdesses eternally dancing in that circle round Keats's Greek vase.

Women and men are not only in a different place now—they are, we now realize much more clearly than before, in *different places*, with needs that change over time. The house is like that immovable object against which an irresistible, irreversible force—the evolution that surfaced with the women's movement—is colliding.

I keep remembering that the suburban house, which became the great American dream house for us all after World War Two, was not only the symbol of what I called the feminine mystique. That suburban dream house literally embodied in brick or wood or concrete block, as it sat on its 60-by-100-foot, or acre or more, lot, the feminine mystique, and trapped women in it. When we stripped through the rhetoric, that suburban house, linked only by car or station wagon or commuter train to man's world of industry, science, art, public affairs, is what isolated and confined the energies of all us "happy housewives" in those years after World War Two. That isolated house, with all those appliances each woman had to spend all day operating by herself, somehow made us spend more time doing housework than our mothers and grandmothers—and drove our husbands to ulcers or premature heart attacks, in the rat race to pay for them.

And now we and our daughters have to work ourselves to pay for that same house and those appliances. There just isn't any other kind of house, though even with two working, how many can afford that thrice-inflated dream house now? Even though we've broken through the feminine mystique enough to demand equal pay on the job, and some choice in our lives, the fact that we come home to that same kind of house, which we may still be trying to run in the same kind of way, makes us doubly burdened now, forced to be superwomen. This remains true even if our husbands help or share, with more or less resentment—and especially if there is no husband now, only the woman herself, to take care of house or apartment and children, as well as job. Or if the children are grown, or she feels she can't manage now to have children at all, and she, or he, or they, are now living by themselves and doing all of it, lonely and alone, *that house*—or apartment imitating it, which is getting even harder to find, and more expensive in most cities and suburbs—still dominates and controls their lives, and keeps them locked in isolation with these problems.

Of course, it's no longer a secret that the great majority of Americans can no longer find housing that meets their needs at all. The new young families can't afford those suburban dream houses even with two incomes. Traditionally, most new housing was bought by new families, but now only 13 percent of buyers are new families, even though the huge generation of the baby boom is now starting families and needs housing. For the most part, only people who've already owned and sold a house can now afford to buy a new one. But there is literally no housing, at any price, for rent or sale, being built to meet the needs of that 83 percent of Americans who no longer fit the old nostalgic model.

According to a story in the Real Estate section of *The New York Times* ("Housing Troubles in the Suburbs Grow," January 4, 1981), developers and real-estate brokers as well as government and company officials now see this housing squeeze as a crisis threatening the "capacity for continued economic growth" of the suburbs of Long Island, Westchester, New Jersey and Connecticut, which are prototypes of those suburbs nationwide where population exploded after World War Two as the cities' populations declined.

"Victims of the shortage include the young, middle-income families who were the vanguard of past suburban growth," the real-estate report said. "With the trend toward smaller families, single-parent households and more singles and elderly, the single-family house on a large plot—the very symbol of suburbia—is usually inappropriate to the needs of the market."

Yet zoning restrictions, building codes and the very premises of mortgage financing "make it difficult to produce the kind of housing that would meet the needs." Meanwhile the construction of new rental apartments has virtually stopped, and apartment buildings in cities like New York and its suburbs are rapidly being converted to cooperatives or condominiums, which can double their cost to tenants.

"We have built ourselves into kind of a corner in terms of the population we can accommodate," says a Chamber of Commerce spokesman in Connecticut. Westchester County has a "crisis" of population decline, with no housing that meets the needs of "working couples and singles." Bergen County, New Jersey, lost sixty thousand people in the last five years, mainly in the twenty-two-to-forty age group. Young people cannot afford to live in the communities in which they grew up. Senior citizens cannot afford to live in the communities in which they raised their families. Workers necessary to teach in the schools, to repair the appliances, to keep offices and stores functioning cannot afford to live in those suburbs.

In Suffolk County, New York, a survey in March 1980 revealed a large number of abandoned houses built in the early 1970s. "Typically the abandoned or foreclosed house was bought five or six years ago, perhaps with a minimal down payment," the study said. "After the purchase, energy costs and taxes soared, but the family's income may have fallen. Many families split—due perhaps in part to the financial strain."

So what has become common in these suburbs is the "illegal" division of these single-family suburban dream houses into apartments or otherwise shared accommodations for "a suburban population that is getting older with less need for large living space," and to meet "the pressures from younger persons."

"It's a reflection of the unwillingness of government to recognize that the American family is more than momma, poppa and two kids," said a regional planner. He said there were so many such illegal apartments in houses on Long Island that "we stopped counting them."

What was needed, planning and housing officials said, was not more of those suburban dream houses, but new kinds of financing to build "multifamily" housing, innovative use of existing buildings such as abandoned schools, more flexible zoning to build clusters of apartments or townhouses. But such proposals "invariably encounter strong opposition."

For many years now I've been aware that to *live* the new equality women are seeking means a *new kind of housing*. When I spoke at schools of architecture or conferences of urban planners or home economists in New York or California, Florida or Texas, on the implications of the women's movement and the sex-role revolution for home and city, I suggested that it required a change in the whole concept of the isolated single-family house or apartment.

What I had in mind was ways people could live, with the kind of privacy and individual control of our own space that is the American dream, and yet with some sharing of services like laundry and child care and access to common dining, or library, or music rooms, or other socializing places; services or amenities too burdensome or expensive—and lonely—for working couples or housewives, single or divorced parents, singles, young or old, to carry alone. A new kind of space for living that would be more human and less impersonal than city high-rise, low- or upper-income apartment grids, and not so separated from the workplace, not so isolated as the suburbs.

I went around Europe looking for such housing or community design. I certainly didn't find it in Communist countries; their apartments, crowded, shoddy imitations of our own public housing, had fewer amenities than ours—and nothing at all was being done to develop new designs for the new domestic services needed when *all* wives and mothers work.

Even in Israel, in the kibbutzes, there was no attempt at sex-role revolution. So women were still doing the laundry and the child care, and doing it en masse, without the prestige of the work that men were doing in the kibbutz. They began to resent the loss of the control and power they'd had in their own homes, and they wanted to take the children out of the "children's houses," or even leave the kibbutz altogether—not for the children's sake, but for their own. (See Melford Spiro, *Children of the Kibbutz.*) Architects had not even thought of applying some of the spatial arrangements on the kibbutzes to housing in cities.

I found, in Habitat, built for the Montreal World's Fair of 1970, and at Arcosanti, in Arizona, physical spaces and concepts that would lend themselves to the dream. But in a big city or suburb in the United States, spaces for jointly shared services—not only child care but kitchens, laundries, dining rooms—while certainly less costly for the individual than each one with his-her own washer, dryer, vacuum cleaner, microwave oven, Cuisinart (to say nothing of grand piano or nursery), would only be feasible if built into clusters of new buildings, or old neighborhoods, of some density. And that would require drastic restructuring of zoning codes, building codes, mortgage financing.

In Sweden, I found such a concept in "service housing." People had their own apartments, pleasant living rooms, bedrooms, balcony terrace, and small kitchenette, but they also had a common child-care center, a nursery for babies, and an after-school program. There was a common kitchen and dining room where all could take their meals—or pick them up after work to eat in their own apartments. They shared cleaning and gardening and laundry services, instead of each doing it separately.

When I was last in Sweden, there were long waiting lists for such "service housing." Single parents and people living alone found the family benefits of that common dining room very warming. Even couples with children, whether or not the mother worked, tended to eat dinner more often in the common dining room than they were required to by their contract. It was simply more lively, more sociable, and, of course, less work. The children, and their various parents, and the singles acquired new extended familylike bonds.

The Swedish feminists—who were as likely to be men as women, and who no longer used the term "women's movement," but rather "sex-role revolution"—were trying to get such services required by law, in new buildings, and even provided in some form in existing neighborhoods. It was they who taught me that without such practical restructuring of domestic work—embracing a new family role for men as well as women—without new kinds of home and child care, equality is "just talk."

But in the first stage of modern American feminism, housework and home only figured as something feminists wanted liberation *from*. Or so it seemed, and was made to seem by our enemies, our own extremists, and the media.

The second stage, I'm convinced, has to focus on a domestic revolution within the home and extending, in effect, the concept of home. We have to take new control of our home life, as well as work life, with not only new sharing of roles by women and men, but physical, spatial design of new kinds of housing and neighborhoods that take into account the changing, shifting needs of women and men, in couples or singly, with or without children, over time, with mortgage financing and building codes and zoning that encourage the new combinations of private space and shared communal spaces and services that are needed.

We've had pieces of it right, all along. But it's hardly insignificant that there's been this blind spot or split that's kept the feminist battle for equal rights with men in jobs or politics from seriously moving to real defense of the family and restructure of the home. It's happened before, fifty years ago and more. For I am not the first feminist to realize that that either/or split is what really holds women back, and to call for restructuring, not abandonment, of the home.

More buried in history than any of the other strands of women's passionate, unfinished journey to full human freedom is the story of three generations of feminists, between the end of the Civil War and the Depression, who concerned themselves with winning control, recognition and reward for "women's work." They challenged two characteristics of industrial capitalism: the physical separation of household space from public space and the economic separation of the domestic economy from the political economy. The history of these "material feminists" has now been pieced together by Dolores Hayden in *The Grand Domestic Revolution—A History of Feminist Design for American Homes, Neighborhoods and Cities* (MIT Press, 1981). It is certainly a welcome study, because even more than other lost women's history, the virtual burial of domestic, or material, feminism—Charlotte Perkins Gilman's *Women and Economics* had been out of print for decades when I wrote *The Feminine Mystique*—has distorted feminist ideology as a whole. (The following discussion draws extensively from Hayden's book.)

To overcome patterns of urban and domestic space that isolated women and made their domestic work invisible, the material feminists developed new forms of neighborhood organization, including housewives' cooperatives as well as new spatial design and building types, such as the kitchenless house, the day-care center, the public kitchen, and the community dining club. They also demanded "economic remuneration for women's unpaid household labor."

While other feminists concentrated on women's equal rights to the rewarding men's jobs in professions and industrial production, and to the vote, the "material feminists" argued that women must assert control over the important work of reproduction of society, which they were already performing, and reorganize it to obtain economic justice for themselves. Marxist socialists who talked persuasively to male industrial workers about seizing the means of production ignored women's work in the household and reproduction, which the material feminists saw as the key issue in the battle for women's autonomy.

They got architects and planners to design—and even build—revolutionary structures whereby couples, families and single people might inhabit a mix of kitchenless and conventional "homes," sharing common parlors, dining rooms, kitchens, nurseries and other services. As a result of feminist pressure, the "apartment hotel" started out in cities like New York as such a revolutionary structure, though its descendants are strictly profit-making ventures. There was an optimistic belief that advances in technology applied in new cooperative spaces and services in cities—such as central heating, which took away that laborious necessity of building and tending a fire in every room—would be used more and more to give women real control over the domestic work that trapped them in isolation and would free them for more human activities in their families and communities, and for their own growth and greater participation in public affairs. If central heating, why not central kitchens?

Melusina Peirce, a Harvard professor's wife, organized housewives in Cambridge in 1868 to take control over their lives by reorganizing "the dusty drudgery" of unpaid, unspecialized domestic work, and cooperatively buy specialized mechanical equipment for cooking, baking, laundering and serving. For their "cooperative housekeeping" they would charge their husbands—cash on delivery. The Cambridge Cooperative Housekeeping Society attracted Harvard wives and daughters ranging in age from mid-twenties to late sixties, and influential husbands, including the Dean of the Divinity School and the curator of the zoo, to its first meeting, which got much publicity. But the Society didn't last long. They rented a house, and Peirce herself ran the laundry—but only twelve of forty member households actually used the laundry or ordered their own meals from the service. Most of the men "laughed at the whole thing."

The new professions of social work and home economics took up and broadened the definition of cooperative housekeeping. Jane Addams's Hull House not only provided a cooperative kitchen—food preparation, dining and children's day care—for the immigrant poor, but incidentally created new structures of living for the idealistic women, and the few men, who lived at Hull House themselves. The families and individuals who rented Hull House apartments could order food served in their own quarters by the central kitchen but many residents dined every evening in the Hull House dining room, where "lively discussions of the science of society, and political equality were likely to take place."

But the professionalization of women social workers and home economists took the whole idea further and further away from the feminist aim: women taking control over their own lives. Because they were doing "women's work" in professional form, social workers and home economists were relatively low-paid. Instead of redoubling their previous material feminist efforts at restructuring and putting a value on "women's work," they tried to clear their skirts from feminist contamination, and began contemptuously to distinguish their "scientific" work from that of "the ordinary housewife." Shaky in their own professional confidence, they became patronizing and condescending, not only to the poor immigrants they made a career of "helping," but to ordinary housewives, whose isolation and insecurity they profited on, cultivating the notion that housewives need continual "expert" counsel in wise "consumption." As Hayden points out, this served their own careers and the industrial capitalists who financed their work.

But Charlotte Perkins Gilman, in *Women and Economics* (1898) and subsequent books, articles, and lectures, used the new doctrine of evolution to argue that women were holding back human evolution because of their confinement to isolated household work and child care. She envisioned a world where women would enjoy the economic independence of work outside the home for wages and the social benefits of life with their families in private kitchenless houses or apartments connected to central kitchens, dining rooms and daycare centers. She also argued that these would be good business! Her vision of "the feminist home," considered very radical by the enemies of feminists, was based on American concepts of individualism, privacy and free enterprise:

If there should be built and opened in any of our large cities today a commodious and well-served apart-

ment house for professional women with families, it
would be filled at once. The apartments would be without kitchens; but there would be a kitchen belonging to
the house from which meals could be served to the families in their rooms or in a common dining room as
preferred. It would be a home where the cleaning was
done by efficient workers, not hired separately by the
families, but engaged by the manager of the establishment; and a roof-garden, day nursery and kindergarten, under well-trained professional nurses and teachers, would ensure proper care of the children. . . .
This must be offered on a business basis to prove a
substantial business success; and so it will prove, for it
is a growing social need.

In suburban homes this purpose could be accomplished much better by a grouping of adjacent houses,
each distinct and having its own yard, but all kitchenless, and connected by covered ways with the eating
house . . . common libraries and parlors, baths and
gymnasia, workroom and play-rooms, to which both
sexes have the same access for the same needs.

Charlotte Gilman, in her writing and lecturing, took her
message beyond the small numbers of women then in the
suffrage movement, to middle-class married women and men
living in small towns all over the country as well as in big
cities. But she was ahead of her time. It would take another
century before women were earning enough to have clout
behind their demand for equality, and get their husbands to
share housework and put a value on it. In 1910, only 25 percent of all women were employed, and 10 percent of married
women. The majority of professional women did not marry.
Further, 40 percent of all employed women were still domestic servants (and most of those early feminist designs—as
well as women's own free time—rested on the cheap labor of
those women servants.)

But in towns like Carthage, Missouri, in 1907, community

dining clubs were organized and cooperative kitchens got underway, serving three meals a day for three dollars per adult per week (half price for children)—steak, stuffed baked potatoes, salad and dessert. The member families jointly furnished a comfortable reading room as well, in their club, and the two single schoolteachers in one group lived there, finally social equals in the community despite having no spouses or households of their own. Their cooperative birthday parties and teenage dances were very popular—and the women turned their own dining rooms into offices for their suffrage work. The cooks and waitresses at the clubs got higher pay and better hours than as servants in a private house. And even the husbands liked it.

By now the women's magazines—*Ladies' Home Journal, Good Housekeeping* and *Woman's Home Companion*—were enthusiastically covering these "cooperative housekeeping" experiments. There were at least thirty-three community dining clubs or cooked-food delivery services, some of which lasted as long as thirty-three years. In both small towns and large cities they attracted middle-class families where wives were now engaging in outside activities, and many single men and women as well. One in Warren, Ohio, was particularly successful. Each member—men as well as women—managed the menu and budget for a week at a time, supervising the paid cook, dishwasher and two waitresses. The club continued for over twenty years, with a waiting list for membership.

In 1919 the *Ladies' Home Journal* sponsored a contest, giving prizes for new schemes for living involving community kitchens, laundries and day-care centers, as well as kitchenless houses and apartment hotels. "The private kitchen must go the way of the spinning wheel, of which it is the contemporary," said the *Journal,* assuming that more and more women would choose to work outside the home. Unions began building housing cooperatives with common nurseries and dining rooms. Architectural experiments in Sunnyside, Queens, and Radburn, New Jersey, advanced

these ideas. There was also a boom in apartment-hotel construction in cities like New York.

After the winning of the vote, Ethel Puffer Howes—one
of the leaders of the suffrage movement, a philosopher with a
Ph.D. from Radcliffe, who married at thirty-six and had two
children in her forties—decided to spend the rest of her life
overcoming the attitudes and barriers that forced women to
choose between motherhood and serious careers. Working
with the editors of *Woman's Home Companion*, she ran a contest
for "The Most Practical Plan for Cooperative Home Service
in Our Town." A pledge with each entry had to be signed by
at least six women: "Resolved, that it is the duty of the
women of this country to free themselves of irrational drudgery for the sake of their higher duties as wives and mothers
and individuals. As a means to this end, we will organize
here and now some form of cooperative home service."

Howes also warned that commercial labor-saving devices
"won't collect and sort the laundry, or hang out the clothes
or iron complicated articles; the dishwasher won't collect,
scrape and stack the dishes; the vacuum cleaner won't mop
the floor or 'clean up and put away.' " Unlike other feminists
of her time, Howes did not see the vote as the end of the
struggle. "Housewives," she said, "must organize themselves
to earn economic equality and respect for their work."

She even developed a research institute at my own college,
Smith (the institute had been officially forgotten by the time
I went there in the forties), enlisting home economists, housing experts, child-development specialists and counselors to
do research here and abroad and start demonstration projects
in Northampton in cooperative food service, child care and
part-time careers. Each of these services was developed to be
run either by business for money or by cooperating neighbors—food in return for cash, for instance, and child care in
return for personal participation.

And then, suddenly, it all ended. At the end of 1920, the
women's magazines abruptly stopped warning women
against domestic appliances which did not meet their real

needs and stopped advocating cooperative housework services. Hayden reveals that advertising and marketing firms
spent one billion dollars in 1920 to promote the glories of the
isolated domestic housewife—and the science, or new religion, of mass consumption. Ads for vacuum cleaners and
toasters to make women "free"—using the very language of
feminism to undo it—were strengthened by new consumer-
credit systems to encourage the housewife to buy. Corporations paid Lillian Gilbreth, an early superwoman "industrial
engineer," who herself had eleven children, to explain how
housewives could "efficiently" do all their own work at
home. Much more openly agents of corporate masters than
Phyllis Schlafly and her sisters today, she and her colleague,
Christine Fredericks, in a book called *Selling Mrs. Consumer*
(1929), promoted "consumptionism" as "the greatest idea that
America has to give to the world, the idea that workmen and
the masses be looked upon not simply as workers or produc-
ers, but as consumers."

World War One had ended. The Russian Revolution and
the advent of communism had made America's robber barons
very uneasy indeed about the spread of labor organization
and worker unrest in the United States. Feminists, with
nearly two million women organized in those militant organizations that after a century of battle had just won the vote,
were seen as a serious threat with their talk of "housework
cooperatives."

As after World War Two, defense industries needed new
markets; they saw vacuum cleaners and washing machines as
their best bet. But women had to be at home to buy these
machines on a mass basis and to run them, one for every
home. With the Depression threatening serious revolt among
workers, President Hoover organized a national Conference
on Home Building and Home Ownership in 1931 to promote
the single-family suburban house on its own plot of land as
United States national housing policy, "to foster political stability and conservative habits among men." This plan, which
came to real fruition only after World War Two, with gov-

ernment-sponsored G.I. mortgages and tax deductions for
homeowners, required that women be kept out of the paid
work force and be kept busy "consuming" as full-time unpaid housewives and mothers.

And a massive Red-baiting campaign was launched
against all feminists. In the "Red scare" of 1919–20, a
spiderweb chart of feminist activists and organizations was
circulated by the Navy Department, indiscriminately smear-
ing the General Federation of Women's Clubs, the Women's
Christian Temperance Union, the YWCA, the American
Home Economics Association, the American Association of
University Women and the League of Women Voters, which
was the successor of the great suffrage organizations. But
their attacks were especially venomous against the material
feminists, who they claimed were advocating "free love,"
"unnatural motherhood," "futurist baby-raising" and "social
hot-beds" like apartment hotels, which would undermine the
family as "an institution of God" if women did not stay home
and stick to their own housework.

In the hindsight of history, Herbert Hoover should be
awarded a posthumous medal of honor by the manufacturers,
builders and profiteers of all those tract houses, cars and appliances. In the largest political sense, it was a brilliant way
to tame the worker: get him saddled with a house that would
require a full-time housewife to support—and to buy the
things that would keep him strapped to pay for—and even
give him credit and mortgage help to get him in so deep he'd
never get out.

Beginning in the 1920s, and accelerating in the 1950s and
1960s, advertising became one of the major American industries, promoting appliances, cars and other products in the
setting of the suburban "dream house." By the 1970s, suburbs contained more of the United States population than
the old city centers. There were fifty million small houses
and over one hundred million cars. Seven out of ten households lived in single-family homes. Over three-quarters of

AFL-CIO members owned their homes on long-term mortgages.

And the feminist challenge to architects, planners and designers and developers of technology—to free women for greater control of their own lives and work—was buried. Instead of built-in vacuum systems that automatically cleaned those apartment hotels, as earlier material feminists dreamed, individual vacuum cleaners that required a housewife to run them every day were promoted for great short-term profit, and ultimately to contribute to the energy crisis.

The evolution of housing from the simple to the complex was turned around by those crude suburban appliance-boxes, which by the 1970s required increasingly hazardous and costly energy sources, such as nuclear power plants. What I later called the feminine mystique, as it emerged full scale in the mass media after World War Two, preserved a century beyond its time the isolated household, designed around the ideal of woman as full-time homemaker. As a result, the housewife's hours of work increased rather than decreased after the 1920s despite labor-saving devices.

That institute at Smith was shut down. With the timidity that too often afflicts insecure "exceptional" women aspiring to academic and professional status, the Smith establishment was easily convinced that it was "unprofessional" for an academic institution to study such mundane matters as "domestic" technology. And so, at such institutions, the brightest young women were explicitly or implicitly presented with that either/or choice between motherhood and career—which left them very vulnerable indeed to the feminine mystique, in the 50s and 60s, and then the feminist superwoman reaction in the 1970s.

The most shameful episode in this buried, illuminating chapter of our history, to me, was the way the very same feminist leaders who had led that final victorious struggle that won the vote cleared their own skirts of the Red smear by acquiescing in the subversion of "the grand domestic revolution." The League of Women Voters invited Christine

Frederick, the Phyllis Schlafly of her time, to run a contest
on "the future of the American home." In choosing the winners, they replaced the vision of "cooperative home services"
with better "trained" servants and more "efficient" housewife consumption.

Even today—as a hidden consequence of that exploitation
and denigration of women's domestic work which underlies
its pseudoglorification in the feminine mystique—feminists
have been shying away from issues of restructuring home
and family life. Feminists today have been concentrating too
exclusively on equal rights with men. We have advanced the
argument beyond Charlotte Perkins Gilman and Ethel
Howes. We do not accept "women's sphere"; we negotiate
with men about sharing these household chores. But we do
not question the spatial design of those "modern" appliance-
filled houses, which earlier feminists would have described as
"enemy outposts in the domestic revolution."

The power of "women's sphere" in shaping political as
well as personal consciousness has clearly been underestimated by feminists today. In effect, we sometimes seemed to
have abandoned that sphere to the Phyllis Schlaflys. But in
another sense, modern feminists—and the necessities of advanced capitalism—have brought about a crucial redefinition
of women's sphere. Few of those vehement feminists a century ago ever suggested that men share the housework, or
that boys and girls be trained equally in domestic skills.

As Dolores Hayden points out, the exclusion of men from
responsibility for domestic work, either private or socialized,
ensured that most cooperative housekeeping experiments
failed after a few months or years. Even exploiting the
women of other races or lower classes to do the communal
housekeeping at low wages wasn't so cheap—or deferential
to a man's personal whims and schedule—as an unpaid wife.
Hayden writes:

Male-dominated private life and corporate-dominated public life are mutually reinforcing. Not only did corporations support male home ownership, believing that "Good Homes Make Contented Workers," but they also needed "Mrs. Consumer" to purchase and maintain mass-produced homes and consumer goods and to rear a new generation of male and female children for this same way of life. . . .

Unpaid domestic work performed by housewives in the private home was promoted as a *social and religious duty*. The extensive Red-baiting of feminists in the 1920's underlines the importance of the housewife, as an unpaid worker, to the structure of the capitalist economy. Women are not only a reserve army of labor during economic boom periods and wartime. They are constantly performing domestic labor, and without that unpaid labor, the entire paid work force would stop functioning.

But the irony is, feminists then, as now, did not get their ideas from the Communists. The Communists themselves did not include women's work in their concept of organizing the industrial proletariat—the male workers of the world—to take over "the means of production." (If anything, orthodox Communists today are more blindly contemptuous of "women's sphere" and "women's work"—and more threatened by feminism—than advanced capitalists.)

Communism, the Stalinist-Leninist brand, ignored the work that was done by half the human race—ignored women's unpaid domestic labor and saw only man's industrial labor, taking over this split and this structure from the capitalism of a century before. Communism was to liberate women from the "bourgeois" family and home by pushing them into the male industrial work force—which left them to do all that other work at home, on top of their paid jobs in industry, with fewer conveniences than their capitalist sisters. Since the Communists did not really include "women's sphere" or the family in the concept of revolution, they did not suggest that men share the housework, nor did they make any serious attempt to create those new socialized housekeeping structures that early feminists dreamed of. (The only exception was child-care centers, which were absolutely essential if all women were to be used in the work force.) The women themselves were thus too harassed by their double burden to move to leadership in the commissariats and to demand, design and give priority to such services.

Without feminism—without a conscious campaign against sex discrimination culminating in a sex-role revolution, redefining the roles of men and women, that would lead to restructuring of work and home—communism became in many ways more dehumanizing and depersonalizing and destructive of family life than the capitalism it mirrored. Because capitalism, at least, took women seriously as consumers, it had to concern itself in some ways with their needs, if only to manipulate them for profit.

We must carry a Marxist premise further than Marx did to understand the economic structure that forces us now into the second stage. As capitalism itself created the conditions that could overthrow it, by creating the vast armies of exploited industrial workers who a century ago saw communism as their liberation—so capitalism, in its advanced stage, has created the new, irrepressible armies of feminism.

Those millions of women, after World War Two, with more and more education—and that all-pervasive mass-media indoctrination exhorting their *power to choose* in buying things —were not only isolated in their suburban homes and frustrated in their need to use their abilities actively in society. The very needs for the things those millions of dream homes now required—whether or not they actually served the best interests of the family—helped create the inflationary and energy-wasting cycle that accelerated year by year until it not only chained the worker to his mortgaged house, and the conservative politics that supported it, but forced the women out to work as well.

But, on the way from there to here, the women's movement—and women's new independence—changed more than consciousness. The family—which both communism and fascism tried to abolish, subvert, or control, and which capitalism itself has always subordinated to profit—has been newly strengthened by women's moves to equality. Women's moves to their own authenticity—and their concrete sharing of the earning burden—has somehow helped liberate men to greater independence and new human values and priorities.

It is a myth useful to the Right—and folly for feminists to acquiesce in—that equal rights for women threaten the values of the family. In the second stage, with all those separate little houses and their appliances now requiring two incomes to purchase and support—and no housing of any kind available to meet the human needs and economic capabilities of most young and old, single or nonparenting families today, in cities or suburbs—the grand domestic revolution may be joined, by practical necessity, by men and women who never thought of themselves as feminists and never went near a commune.

Of course, the government could, in the name of conservativism, take Herbert Hoover's idea one step further, and offer new kinds of mortgage guarantees and tax incentives—changing zoning codes accordingly—to get builders to build or renovate new multifamily housing and apartments, in cities or suburbs or empty land beyond and between, to meet the new needs of two-paycheck parents, single parents, single, divorced and widowed women and men, and older couples and singles whose very needs for family and housing are no longer structured by childbearing.

What "special interest group" or combination thereof will exert the political pressure for such housing aids? If the women's movement breaks out of its own ideological straitjacket, it could join here with labor unions and with enterprising builders—and with entrepreneurial investors whose concern to meet the housing needs of this huge new market

—the 83 percent of Americans who don't fit that old dream-house family—would be, of course, their own profit.

Union pension funds would be better invested in such housing than in shoring up the failing companies in which their members work or in buying municipal bonds that banks won't touch. So far, the conservative approach to rental housing in the city is simply to abolish rent control, to make apartment building more profitable for owners, or to help them in the profitable escape of selling the decaying apartments at huge profits to tenants who now have to provide their own fuel and other expensive services.

But as those already too expensive apartments are sold to tenants as condominiums or cooperatives, the stability and stake are there for *people*— not only women—to begin, in city apartment buildings or suburban neighborhoods, to organize some of the new services they need. Not the kind of experiments that failed seventy or a hundred years ago because "an unpaid wife" was cheaper. Today, such services will be organized to meet the needs of men as well as women, not only the officially poor, but also the harassed middle-class majority that occupies decaying city buildings and suburban neighborhoods.

Of course, another route is simply for women and men to put in more and more hours of work to pay for increasingly expensive, and scarce, housing of the old, conventional kind —feminine-mystique suburban homes, or high-cost dehumanized, anonymous dormitory high-rise city apartments. Assuming, of course, that they can find the jobs and work overtime or can moonlight to pay those mortgage rates. Or young couples will simply stop having children; and older people, whose pensions won't finance those profitable "leisure worlds," will be kept out of sight somehow if their kids can't take them in.

But the very state of the economy, and the widespread revulsion against "big government," inflation and other threats to "the family"—and our dwindling core of human autonomy—leave crevices of possibility for second-stage solutions.

Again, the house brings us to reality. What kind of houses —or new homelike, family-type structures—will meet the needs of those women and those men in their twenties and thirties, single or living together or starting their families, in this new, fluid equality, sharing wage work and parenting in various combinations, working out their own balance of power and responsibility in the family as they go along, not even aware how the space and structures available (or not available) to them impose perhaps unnecessary strains, or foreclose certain life-nourishing possibilities? What kind of structure can take the place of that dream house for all of us now living alone, old or young, who need new spaces for intimacy and support, caring and privacy, and our human identity?

The hold of the old forms is strong.

"Home" and "family," which were our childhood source of warmth and security, were cast in the model of that suburban dream house. And if our childhood homes fell short of that dream—for whatever reason of economic, social or emotional deprivation—we truly embraced the chance to create such ideal "homes" for our children, in those houses we could buy on the FHA mortgages, under the G.I. Bill. They met, and created, real needs, those homes—even if it was at an enormously wasteful cost of energy; even if, for a time, they seemed to trap the housewife-mother in one way and the breadwinning father in another. That same house is too big and drafty and expensive, with the children gone, and almost impossible to run if its owner/owners must work too, or if the owner is a single parent—or if the owners are just starting to have children, and both have to keep on working to pay the mortgage. Too lonely, too hard and unpleasant to do the chores and cook and eat the holiday dinner, all by herself, or himself, if they are divorced, or not married, or widowed, or alone. What other kind of house could there be for us?

•   •   •

I touch base here with personal truth again. In the years since my divorce, I seem to have created a new extended family that consists not only of my own children but friends on whom I can always depend for a bed and caring ear, if I am in their city, or reciprocate if they are in mine. Although I live alone in my little house on Long Island—or my office-apartment in a midtown Manhattan tower—I like to think my family stretches from California to Cambridge. There is almost always someone occupying my daughter's deserted bedroom—friends, women and men, with whom I've worked, fought, loved and suffered over the years. I suppose I still have a secret dream of remarrying, but the life I live has its own strengths and nourishments—within limits.

The limits are partly imposed by those old forms. As our children grow up and leave home, as more of us struggle with the problems of husbands' strokes and heart attacks, or the unsettled loneliness of divorce, or our own illnesses, we admit our needs and fears and vulnerabilities to each other, and we give each other love and support—almost like a family. But it is not the same.

Shortly after my divorce, being equally afraid of remarrying and of loneliness, and even of coping with holidays and vacations for my children all by myself, I started a sort of respectable, non-hippie commune. A half dozen friends—women and men, divorced or unmarried, some with children, some not—rented a big house on the tip of Long Island, which we used weekends and during the summer, and at Thanksgiving and Christmas.

In one form or another, it lasted almost ten years. Our "extended family of choice" required almost as much work as an individual household; it was not so much physical labor (though there were continual battles as we worked out by trial and error the sharing of the chores and the expenses), but the emotional problems and nuances which were difficult to deal with. Nothing could be taken for granted.

The physical space, in houses large enough, did not perhaps meet our needs for both privacy and shared work and company. The living room was too big and formal; we almost always congregated in the kitchen. The bedrooms weren't big or pleasant enough to use as our own apartments when we didn't want to be together. But what was the point in spending money to fix up a place we only rented, and which was a temporary residence anyway? We couldn't get the lease renewed for one house we occupied because the zoning didn't permit more than three unrelated people living together. "What this place needs is a wife," another landlady exploded, agitated over a torn slipcover no one had taken the responsibility to replace. When one house we all loved came up for sale at a price which jointly we could have afforded, there was no legal way to buy and get mortgage financing for a house for five or six unrelated partners, and to write in legal provisions for any one's getting out of his or her share, if need be. And with this sort of extended family, there was necessarily much more changing of size and shape—as people got married, or couples broke up, or job locations were changed—than in a conventional family.

By now, we have all moved into separate houses—within a ten-mile radius—in the country. But we still share Thanksgiving or Christmas dinners, often travel together, celebrate birthdays and births, succor each other in loss or sorrow or sickness. The "commune" was more trouble than living alone, I tell myself. But maybe it might have been worth the trouble if we hadn't had to move each year into increasingly expensive and unsatisfactory structures that we never had the right or real possibility to make "home."

Several years ago, at the International Design Conference in Aspen, Colorado, industrial designer Niels Diffrient invited me to discuss the implications for architecture and design of the women's movement and the sex-role revolution. After presenting the theoretical implications, with the help of California architect Frank Gehry, I invited those interested to spend the afternoon in a "game," in which they would begin to design new kinds of structures to meet new family problems.

When the people assembled that afternoon in Aspen, I told them this news: A secret meeting had been called, on some unnamed island in the Pacific, of the Pope, the President of the United States and the prime ministers of Britain, the Soviet Union, France, Germany and other nations. Their concern was the crisis of the falling birth rate; in the advanced industrial nations of the world—Communist and capitalist—almost no women were having children. Not enough children were being born to do the work of society or take care of its aging citizens, much less fight possible wars. At the present rate, the crisis would reach staggering proportions before the year 2000. I had been invited to the conference, I told them, because some of the political leaders present blamed the women's movement for this population crisis. But I had come back from that island to meet here with the architects, urban planners, and designers because the real problem was that the forms of housing available today made it virtually impossible for women to have children if they also had to work—as most women now did. They couldn't meet the job standards originally set for men who had wives to take care of home and children, and at the same time take care of children in houses designed for the full-time unpaid service of a lifelong housewife.

The architects, planners and designers were then to divide into groups of twelve to fifteen, and design a new plan for living for one hundred families and/or individuals on ten acres in an area within commuting distance to midtown— and they were to design it taking into account changing sex roles and women's demand for equality in work and home. One group was to deal with the needs of single parents; one with two-paycheck families with children; one with a mixture, including many singles; one with people beyond the childbearing years; one with ethnic and blue-collar families; and one for artists and for architects to express their own dreams for themselves.

Every group knew the answer had to be some sharing of services, some communal living or eating or child-care space. But in every group, a sizable number absolutely insisted on a separate house for each family. A California architect tried desperately to get the artists to treat the whole ten acres as a single living space, most of it roofed over in a great solar dome with studio-bedrooms for each adult, dormitories and nurseries for the children, common dining room, kitchen, library, music room, etc. But the individualists were so vehement that the architects and planners ended up designing fifty separate houses as well as communal service, eating, dining, child-care and recreational space. The architects for the single-parent families were also so wedded to the idea of separate detached houses that their only innovation was a kind of attached second houselet—like a large doghouse—for the grandmother to live in and baby-sit!

A few years later, at the National Assembly on the Future of the Family held in 1979 by the NOW Legal Defense and Education Fund, public awareness of the new shape and size of the majority of households (and the emergence of serious women architects) made it possible to advance, at least, to a recognition of that large and growing new market for new kinds of housing—and the realization that existing suburban housing and city apartment design didn't meet it. Architects, designers, builders, experts on zoning codes and financing began to talk about the need for new combinations of private living space and new kinds of shared space for eating, cooking, socializing, doing chores, taking care of children—for people now living alone, old and young, for divorced and single parents, even for conventional families with the double burden of parenting and work.

It could be profitable to design and build for this market which now comprises all but 17 percent of American households. But it would take new concepts for zoning and for mortgage financing—extending aids that were once available to young families to buy that single suburban house to families of different shapes and sizes and ages and needs, in forms that would permit more homelike, and less time-and-energy-wasting, sharing of space and services than either the city apartment or the isolated suburban house. Such structures would, for instance, be more nourishing to needs for intimacy and communality than the singles bar, and yet would have to respect that strong American need for individual space and privacy and control—a home, a room of one's own.

There has to be a second-stage kind of fluid tension or balance between these poles of individual privacy and needs for new forms of family and for sharing of space and work. It becomes clearer now why that appeal to the independence and the autonomy of the family resonates among Americans, who have indeed in recent years lost too much of the control of their own lives to the corporation, the bureaucrats of business and of government. It is also clear why that little house —that last sphere of privacy where one still feels in physical control of one's life and physical roots in community—has been so important to Americans; it is a hedge against that frightening powerlessness, the anomie that finally becomes apathy, that is becoming our characteristic political mode. The real appeal of the women's movement, and the nostalgia for the sixties of that aging youth generation, was precisely the new roots in community that active participation in reshaping our destiny gave us, in contrast to the increasing bureaucratization, professionalization, depersonalization, media manipulation and trivialization of national party politics. Hence also the current nostalgia for a return to local or community control, or even the old kind of flesh-and-blood political machine.

We may find new strength for the second stage, new solutions for the real national problems—inflation, pollution, housing, child care, health care, security—by truly moving to a new guerrilla type of community resistance. Not being able to rely on big government programs, we may find, in the process of organizing at the grass-roots level for innovation of needed services, a true focus on the new needs and strengths of all our families—and forge a new political base.

In a crumbling, unpredictable economy, underlying the appeal of some conservative slogans and ignored or misunderstood by hidebound liberals and rigid feminists, the new urge of both women and men for meaning in their work and life, for intimacy, yes, for love, and roots in home and family —even though it may not resemble the ideal family that maybe never was—is a powerful force for change. I'm not even altogether sure that the women's movement as such will be the main agent of this next stage of human liberation. But if we don't want to retreat—with women and men withdrawing into tired, lonely disillusionment and backlash, and finally apathy to rigid, fascist-like order, decked in false colors of family, flag and God—we must somehow create a new, flexible, second-stage movement of women and men, with new kinds of union and corporate, volunteer and church, public- and private-sector leaders who are in tune with the evolving needs of human life and truly put those needs of life first.

10 Human Sex and Human Politics

 I would like now to hint at certain far-reaching implications of the sex-role revolution which will become clearer in the second stage. For beyond the current confluence of economic turmoil and political reaction, beyond the seemingly irreconcilable polarities and defensive extremes of first-stage feminism and antifeminism, and beyond sexual politics—the basic evolutionary trends manifest in advanced industrial technology, the longer life span and the increasing control of our biology insure that the sex-role revolution which started as the women's movement will continue.

Should we then fear a continued increase in rape, sadomasochistic pornography and violence against women, escalating homosexuality, male impotence, divorce and ultimate extermination of that classical family of Western nostalgia, all of which are now supposed byproducts of the women's movement toward equality? And what about those other fears, not expressed so widely as they used to be? Now that so many women are performing previously masculine breadwinning roles, from engineer to executive, artist and athlete, and now that so many men are sharing that previously feminine nurture of the children—will women lose their femininity and will men lose their masculine potency in dreary, sterile unisex? (The wish-fear behind these specters is that men will reassert their sexual superiority and omnipotence and put women back in their place again, to "save" the family and the race.)

But if those excesses of sexual violence and pornography can be seen as the pathological end result of that vicious cycle of sex-role polarization, their very excess hints at enormous creative energies to be released in the service of life, once that vicious cycle is reversed. The extreme reactions and reversals —Superwoman and Total Woman, Househusband and Urban Cowboy, the strident messiahs of the New Macho preaching sexual punishment from pulpit and podium, or playacting it in leather, whips and chains with sexual partners, male or female, and the obsession with pornography in general—hide the quiet, healthy shoots of the second stage: the truly new possibilities of lives and families based on sharing work and nurture.

There will be, I think, a profound liberation of human sex and human politics in the second stage of the sex-role revolution, but it will bear little resemblance to the sexual politics of the first stage, or to the sexual pathologies and reactions that are still playing out that old vicious cycle of sex-role polarization.

It was a man, the great anthropologist Gregory Bateson, who first drew my attention to anthropological data from studies of many cultures which indicate that the more isolated and polarized the roles of men and women—as, for instance, in those societies where women are shrouded in veil or chador, walled in the harem or sexual ghetto and not even allowed to move in the city at all, their only point of contact with men the sexual act itself—the more sex becomes an obsession and is defined as "dirty." (The excesses of Victorian or puritanical sexual repression and the pornographic excesses of sexual reaction today express that same sexual obsession or revulsion.) And in such societies, where basic human sexual needs for intimacy are alienated, violence breeds.

The psychodynamics of this process were sketched in

early warnings almost predicting the excesses of fascist Germany and Stalinist Russia—and predictive of certain phenomena of sex-and-violence we see in the United States today—in the early work of Wilhelm Reich (see *The Mass Psychology of Fascism* and *Listen, Little Man*). In war, the seclusion of men from intimate daily relations with women as a virtual condition of the necessary violence has been taken for granted through history, as well as the prevalence, and condoning, of rape among warriors.

In an obscure study called *The Glory of Hera*, the psychologist Philip Slater shows how the isolated, denigrated position of women in ancient Greece—where only *free men* took part in the activities of the polis that left a mark on society, and women and slaves did the subhuman animal labor (necessary for life but leaving no human mark)—led men to look for intimacy to other men, their comrades in the polis. Sharing their real tenderness with male lovers, they finally took wives, contracted for as children, merely to carry on the family. Those lonely, isolated, frustrated, denigrated wives then focused all their love-hate, and their own vicarious needs to leave that human mark, on their sons. The vainglorious, empty machismo of the narcissistic hero nourished by such a mother—and an absent father—led him to be driven to seek "vain-glory" in exploits like the Trojan Wars. A similar drama was played out by the suburban mother and absentee corporate father of the fifties, as dramatized by a plethora of case histories in mental-health centers and clinics from Westchester and Grosse Point to Pacific Palisades.

Many psychologists have traced the psychodynamics of the inauthentic sex role-playing of women and men in modern industrial society, where the dependence and mutual hostility and torment of the women and men "playing feminine/playing masculine" masked itself as "love" in the family and led to pathology in its children (see R. D. Laing, *The Politics of the Family*, and Jules Henry, *Pathways to Madness*). The way capitalism has exploited the alienated human needs for love and dignity, and has, above all, exploited the resulting sexual obsession for profit or power, has diverted people from paths toward true autonomy. This exploitation has been pointed out by psychologists, economists and political scientists whose point of view was hardly feminist and who may or may not have seen the conflicting, unequal sex roles of men and women as central to the vicious cycle. (See Herbert Marcuse, *One Dimensional Man* and *Eros and Civilization;* Philip Slater, *Pursuit of Loneliness;* Norman O. Brown, *Life Against Death;* John Dollard, *Frustration and Aggression;* Richard Hoggart, *Uses of Literacy.*) The antisexual stance of Stalinist and Maoist communism may perform the same function. It is significant that the ideology of feminism and sex-role revolution seems as threatening to Communist commissars of the reactionary Left today as it does to reactionaries of the capitalist Right.

Thus, sex-role polarization and inequality lead to and are reinforced by sexual obsession-revulsion, which leads to and is reinforced by sexual dehumanization and alienation from the core of generative, authentic human love and life—and this feeds violence. And the political and economic exploitation of sexual frustration, obsession and alienation further feeds and is fed by sexual dehumanization and violence. In some profound symmetry, which Freud and others have depicted as "life force" and "death force," there is a basic energy, which, if thwarted in its service of life and growth, ultimately serves death.

I am not comfortable with metaphysical speculation, but I do know that in the women's movement we have basically served the interests of life. We have opened up life for women, and thus for men and children. But we have also threatened that sex-role polarization which has been seen as basic to life, to sexuality, and indeed to identity, by some men, and even more by women. I understand now why Margaret Mead, whose early work did so much to break through sex-role stereotypes, stopped in panic to question whether the very process of sex-role polarization might not be basic to life itself. I have been thinking a lot lately about that mysterious, ever-changing, circular process of masculine-feminine definition—the bonding, need, love-and-hate of men and women circling and changing in parallel symmetry, like the endless, infinitely various permutations of the double helix of the DNA and RNA which carry the code of our identity, our selves, in every cell.

Throughout this book I have suggested that sexual politics has been a red herring, an acting-out of feminist reaction, a diversionary tool with which the forces of political, economic and religious reaction—whose power is indeed threatened by women's movement to equality—seek not only to beat women back but also to distract people generally from their economic-political exploitation and divert them from their own autonomy.

But powerful life forces are also served—and threatened—by the real sexual implications of the women's movement, and even by the sexual politics, in ways that we must understand more clearly as we enter the second stage. In the first stage, the women's movement was dealing with the symptoms when it focused on rape and pornography, and those marches to "take back the night."

In the second stage, when women and men share the work of their *days*, on the job and at home, with new equality and autonomy, authentic feelings, on the part of both women and men, will replace the role-playing and the torturous stifling masks imposed by that excessive dependence, need for dominance, and the resulting buried hostilities in the family. There will be less alienation, less sexual obsession-revulsion, a diminishing reservoir of frustrated life energies to be exploited by either capitalist, corporate or Communist bureaucrats, for their own profit or power, or to be channeled into sadistic pornographic fantasy or actual violence.

Of course, psychologists, psychoanalysts and all who deal with emotional pathology have been telling us for years that it is denial of tender loving mother's touch and sensitive care that creates those monsters who cannot give love, get love, or even relate intimately to another human being, and thus rape, or murder—or batter their own children.

If a mother cannot love herself enough truly to love another, and her son suffers too much the pain of needing and being denied that loving touch—he has to turn his own sex, and its object, into a machine. He has to render the object faceless, even destroy it, rather than risk that pain. And a daughter, struggling to free herself from the terrible dependence that made it impossible for her mother to love herself, much less another, might for a while put on that same armor against her own vulnerability and his, divorcing sex from the power of these soft feelings, turning sex, and her lover, into object, machine.

Psychiatrists and anthropologists like Laing and Henry are hardly feminists. They do not ask why, in such families, the mothers have so little sense of self, why they are forced to act out that inauthentic love. They do not ask how or if, in fact, complete dependence (economic, social, psychological) can ever lead to authentic love of husband or child, or let a woman pass on a core of confident female identity to her daughter, or confident trust in other women to her son? Certain accepted psychological facts—truisms like the "normalcy" of masochism (or passive frigidity) in woman's sexuality—were not questioned for all the decades they were diagnosed, analyzed or treated by men, and by the women they trained who could not transcend that self-denigration of women built into their culture enough to say "no" to the male authorities and define their own sexuality. No one asked why depression was so common after childbirth in all those women who were supposed to find their total fulfillment and self-definition as mothers. But such depression is hatred, rage, aggressive energy turned against the self: how could a mother smothering that rage, writhing in that self-denigration, truly, joyously, spontaneously touch with love that child, or man, no matter how correctly, sweetly, dutifully she "played" her role, and how effusively she protested her "love" ? How could she feel that genuine love when she had no control over her life, especially if that "act of love" could lead to pregnancy with its risk of death, or another child to take care of no matter her own wishes, circumstances or capabilities. It would be surprising if such a woman's unwelcome daughter ("another one like me") or resented (envied) son did not somehow get the feeling, and pass it on, that sex was dirty, sinful, and want indeed to "punish" women from whom they might not ever expect to get that truly loving touch.

In the decades since Kinsey and his colleagues have been measuring "human sexual response," the increase in female experience of sexual orgasm has precisely paralleled the increase in woman's power to control her reproductive process and her advance to equal rights and opportunities in society. The most significant sexual change since the sixties may be the unsensational fact that in the decades since the women's movement—despite the reaction, the hostility, the sexual politics and the dehumanizing acting out of sexual obsession-revulsion in pornography and rape—the majority of American husbands and wives have been found to be having sex more often, with their *own* wives and husbands, than ever before. Between 1965 and 1975 there was a 23 percent increase in the average frequency of sexual intercourse within marriage among a national cross-section of 3,000 American wives studied by Charles Westoff and James Trussell of the Office of Population Research at Princeton.

Behind sexual politics it is precisely the consciousness of "choice" and of "equal rights" and opportunities that is resisted by women, or men, whose identity rests on passivity toward authority, inequality and hierarchy, no matter the resentments and human potential suppressed. It is not a coincidence that these same forces of the fundamentalist far Right are organizing with new militancy against "humanism," and against the scientific study of evolution in the schools, and are encouraging or inciting use of handguns and firebombs against planned parenthood clinics. (The shooting of the maker of those songs that led the greening generation

to "make love, not war," and even of a conservative President, are on a certain level expressions of the pathology.)

It's as if the forces of extreme reaction are making a final
stand, in the terms they themselves proclaim, against "humanism," "evolution," "equality," and "choice"—against the
human evolution that seems to us, and to philosophers and
theologians of all the great religions, the expression of creation, the divine spirit. They take their implacable stand
against the liberation of human sexuality in love and intimacy and chosen childbearing, and condone violence, beating and rape of women, children, and all growing things.
Many observers have puzzled over the apocalyptic terms in
which the so-called "pro-life" leaders crusade against abortion. Many have noted that while men often seem to be
manipulating them, it is women who show the most intense
feelings over these issues. And indeed, it is women who are
undergoing an apocalyptic change in the very basis of their
identity at this time: a leap in human evolution—which is
what "equality" and "choice" mean for women. The personhood of women, which is what the first stage was all
about, is a liberation of women from that old passive biological destiny and unequal subservience, God-given or manmade, to new humanness. And women are not the first people in history to show a desire to escape from freedom—as
well as that strong drive toward it.

All women, for whom that marriage-and-childbearing
"destiny" used to be the main source of identity, prestige,
financial support, have suffered an apocalyptic change in
their being. They can't escape that change. It is, in the most
profound sense, a change in the direction of *human* liberation.
As contraceptives liberate sexuality from consequences in
unwanted "punishment" childbirth, a longer life span and
fewer children mean that the function of sex and marriage
shifts from biological reproduction to human companionship
and sexual intimacy—*human sex*.

With most married women now working, fewer men can
rest their identity and authority on being the sole provider

for the family, and more women have a source of identity in work outside the family. With so many more women educated, the lack of good jobs or professional openings still limits the extent to which women can rely on work as a primary or alternate source of identity or income. As even the most traditional, submissive women can no longer completely deny, the steep rise in the divorce rate leaves women who are still completely dependent on a man's support particularly vulnerable, economically and psychologically. This same vulnerability is also denied by feminists, who sometimes profess more equality than they really have, especially those whose own, not necessarily high-paying "careers" are augmented by a successful husband's support. And their pretensions can truly provoke apocalyptic rage or contemptuous scorn from antifeminists who enjoy, and still stoutly hold on to, that "unequal" male support, sometimes pretending a subservience that is also not quite what it seems.

The transcending of sex-role polarization is indeed an apocalyptic change—but it does not threaten, it *serves* the interests of life. It is somehow the resistance to this evolution of human life that leads to apocalypse: as if the demands of growing life, violated, lead to death, or its projection in apocalyptic fear.

The trouble is, a secure sense of personhood in women seems to be essential to enable a woman to love, to actively and/or passively enjoy her sexuality, and to freely, joyously, responsibly, responsively give that crucial tender loving "touch" to another—man or child, and especially to another like herself. That sure sense of personhood cannot be passed on to daughters by mothers who did not themselves enjoy it. Whatever ideology women embrace, that sense of self can no longer rest solely on that old role of lifelong-supported wife and mother without denying the realities of survival and the possibilities for growth of our eighty-year life span. Nor can it rest solely on work, eschewing those bonds of intimacy and family support which the very precariousness of work today, and the anomie of life, render as essential for the purist ideological feminist as for the most willingly submissive "total woman."

At the end of a debate with Phyllis Schlafly in North Carolina this spring, I was handed this note from someone in the audience:

> When one looks at the pictures of the women who are active in "pro-life" and anti-ERA demonstrations, one is struck by the violent expressions on their faces. These are reflections of hate, not love, for women and babies.
>
> This violent energy has no rational basis. When there is no rational basis there has to be a psychic inversion. Could this be a transferral of unacknowledged, unrecognized resentment of women's put-down by our society—a transferral of self-hatred for being women, and hatred of men for their part in this put-down? A transferral to other women who endanger their ego system by refusing to accept the status quo and demand that these wrongs be acknowledged and recognized and corrected?

That same excess can occasionally be seen at the other extreme—the radical lesbian "separatists." They have given much energy to the women's movement, but their own repudiation of women's relation to men, children and family has been, in part, responsible for the movement's political blind spot about the family and has played into those fears the Right manipulates. Such "separatists" sometimes show the same rage at other women, who evidently threaten their ego system by defining feminism to include men and family, as do the anti-ERA extremists. The hostility that lesbian extremists evince for women who embrace a larger definition of female personhood often seems to exceed their hostility toward men. Their definition of feminism in terms of sexual preference for women is, of course, a reactive reversal of the feminine mystique, which defined women only in terms of their sexual relation to men. Is it possible that such loudly professed love of women by those who repudiate so much of women's identity and experience could mask the same kind of self-hatred, and hatred of other women, that the North Carolina observer identified in Schlafly's extremist supporters?

Sharing my ideas about the second stage with the feminist network in Kansas City in April 1981, I was asked by a troubled sister: "Where does this talk about family leave people like me politically? I'm not interested in child care. I'm a lesbian. If you're going to concern yourself with the family and men, then either you're saying you're not a feminist any more, you're now a humanist or something, or you're telling people like me we can't call ourselves feminists. The family will just split us."

"Why?" I asked. "Don't you have family needs? The family is who you come home to."

"Then why don't you talk more about gay families?" she asked.

"Because it twists the focus to sexual politics," I said. "It gets mixed up with the reaction against the female role, and threatens people who feel sex should be private and are mixed up about it themselves. There has been too much focus on sex in the movement and it's given us a political blind spot on questions like child care, which has played right into the hands of political reaction."

"But what about lesbians?" she persisted.

"That's sex," I said, "not politics. Or it should be. That's not all you are, surely. That's really not the main question, and you shouldn't want it to be, when it comes to politics, or the women's movement, or come to think of it, to families."

"You mean, it's just sex," she said.

"Sure," I said. "Enjoy!" And we laughed, and she gave me a hug.

                    *   *   *

The question of the diversity of families, which has been distorted by sexual politics, goes far beyond gay families today. In fact, in the second stage it will become increasingly clear that people must pool their emotional and economic resources and feminists give up some of their newly won independence for interdependence in patterns that go beyond marriage, both before and after child-rearing years, and on bases that are not always even sexual.

While the Moral Majority now seeks to blacklist a television program called *Three's Company*, in which two women and a man are forced by the high cost of housing to share a home, the business world is pragmatically coming to terms with these new family patterns. The only bright spot in the housing market this past year was the great increase in sales of homes and mortgages to single women living alone. But since, in fact, it almost always takes two incomes to buy a house or condominium apartment these days, banks and mortgage-loan officers and condominium boards will increasingly be faced with requests for mortgages or leases for two, three, or more persons unrelated by blood or marriage.

The speed with which the corporate sector is accepting "family diversity" is shown in a recent full-page ad by the conservative *Reader's Digest* announcing a new magazine called *Families:*

Today's family is:

- Mom, dad, and 2.4 kids

- A couple with two kids: his, hers, theirs

- A 26-year-old secretary and her adopted son

- A couple sharing everything but a marriage license

- A divorced woman and her stepdaughter

- A retired couple raising their grandson

- All of the above.

The extremes of sexual politics may have helped some women free themselves of that excessive dependence on male definition and the smoldering, impotent rage. But to spend one's energies railing against or reversing or aping male definition is still to be defined by it. It does not transcend the polarization, it does not lead to full personhood, wholeness, authenticity as women. In a fascinating study of women at the huge government-sponsored National Women's Conference in Houston in 1977, the eminent sociologist Alice Rossi found that feminists who were involved mainly in sexual politics did not show a general increase in political competence or self-confidence sufficient to risk mainstream politics. This was not the case for feminists involved in the battle for equal opportunity and changing women's condition in society. But actual experience in the professional work world or the mainstream political world—as one's own person, not as wife —brought the greatest increase in that competence, which is, of course, both political and personal.

A young Wall Street lawyer, deciding finally to have a baby, described her personal evolution in this way:

> I never had any confidence in myself before I practiced law. I think the women's movement not only gave me those opportunities—it helped me respect women a lot more—and respect myself as a woman. I like the self-confidence, the ability as a problem-solver and the courage to speak out that I got in law. I've lost a vague, tentative, ethereal quality I used to have. But my style in work is not like a man's. I'm very determined but I'm not aggressive. I'm not put off by a blowhard. I let them rant and rave, then quietly handle their points, one by one. It works every time. The men in my firm go for the jugular, take every punch, always on the aggressive. I was put off by that, I wasn't sure I could be that aggressive. It seemed to be the only way, at first, but it's just not me.
>
> When I began to handle my own cases, I began to

find my own style. I think there is a difference between men and women. I don't try to rant and rave in court like the men.

A few years ago, when I was pregnant, I felt having a baby would interfere with my career. I had an abortion. Today, I go into court and see a lot of women in their thirties with pregnant bellies way out to here. And I think they look just beautiful, handling their cases with confidence and professional skill and confident enough to have the baby too.

Thus, as we transcend sex-role polarization in the second stage, that new healthy core of self in women, replacing the conflicts and denigration of the either/or split, will stand firm on the two roots of human identity: love and work—in ways that may or may not be different from the meshing of new values in life, family and work for men. One thing seems certain already: the more authentically a woman, or a man, is free to know, and become, herself or himself, the more surely, uniquely, she is *herself*, he is *himself*. The second stage is not unisex. It is human sex, for women as for men—active or passive, responsive, responsible, playful or profound, no longer an acting out of eroticized rage, or manipulation of covert power, joyless dues for economic support, or brutal revenge of love denied.

Fully self-realizing people, as psychologist Abraham Maslow found, can reach "peak experiences" akin to religious ecstasy in sex, but they are no longer driven by it. They need it less and enjoy it more, or differently. In the hierarchy of needs, when we are no longer driven by needs for bare economic subsistence, by needs for food and physical shelter, by needs for security, sexual intimacy, for status and success, we are freed for the expression of higher needs.

When we are no longer driven by powerlessness to excessive need for power, we can express our human potency in many ways—human sex, human politics, the creative further reaches of the human spirit. The most important effect of

transcending those old sex roles may be an evolution of morality and religious thought, as the concrete, flexible dailiness
that used to be reserved for female private family life is wedded to the noble grandeur of spiritual vision and higher
moral principles as formerly preached from pulpits one hour
a week by male priests, ministers and rabbis. In the second
stage, that same wedding of the abstract and the concrete will
transform the discipline and practice of every profession. It
is happening in the churches, not just because women are
becoming ministers and rabbis and priests, but because the
male theologians are now living the problems in the family.
The younger man and woman of God are becoming conscious of their own Beta mode in response to the rigid fundamentalism of the far Right, as it denies the freedom and generative power of the religious spirit itself.

In private life, the new woman, strengthened by her participation in the rewarded work of society, strong enough as
a woman now to take back control of her days, will be able to
share flexibly with her man, or intimate others, that life-sus-
taining, self-nourishing, loving nurture of the young and old.
She will no longer require complete control of the family to
assuage her complete powerlessness in society. She will be
strong enough in her own identity so that she is not so easily
exploited by the insatiable drive for things, or so docile to the
demands of corporation or church. He will have the strength
of a human identity that is not defined by bread alone, nourished by authentic feelings in and beyond the family. And
together they will raise sons and daughters strong enough to
know and meet their own needs.

Can capitalism survive the loss of this reservoir of frustrated human needs so easily channeled into that insatiable
desire for "things"? Can capitalism survive the new strengthened family that is already emerging from the sex-role
revolution?

"Tomorrow Begins Today," a study issued by the Security Pacific National Bank of Los Angeles, states: "Currently,
80 percent of all families earning $20,000 or more are two-

wage-earner families. . . . Two-wage earners place less emphasis on careers and increased value on leisure activities, child care and household service. Career roles are less instrumental than the search for self-identity and good health."

But, then, capitalism surely has enough flexibility to retool itself to meet the new hierarchy of needs, to its own profit.

Certain forces are now manipulating a genuine disaffection with the dehumanization and loss of personal control over our lives into a simplistic and deceptive disillusion with all governmental and political solutions to problems—masking the corporate responsibility for much of the alienation—and, in fact, with the new intent of using governmental and political power merely to unleash private corporate greed, with no control or concern but profits, and with disregard for real human needs.

The challenge of the second stage is to tap our own wellspring of generative human power, accepting the political responsibility to restructure the system as it dehumanizes both work and home—using the capitalist system to meet the new needs of individual growth and family, with a real choice to have children, and to engage the evolving human urgencies of both men and women for meaning and purpose in life. The mode of the second stage transforms the very problems into solutions, liberating those frustrated life energies from the passive service of demagogue and profiteer, pornographic escape or deadly violence. For above all, it frees us for new kinds of political participation: *human politics.*

The exercise of generative political power is its own reward, as the ancient Greeks—the free men—and our forefathers of the American Revolution knew, and as we learned in the women's movement. Maybe that is what Marx meant when he foresaw the "dictatorship of the proletariat" leading to the "withering away of the state." In that regard, the Poles rebelling against Communist bureaucratic control of their days and the Americans to whom Reagan appealed, rebelling against capitalistic "government" bureaucratic control of their lives, have a lot in common.

But not even dissident Communists in Poland concern themselves with "women's sphere." Women are only 23 percent of the membership of Solidarity, though they are 45 percent of the Polish labor force. The Polish sociologist (female) who told me this thought it must be because "women are too busy"—or maybe Solidarity wasn't dealing with women's interests. It is, after all, in capitalist America that the flexibilities inherent in our own system, our democratic tradition, even our individualism, could produce the women's movement as the first stage of the sex-role revolution.

As feminism defined as political the details of daily and family life that had never been seen as political before, so the agenda of the second stage, going beyond feminism, may make the concerns and process of politics more human and personal than we can now conceive.

The abstract political rhetoric, media manipulation and poll-pandering games of old political power that were played out in recent years by both political parties and the old slogans of the Right and the Left leave us apathetic and paralyzed now, increasing impotent rage because they do not really touch the concrete urgencies of our own lives. In the Reagan campaign, the far Right clearly played to and diverted our rage, using then the power of government to subordinate the interests of people to profit, and subjecting our lives even further to authoritarian or corporate control, while pretending to do the opposite.

It is important here to ask just why feminism was, and is, so threatening to the rigid authoritarian powers of the far Right and the far Left, who stamped it out under fascism and communism, and to those who today would replace humanistic and ecological concern and the freedom and spontaneity and diversity of religious conscience and democratic dissent with authoritarian control, in advanced capitalism.

The totalitarianism of the fascist Hitler regime in Nazi Germany was clearly based on polarized, airtight, separate sex roles and authoritarian power in the family. This was spelled out in Hitler's own speeches, which Gloria Steinem has brilliantly culled in *Ms.* (October–November 1980) in apposition to proclamations of the leaders of the fundamentalist radical Right in America today.

"If the man's world is said to be the state," Hitler told the National Socialist Women's Organization, in 1934, "her world is her husband, her family, her children and her home. . . . Respect demands that neither sex should try to do that which belongs to the sphere of the other."

Feminism had become very strong in the Weimar Republic before Hitler and the Nazis came to power. German feminists, after winning the right to vote, had elected thirty-two women deputies to the Reichstag in 1926 (compared to fifteen in the British Parliament and three in the U.S. Congress), and had gained popular support for women in industry and professions, for the rights of contraception and abortion "preserving the freedom of the individual over his or her own body," and for "a new morality" of equal rights for women and men, in or outside marriage. But after Germany's humiliating defeat in World War One, the devastating realities of inflation and mass unemployment led to a spirit of national impotence that was denied by imposing a rigid hierarchy of race, sex and class that scapegoated women along with Jews, Communists and any group that challenged "natural Aryan" superiority.

Hitler was elected by appealing to a backlash against feminism as well as anti-Semitism, promising to restore male and "Aryan" supremacy. One of Hitler's first acts after he came to power was to disband feminist organizations and close down feminist publications. In 1933, feminists were removed from teaching and other public posts by the same law that removed "non-Aryans" from such jobs. All women were banned from the Reichstag, from judgeships and from other decision-making posts. Married women were to stay at home and leave paid jobs to men. Magazine ads for contraceptives were outlawed as pornographic. Birth-control clinics were padlocked. Under Hitler, abortion became sabotage, a crime punishable by hard labor for the woman and a possible death penalty for the abortionist. "The right of personal freedom," Hitler told women in *Mein Kampf,* "recedes before the duty to preserve the race. . . . The sacrifice of personal existence is necessary to secure the preservation of the species."

Nazi totalitarianism that declared the very idea of individual rights to be dangerous was based on the patriarchal family as the basic cell (*Keimzelle*) of the state. But the fascist movement to return women to *Kinder, Küche, Kirche* and thus to restore the male-dominated family as the model of authoritarianism and male supremacy—and as metaphor for the vanished superiority of "the Fatherland"—had arisen earlier in Germany, and is rising again, in the resurgent religious fundamentalism of Moslem nations—and in the United States.

In America today, equal rights for women—and our independent personhood, our control of our own bodies—are profoundly threatening to those who seek to escape from freedom and choice through rigid authoritarian direction from above. That tendency is exacerbated when old national and individual, political and economic sources of self-confidence, security and control are threatened. The United States defeat in Vietnam, our loss of superpower omnipotence, our new reliance on foreign sources for energy, the movements to equality of opportunity of previously "inferior" races, classes, sexes, and the insidious seeping inflation shake many Americans' sense of control. But does our tradition of democracy and diversity and individual freedom, and our real strength in the world, which was built from that tradition, really require or even permit superman superiority? Only for the very rigid—who are very insecure—do threats to potency lead to demands for omnipotence and require a truly subordinate race, sex or class against whom to vent the rage and sustain the phantom of superiority. (The new rise of violence, vandalism and "hate" propaganda against Jews in America seems to be incited by some of the groups who are spreading virulent hysteria about ERA and abortion. A leaflet sent to each Illinois state Senator, just before the legislature voted on ratification of ERA in May 1980, reproduced a news clip of a Hollywood fundraising party for ERA, with arrows pointing to all the "Jewish names." The leaflet said: "More *Proof* that ERA is a *Plot* to wreck Christian Homes—and is Promoted by *Anti*-Christians, Jews, Anti-Americans and Subversives.")

The comfortable American niceness of Ronald Reagan's charisma seems the stylistic opposite of the Hitlerian goose-step. But as various political scientists have suggested, if fascism comes in America, it will be a "friendly fascism." The smooth new men who have assumed power in the United States hardly invite such sinister comparisons. And yet there is that authoritarian dismantling of programs, sometimes without even bothering to change laws, that protected the young and the old, the weak and the poor, the equal rights of women and minorities, our air and water, forests and wilderness and flowering arts, and our democratic freedoms. There is that no-longer-to-be-questioned buildup of deadly arms. And there is that strange, paralyzed acquiescence. Talk of "the will of the people" echoes in terrible silence.

If inflation gets worse, and unemployment spreads, and there are too few jobs or openings in professions, or fewer student loans for men or women, the impotent rage will increase, and along with it the need to vent that rage on scapegoats. Max Scheler, an eminent sociologist who escaped from Nazi Germany to France, postulated a state he called *ressentiment* —a frustrated rage, buried very deep, by those wanting to identify with the master class or race that is, in fact, causing their misery. Instead of directing that rage against those responsible for the degrading, frustrating conditions that truly threaten their control of life, the increase in frustration leads them to vent their rage at any who dare themselves to be free, or to speak the truth about the real situation, threatening their own ability to remain safely obsequious.

They vent their rage on any people they see as threatening their own precarious illusion of superiority, as long as

their victims are weak enough to attack safely. The scapegoat
has to be, or be made, vulnerable enough, by actual weakness
or by difference, isolated enough, to safely move against. As
Jews in Germany, blacks in America—the handicapped, the
poor—and everywhere, women. But in America, those who
move to attack women's rights, and to find scapegoats among
the young and old, the poor and the "different," in the name
of an absolutist God, an authoritarian family and an omnipo-
tent flag, may or may not so easily succeed. Americans are
not that rigid, not that insecure. Our very system is based on
diversity, flexibility, mobility—the individualism that Reagan appeals to. It is the best testimony to the strength of that
system, and hope of saving it, that women, once the least
secure and most rigidly conservative, have moved from political passivity to active individual autonomy.

In looking at the larger danger to our rights in America
today—as in dealing with the problems of living equality in
the second stage as best we can, personally and politically—
we must, above all, hold on to the *concreteness*, the changing
realities of each situation, and our own and others' experience of it, so that we neither overestimate nor underestimate
the real possibilities of movement or the dangers and resistance to it. In the face of larger political danger, we must
move in new ways according to that flexible, life-attuned,
Beta political mode that was the strength of American feminism, and is the unrecognized, still not fully realized strength
of American individualism and pragmatic democracy.

For, of course, feminism is threatening to despots of fascism, communism, or religious fundamentalism, Third
World or American brand, because it is an expression of individualism, human autonomy, personal freedom, which, once
fully experienced, can never be erased or completely controlled. The concrete experience of such individual autonomy, feminist style, is more powerful than its own or others'
revolutionary rhetoric. Because this experience was shared
by women across the lines of generation, class or even its
own definition in special-interest or single-issue terms—and

because that experience was transmitted through the family itself to men and children, and catalyzed their experience of greater autonomy—there is a base for continued movement in the second stage, despite the seeming dominance of current reaction.

In dealing with the concrete problems of restructuring home and work in the second stage, we are stronger than we think, and we can tap our real strength, because, in fact, so many millions of women and men are concretely experiencing the same problems.

The final battle for the Equal Rights Amendment, as both symbol and substance of women's rights, brings us to the end of the first stage. After June 1982, whatever our outrage, and eventually our passionate glory, when women's rights are finally written into the U.S. Constitution (and the battle has now taken on new political importance), the ERA will no longer be the single issue uniting disparate groups of women.

The rights that women have struggled to win in the last decade are in deadly danger now, with the right-wing groups in control of Congress moving faster than anyone anticipated to abolish laws against sex discrimination and legal abortion. The historic, and brilliant, appointment of a woman to the Supreme Court—even a woman who seems to have supported equal rights for women and legal abortion—does not blind us to the ominous reality of the Reagan Administration's executive orders, Congress's moves and a conservative Supreme Court's recent decisions backtracking on equality for women and minorities. The decision that military wives who have followed husbands from post to post, never able to accumulate their own seniority or pension rights, are not entitled to any share of their husband's pensions in the case of divorce was especially frightening. With the divorce rate now exceeding 50 percent, women are suddenly realizing why the Equal Rights Amendment is necessary. A poll by Louis Harris in spring 1982 showed 85 percent of women who want to work for money (but can't find jobs) now supporting ERA. And President Reagan actually joked that there wouldn't be unemployment if the women would just go home!

But women, in the battle for their own rights, have discovered a strength, and a power, a new political independence and confidence in their own values that is now the cutting edge of American politics, portending a fundamental realignment in the two-party system. "We are women to match the mountains," former housewives sang in the hills of Asheville, North Carolina, in May 1982, as diehard political bosses began to play hard ball on their issues. Political analysts of all persuasions have begun to identify this new pattern ("Reagan's women problem," some called it) as it became clear that in the 1980s women, far from following men as they always have in the past, are now voicing a clear and unprecedented "women's vote" on issues beyond those of their own rights—concerns of family and human survival, issues of care and responsibility for life.

For women's rights and reproductive freedom are now supported by almost as many men as women. And women are now pulling out in front on the larger issues of war and peace (a poll in 1980 showed 50 percent thought Reagan "reckless about war") and the economy—by a margin of 2 to 1, women in 1982 advocate a reversal of Reagan's economic policy that takes away services essential for children, the elderly, students, the sick and the handicapped, and the environment, while building up nuclear missiles and corporate profits. Women disapproved of the way Reagan was handling his job by virtually the same, and opposite, margin by which men approved it—53 to 41 percent (*Washington Post* —ABC News poll).

By 1982, the fear of war, which had led 54 percent of women to vote against Reagan for President, was now igniting concerned men—doctors, scientists, students, and others previously nonpolitical or apathetic—in support of a nuclear freeze and disarmament. Patrick Caddell, formerly Carter's pollster, said that where before men used to chart the forward positions in the political mainstream, and women followed, now women are taking the new positions first, with men following.

Pollsters find that women are leaving the Republican Party in great numbers. In that same poll, only 17 percent of the women polled considered themselves Republicans; 55 percent said they would vote Democratic in the next elections.

Women, of course, are suffering more from the cutbacks in social programs. Experts, in fact, were beginning to talk about "the feminization of poverty." For 93 percent of all welfare recipients are women and their children; 80 percent of all families receiving Aid to Families with Dependent Children are headed by women; more than two-thirds of those receiving Medicaid, food stamps, government-subsidized housing and legal services, and 90 percent of those receiving the minimum Social Security benefits of $122 a month are women.

Women who are divorced, widowed, and single heads of household—and women whose husbands have been laid off— are hit the hardest. But even upper- and middle-class women, in contrast to their husbands, were turning against Reagan's "new federalism" as their volunteer and church organizations were being asked to compensate for the social services formerly provided by the federal government. These are traditional women's concerns: compassion, love, and responsibility for life. But they have never before been expressed in a different political voice from men's. These new political concerns presage a turning point in American politics that goes far beyond women's rights, but it's clear to me that women's rights—and the women's movement generally— gave women, for the first time, the confidence to vote their own needs and values, independently of men.

How this new confidence will translate itself into mainstream politics is not yet clear. The Republicans have not even bothered to mask their disdain for women's interests. As a young woman wrote in the *Harvard Political Review* (Summer 1982), "You don't have to be a militant anything to recognize that no woman occupies an important policy-making office in the Reagan Administration." But it remains to be seen whether the Democratic Party can replace the superficiality of its rhetoric with a long-absent, gut-level commitment to women's needs and interests. Some leaders in the women's rights movement, and the antiwar movement, were talking of organizing a separate "women's party." But others, recognizing that growing numbers of men share these same concerns, were thinking instead of a new kind of political coalition, with men, of which women would be the clear cornerstone. Its agenda would not be a mere replay of New Deal —Fair Deal—Great Society slogans. The protection of women's rights—and the second-stage issues of women's larger concerns—would be at its core.

Will labor leaders—forced to an impasse, and even a retreat, on wage demands as unemployment mounts, and a permanent shift takes place in the labor market in the direction of service jobs mainly held by women—move in the interest of their own survival to the new thinking such a coalition will demand? Will Democratic politicians be able to understand that the women's voting bloc, now larger than its traditional ethnic and blue-collar base, could be their hope for power again in this century, but only if they mobilize real political muscle, expertise, and courage in behalf of women's concerns? Will moderate Republicans begin to fight for women's interests to save their own political lives?

To bring about such a second-stage political movement, the seemingly apathetic "me" generation of students would have to be aroused as they have not been since the Vietnam War, the daughters to insure the opportunities they now take for granted, the sons to move beyond a passive, fearful careerism to their deeper stakes in life. The women who have learned assertiveness training and to dress for success would have to apply their new skills, and hard-earned dollars from their own careers, to the larger political movement necessary now if these opportunities are to be lived. The women afraid of divorce would have to join the fighters for rights to insure themselves and their families against financial disaster. And leaders of single-issue, special-interest groups—for the rights of blacks, Jews, children, the aged, homosexuals, the handicapped, the environment, even the rights of women—would have to address, and transcend, those special interests in this new politics of human concern. We will still need our separate caucuses. But the unfinished business of women's rights and choice would thus become a priority, in the second stage, for all who move to a new human political tune, leaving behind the macho old men of reaction and their female imitators.

As we are forced now to move in response to concrete needs in a truly flexible Beta style, responding to each situation according to its own pragmatic demands, we may, surprisingly, find common ground with those who, in the abstract, we have seen as enemies. And the great voluntary service organizations—from Girl Scouts, Junior League, YWCA, women's clubs, girls' clubs, to the religious sisterhoods, Catholic, Protestant, Jewish—may be as important here as old-style liberal and civil rights groups.

I was continually surprised, for instance, in the last ten years to see women organizing in Europe and Latin America, under repressive regimes, as for instance, in Spain while Franco was still alive, or in Brazil, or running women's health centers and dispensing birth control, simply ignoring the repressive laws of church and state, as in Ireland. Is it because women are still not taken seriously enough for that kind of political activity to be considered a real threat, or because the Beta mode is effectively invisible—effective because it is invisible—to Alpha political eyes?

In the first stage, the women's movement almost cut itself off from this enormous potential force by a purist NOW stand against volunteerism. Of course, the women's movement itself was among the most generative expressions of voluntary, activist human politics in history. But, in the first stage, we overprized our link to previous manmade revolu-

tions and disparaged those volunteer-service women's clubs
and groups, school boards and zoning battles, the "municipal
housecleaning" that was in many ways a uniquely American
strength and female tradition. Our mothers and grandmothers experienced leadership, in the Beta mode, in those voluntary organizations, but their own and society's denigration of
women kept them, and even feminists themselves, in the first
stage, from valuing it as "real" leadership.

In NOW's infamous 1971 resolution on volunteerism—
which current NOW leaders would happily forget—women
were urged to volunteer only for social change and feminist
groups, and not in community service where their labor was
exploited (they should get jobs for which they could get real
pay and real professional credit instead) and where the officers and boards were usually composed exclusively or
mostly of men. I myself never liked that stand on volunteerism—though we should indeed have opposed the exploitation
of women, in volunteer work as in office and home, and demanded their representation on those community-service
boards. But that polarization between feminism and volunteerism, as a matter of principle, was as false an expression of
first-stage *reaction* as the seeming repudiation of family.

In that first stage, many of us also objected to wasting our
own feminist energy on "Band-Aid" services, like rape centers or battered-wife shelters or women's health centers,
which, we thought, didn't really change anything. Except, of
course, that they did. But they did because, or only insofar as,
women stopped abrogating their own power in service to
others, and instead used it to generate more life-enhancing
power for themselves and those they serve—not to patronize,
and keep the victims passive.

In the second stage, we will transcend the false conflict
between volunteerism and professionalism because, in fact,
the voluntary organizations will be the only way to provide
the services essential to further social change, and the living
of equality—now that it appears we will have to rely less and
less on government agencies and the courts. And in organiz-

ing for those services which we need communally and cannot afford or provide, even as superwomen, by ourselves—organizing women and men for day care and lunches, for children and the old, and for new service housing, and health and leisure and arts and legal services cut out of government budgets, organizing in new guerrilla resistance ways to protect our own rights and those of others—we will build a new political force.

It was conventional political wisdom, in recent years, which even liberals accepted, that you didn't really need grass-roots political organization to elect candidates now—only money to buy media time and professional political "consultants" or managers. Feminists who ran for office, relying on such "expert" male counsel, and not their own instinct and experience for Beta organization in neighborhoods—not even fully utilizing the womanpower of the movement itself—narrowly lost a number of elections. The organization of neighborhood networks for second-stage service could renew the vitality lacking in American politics since the demise of the old ethnic-machine political clubs. That kind of political vitality has been seen in recent years only on the political periphery: in the passionate participatory democracy of the women's movement itself, and in groups like Moral Majority. *Both* express an urgent need for new communal participation, communal activity and communal roots in America. Mainstream religion is now experiencing a spontaneous turn to small Catholic action ministries and Jewish *haevura* that do not rely on authoritarian priests or rabbis, but their own generative, self-renewing participant-leadership. The mainstream political parties do not meet this need for activism. The apathy they elicit may be a direct result of their reliance on "professionals."

In the second stage, the polarization between social change and service organization and between professional and volunteer leadership will disappear. With most women now working, even traditional community-service organizations can no longer depend on the "free" time of the housewife for leadership and for volunteers. As women and men share the earning and parenting, wage work and housework, in new patterns, they will also be impelled to share volunteer political or community service not just from "compassion" but to meet their own real needs in life, despite their already overburdened days—and as their only hope to relieve some of those burdens.

Partly as a result of the women's movement itself, the traditional volunteer organizations—YWCA and Girl Scouts, church and synagogue sisterhoods, community chests, family service, mental health, child care and arts councils—have also evolved to new activism, feminism and responsibility for social change. The National Council of Churches, the Federation of Jewish Philanthropies and the Community Chest of Peoria, Illinois, as well as ADA and Common Cause, last year had women presidents. In the women's movement itself, from the beginning, women who were already at the top of their professions volunteered professional services that we never could have paid for because their own passionate interests were involved, and housewives became new professionals, innovating new programs and policies to meet their own burning needs and those of other women in, for instance, the crisis of divorce. Now, traditional voluntary organizations know they have to provide women with professional apprenticeships, career credits—and tax deductions for their time— and baby-sitting expenses, as well as clear access to leadership, even to get housewives to volunteer. And feminists must realize that too much organizational reliance on professional experts—like obsessive personal concentration on women's professional "careers"—vitiates the very vitality that was our unique political strength, and the generative power we need to keep alive the dream of equality, and live through its problems, in the second stage.

There is a shock, a disapproval, as women refuse to provide free services in home or office or volunteer organization that other people (men) get pay and professional credit for. Carried to an extreme of reaction, this makes women themselves uneasy, from what I suspect is a true core of generativity, not just that imposed, driven, guilt-ridden self-abnegation. You shouldn't have to pay for, get paid for, loving your children, baking them cookies, reading them stories at night, as one woman put it. You shouldn't have to pay for, get paid for, passionate political effort to advance your own rights, or the well-being of the weak, or the noble cause of justice, art, truth, community, nation, or of God. Some true concern for higher purpose, self-transcendence, creation makes us uneasy when even women begin asking, "What's in it for me?" The time has come when both men and women have to move to larger questions, larger purposes.

When I started sharing these thoughts at a Protestant church convocation in Kansas City, a middle-aged woman ex-volunteer, gone on to her own professional career, said to me in horror, "I've done my do-good service. That's not the answer now, for women to go back and serve the community for nothing—take on saving the world, on top of their jobs and families."

Of course, that's not the answer. But the real point about the "culture of narcissism" was that it was no good for women, men, the children or the community—to keep polarizing, allocating that rewarded work of profession and political power to men, and sloughing off on the women, and thus denigrating, the "selfless" service. Without any rewards for themselves, women wouldn't keep on doing that service with any real vitality. Or they would distort service that should be selfless, such as the care of their children, to fill their unmet needs of self.

But life lived only for oneself does not truly satisfy men or women. There is a hunger in Americans today for larger purposes beyond the self. That is one reason for the religious revival and the new resonance of "family."

For many women, the women's movement itself served all these needs. It had more vitality than most volunteer activity because we were truly acting *for ourselves*. I was always irritated at the accusation that there was something *wrong* with

the women's movement because it spoke to the condition of
"white, middle-class women." That was its strength, of
course, in a country where all women (and men)—except for
the Marxist daughters and sons of the rich—would like to
think of themselves as, at least, middle-class, certainly not
poor (even if they are), and, if they are a minority, would like
at least the chance to enjoy what the majority take for
granted. But, of course, the women's movement, unlike the
effort put into one's own career, was never just for oneself. It
obviously, and consciously, did speak to conditions all
women shared, and inspired minority groups of women to
spell out their special interests: "If I am not for myself, who
will be for me? If I am only for myself, who am I?" It also
met women's needs for communality, for higher purpose,
and expressed our own generativity in a rewarding public
mode.

When I suggest a new passionate volunteerism, I mean a
human politics in the mode of the women's movement, stem-
ming from, and going beyond, the vital interests in life of
both men and women, with the same kind of relevance and
meeting the same need for communality and active personal
participation as did the women's movement.

Human politics cannot truly meet those tests if it deni-
grates our own interests in purporting to serve the larger
cause. If rich liberals like Teddy Kennedy tell us not to be so
selfish as to think of our own interests in our "compassion"
for the poor, we can rightly get annoyed, if we ourselves do
not have that backstop of inherited wealth. On the other
hand, when Ronald Reagan tells us productivity and America are served by giving up our kids' student loans in favor of
tax rebates for the rich—we begin to wonder. For liberals
and conservatives, issues like welfare or abortion for *others*
will not fuel second-stage politics for very long: our own
interests have to be served and transcended for larger purposes by human politics.

In the spring of 1981, I spoke to an extraordinary gathering of the leaders of previously nonpolitical service organiza-

tions, national volunteer and church groups—and some union, business and professional—a spectrum that included American Baptist Women, American Legion Auxiliary, Association for Women Dentists, American Library Association, American Nurses Association, Amalgamated Clothing Workers, Archdiocese of Nurses, Big Brothers, Big Sisters of America, B'Nai B'Rith Women, Child Welfare League and Children's Defense Fund, Federation of Protestant Welfare Agencies, Foster Grandparents, Grey Panthers, Girl Scouts, Legal Aid Society, National Grange, Junior League and J.C. Penney, Stride Rite, Save the Children Federation, Trust for Public Land, Successful Women, Inc., United Federation of Teachers, United Neighborhood Centers Association, United Way, Women with Disabilities United, YMHA and YWCA and the Women's Health Network—and called for a new passionate volunteerism: the mode of the second stage. This National Convocation on New Leadership in the Public Interest had been called by the NOW Legal Defense and Education Fund, but the three hundred-odd organizations responding ran the entire gamut of traditional and feminist volunteerism that has been the generative current of service to life, renewal and gentle change in America. We, they, are the front line now. For grass-roots community organization, as apple-pie American as the Community Chest, will be our guerrilla resistance as we live our dream of equality and move now to save the dream of American freedom, democracy and diversity from the current danger of authoritarian control.

I said we all had to transcend our single-issue, special-interest politics—including the politics of feminists themselves—to break the terrible silence and resist reaction. I said we had to do this, and we could do this, without relying now on courts or government help, or even corporate funds—as we had organized the women's movement itself—drawing upon our own generative power, without any time to spare, by taking back the day, and our own roots in life and the family, our own vision of God.

And the ones who wore pearls and the ones dressed in the suits of success, the women and the men who have been quiet, uncharismatic leaders in the service of the young and old, all growing living things, stood up and applauded, responding to this call to move forward again. For those whose roots are in the service of life have the strength now to ask, if no one else does, what should government be responsible for, if not for the needs of people in life? And the strength to start from these real needs of life, to take back government, for the people. The second stage will reassert our dream of equality —and the dream of American democracy—in new terms of human politics. Its leaders may not seem charismatic in the old mode. Its passion and strength will come from living the questions in concrete dailiness, wedded to the highest reaches of spirit.

"Is it ended, then?" the daughters ask. No, it never ends; and, yes, this part is over. They want to be able to take it for granted; they don't even want to think about it anymore; they've got new problems, they tell me. And yet they can't take it for granted; they still have to pay their dues. And it is very important indeed that they start thinking about the movement in new terms.

The vicious circle has been broken. It has to be reversed, and the healing energies have to be liberated by those who begin in a different place from where we leave off. It is very important indeed that the daughters and the sons hold to the dream of equality in the years ahead. Of course, they have new problems. They can live with those real problems if they don't succumb to false fears and turn back into that vicious circle. The daughters will go farther than we could envision. They will be new kinds of women, different from their mothers, as I was different from mine. And in some ways, they will not be different. They will find themselves sometimes being surprisingly strong, and still acting weak; gutsy and adventurous, and also soft and vulnerable. They can trust their feelings and their strengths. They already have strengths we lacked, and feelings they are not afraid of (partly because of us) as well as opportunities and supports from society itself now, role models and affirmation from other women, and different expectations from the men in their lives.

The daughters don't have to be afraid to let that confidence, that strength, that joy shine through. They can say "no" to superwoman standards—in their work or their homes—because they already feel good enough about themselves as women to trust themselves. Sure, they will have problems, putting it all together, but they won't have as many problems and guilts as we did. Yes, they have more choices—and those very choices may seem like a burden. But they already know that they are strong enough to risk pain, loneliness, rejection; to risk not being perfect—and to risk mistakes. Well, they've had to, learning to be a doctor, lawyer, business person, to do their work. Risking pain, and not always being in control, trusting their own feelings, they still risk falling in love—if that's what they still call it.

In the second stage, perhaps, the daughters will stop looking for supermen. They've begun to understand that their own superwoman drive and assertion of absolute independence is a mask for that residue of soft need to remain dependent. They have begun to realize that a little dependence is nothing to be afraid of, and that they won't drown in it— they wouldn't have to drive themselves so hard if they let themselves have those feelings once in a while. And they have also begun to see that those young men are just as afraid as they are—maybe more afraid, if they're still expected to be supermen. The sons are just beginning to be able to express those feelings the daughters now know are their life's blood.

The daughters no longer have to play games. Their strengths, their ability to earn, their confidence and joy in their work—it is all part of being a woman now, part of female identity, even part of their attraction. It makes it much easier for that new man to enjoy new adventures in life and to be himself.

I expect my daughter will be a better mother than I was. She won't have my guilts and driven-ness, and the self-doubts that kept me from enjoying those years even more than I did. She will simply have the practical problems. I expect the daughters will work those out. Not even the most rigidly traditional institutions can resist evolutionary change, if the daughters don't give up the dream, if they let the men join them in the parenting and the work of restruc-turing. They may not be able to have it all, either their way or even my way, all at the same time. But maybe they won't even want to.

And men will not demand or fail tests of potency in bed, or war, for lack of potency in life. And women will feel good enough about being women not to need supermen to take care of them, or to mask the need by playing superwomen themselves. And our daughters and our sons will be able to choose to have children, and bring them up with self-respect and love flowing from many sources in their evolving fami-lies.

If we cannot, at this moment, solve the new problems we can no longer deny, we will at least pass on the right ques-tions to our daughters and sons. These second-stage ques-tions reflect the most urgent problems now facing this na-tion. Improbable as it may seem, we could bridge the old conservative-liberal chasm, if we realize the true potential of that elusive new male-female, second-stage mode. Strangely enough, some of the new programs proposed by conservative thinkers (the libertarians, not the fundamentalists or radical Right) hint at this Beta mode, which eludes old liberal and radical orthodoxies, though Reagan and his men would surely shudder if any of their approaches were called "femi-nine." But the second stage is going to be full of such para-doxes. Its mode of necessity leaves behind fixed positions of ideological purity. We now have to deal with the problems of the second stage politically, as women and men are already dealing with them personally, with a diversity of fluid, shifting approaches, geared to the concrete demands of the individual situation, with whatever means are available.

The second stage is not going to be marked by magic orthodox "solutions" emanating from one central source—massive public programs from the government, or simplistic ideological dogmas handed down by commissars of the Right or Left or priests of any church. The second stage is going to be defined by a fluidity, flexibility and pragmatism demanding more individual responsibility and voluntary pooling of community resources than has been demanded of American democracy for many years—though it is the essence of American tradition. It is what we demanded of ourselves in the women's movement.

If we can eliminate the false polarities and appreciate the limits and true potential of women's power, we will be able to join with men—follow or lead—in the new human politics that must emerge beyond reaction. And this new *human* liberation will enable us to take back the day *and* the night, and use the precious, limited resources of our earth and the limitless resources of our human capital to erect new kinds of homes for all our dreams, affirm new and old family bonds that can evolve and nourish us through all the changes of our lives, and use the time that is our life to enrich our human possibility, spelling our own names, at last, as women and men.

Afterword:
How to Get the Women's
Movement Moving Again

 This is addressed to any woman who has ever said "we" about the women's movement, including those who say, "I'm not a feminist, but . . ." And it's addressed to quite a few men.

It's a personal message, not at all objective, and it's in response to those who think our modern women's movement is over—either because it is defeated and a failure, or because it has triumphed, its work done, its mission accomplished. After all, any daughter can now dream of being an astronaut, after Sally Ride, or running for President, after Geraldine Ferraro.

I do not think that the job of the modern women's movement is done. And I do not believe the movement has failed. For one thing, those of us who started the modern women's movement, or came into it after marriage and children or from jobs as "invisible women" in the office, still carry the glow of "it changed my whole life," an aliveness, the satisfaction of finding our own voice and power, and the skills we didn't have a chance to develop before.

I do believe, though, that the movement is in trouble. I was too passionately involved in its conception, its birth, its growing pains, its youthful flowering, to acquiesce quietly to

ts going gently so soon into the night. But, like a lot of other
nothers, I have been denying the symptoms of what I now
eel forced to confront as a profound paralysis of the wom-
en's movement in America.

I see as symptoms of this paralysis the impotence in the
face of fundamentalist backlash; the wasting of energy in in-
ernal power struggles when no real issues are at stake; the
nostalgic harking back to old rhetoric, old ideas, old modes of
action instead of confronting new threats and new problems
with new thinking; the failure to mobilize the young generation who take for granted the rights we won and who do not
defend those rights as they are being taken away in front of
our eyes, and the preoccupation with pornography and other
sexual diversions that do not affect most women's lives. I
sense an unwillingness to deal with the complex realities of
female survival in male-modeled careers, with the new illusions of having it all in marriage and equality in divorce, and
with the basic causes of the grim feminization of poverty.
The potential of women's political power is slipping away
between the poles of self-serving feminist illusion and male
and female opportunism. The promise of that empowerment
of women that enabled so many of us to change our own lives
is being betrayed by our failure to mobilize the next generation to move beyond us.

Evidence of the movement's paralysis has been impinging
on my own life in many ways:

• Over the last few years, I've noticed how the machinery
for enforcing the laws against sex discrimination in employment and education has been gradually dismantled by the
Reagan Administration, and how the laws' scope has been
narrowed by the courts, with little public outcry. Professional lobbyists for women's organizations objected, of
course, but there have been no mass protests from the
women in the jobs and professions that those laws opened to
them. In the early days of the National Organization for

Women, nearly 20 years ago, we demanded and won an executive order banning government contracts to companies or institutions guilty of sex discrimination; it was the first major weapon women could use to demand jobs. Some officials in the Administration are proposing the order's elimination. The Reagan Administration is also urging the courts to undo recent movement victories regarding equal pay for work of comparable value.

• The crusade against women's right to choice in the matter of childbirth and abortion, preached from the pulpits of fundamentalist churches and by the Catholic hierarchy, first achieved a ban on federal aid to poor women seeking abortion, then the elimination of United States government aid to third-world family-planning programs that counsel abortion. The Attorney General announced in the summer of 1985 that he would seek to reverse the historic Supreme Court decision, Roe v. Wade, which in 1973 decreed that the right of a woman to decide according to her own conscience when and whether and how many times to bear a child was as basic a right as any the Constitution originally spelled out for men.

At a recent meeting to mobilize women in mass communications to help save that right, I was amazed to hear a one-time radical feminist suggest that abortion should not be defended in terms of a woman's right. "Women's rights are not chic in America anymore," she argued.

• The main interest of many feminist groups in various states in recent years seems to be outlawing pornography. Laws prohibiting pornography as a form of sex discrimination and violation of civil rights have been proposed in Minnesota, Indiana, California and New York. A former NOW leader who practices law in upstate New York was startled, when she dropped in on a feminist fund-raiser, to be asked to support a nationwide ban on sexually explicit materials. When she warned, "A law like that would be far more dangerous to women than the most obscene pornography," she was greeted with incomprehension and hostility.

• At a black-tie banquet at the Plaza Hotel in New York in September 1985, I proudly watched a sparkling parade of champion women athletes as they entertained the corporate donors who sponsor their games and scholarships through the 11-year-old Women's Sports Foundation. The women champions in basketball, judo, gymnastics, tennis, skiing, swimming, boxing, running and sports-car and dogsled racing paraded down the runway in sequined miniskirts and satin jumpsuits, clasping their hands over their heads in the victory gesture. They gave credit to parents and teachers, but not one mentioned the recent Supreme Court decision regarding Grove City College in Pennsylvania. That decision threatens to remove school athletic programs from the protection of the law banning sex discrimination in federally assisted education—which is what provided crucial athletic training to these new female champions in the first place.

• At another reception, one of the many new networks of women corporate executives, a woman in her late thirties, holding a job a woman had never been given before in a large insurance company, told me: "If my slot became open today, they wouldn't give it to a woman. Not because I haven't done a good job—I keep getting raises. But they've stopped talking about getting more women on the board—or in the company. The word has gone out from the White House: They don't have to worry anymore about women and blacks. It's over."

• At a media women's reception for Christine Craft, the last movement heroine to take a case to court against that particular mix of sex and age discrimination that threatens to impose a premature ceiling on the first generation of female broadcasters, women now hitting their forties, many younger women competing for anchor jobs did not show up to support her.

• At one company, executives who faced class-action suits a decade ago now boast that their best new employees are the women. They were shocked when one of their star superwomen, on a rung very near the top, became pregnant with her second child and announced she was quitting. The boss even offered her an extended maternity leave, which is not required by law or union contract, but she quit anyway. "You may never have another chance like this," her colleagues, male and female, protested. "I'll never have these years with my children again," she answered. Most of them did not understand. They figured that whatever guilt or pressure she suffered trying to juggle baby and demanding job was her peculiar "personal problem." That sort of thing is not discussed as a women's movement problem, requiring a political solution, in her professional network.

• Another longtime feminist mother, with three "yuppie" daughters—banker, lawyer, talent agent—says, regretfully, "They're not feminists . . . they take all that for granted." She goes on to tell me that "Janey's problem is her love life and her job, and Ann's is her kids and her job, and Phyllis thinks maybe she should go back and get an MBA. With all that and exercise class, they don't have time for the meetings we used to go to. Why do they have to be feminists when they never had to suffer like we did?"

But the center for displaced housewives where this mother works—in a not-too-secure administrative job—may close down soon because of a cutoff in government funds for job training. Seeking a part-time typist at $6,000 a year, the center was amazed to get more than 100 answers to a single ad, including women with degrees and years of job experience. Among the applicants was a long-divorced woman of retirement age who had served as a role model for feminist independence, enjoying brief celebrity for the self-help book she had written about her first brave years alone. Now she is applying for "any kind of job, typing, sales"—and has begun studying the ads for "household help." She is, to put it bluntly, desperate.

• I have breakfast with two of my younger colleagues in the movement, the best and brightest, the kind that should be moving now into national leadership. One tells me she is leaving for a new job in foreign affairs. She has developed her women's rights office into such fine professional shape that "any good pro can run it now." She needs a new purpose, room to grow. The other, barely thirty, has the professional skills, honed during ten years of service to the women's movement, but is not interested in the movement job. "What's the use of all this professionalism if the grass-roots movement isn't there?" she shrugs. "What's wrong with it?" I ask. "There's a yearning for the same old music, the same old marches, by the ones who still meet in the church basements," she says. "But they are the desperate ones, the lonely ones and the pros like myself who still make some kind of living off the movement. Let's face it, the yuppies—I hate that word—who are in the halfway decent jobs that the movement opened to women don't relate to the old rhetoric. The new professional networks, which supposedly help them get ahead, don't even pretend to be feminist anymore. When it comes to the yuppies' new problems in life, and mine, we're just as alone as the women you wrote about twenty years ago."

Thinking of my own daughter-the-doctor and my daughter-in-law the editor-mother, I realize how much more complex, confident, vital and pressured their lives are than ours were. Their problems, putting it all together, keep them too busy to go to meetings. But are their problems as serious as those of the desperate housewives and the invisible women in the offices twenty years ago? Or as serious as those of the women struggling alone for economic and emotional survival today? Do women who are moving ahead in their own lives have less in common with the desperate ones? Do they even want to deny the very possibility of that desperation? (We were all pretty desperate then.)

This last year, books, articles and notices of television programs have been piling up on my desk about these new problems of "the postfeminist generation." *Smart Women, Foolish Choices*, for instance, and *A Lesser Life: The Myth of Women's*

Liberation. This growing chorus expresses a personal disillusionment with male-defined careers, a faintheartedness about "having it all," a rebellion against superwoman standards, a sense of malaise or guilt or regret about prices paid in marriage or with children—and a recurring theme of "not wanting to be like a man."

• For most of 1985, NOW was locked in a bitter, vengeful internal power struggle. Eleanor Smeal, for whom the limit of a four-year presidency of NOW had been waived for the duration of the equal rights amendment battle, came out of retirement to run against her successor, Judy Goldsmith, in midterm. She blamed her for NOW's depleted treasury and loss of members, and demanded a return to street demonstrations for ERA and free choice in abortion. Many older feminists, who thought both had been good leaders for their time, deplored the waste of energy in such a clash, as powerful enemies were closing in. Futile nostalgia for the radical marching tunes of another day will not enlist a new generation, in different circumstances, to save the rights now being taken away. But the weakening of the organization and the longing for the old sense of empowerment are real enough—and not likely to be solved by recriminations that, unfortunately, continue to divide NOW since Eleanor Smeal's return to power.

Aware of these symptoms, and yet denying my own sense that the American women's movement was over, not ready to admit defeat but wanting to move on to other things myself, I went to Kenya in the summer of 1985 out of a sheer sense of historic duty to see the thing through to its end. Most card-carrying American feminists were not even bothering with the meeting in Nairobi. NOW had scheduled its own convention in New Orleans at the same time as the United Nations World Conference of Women.

Ten years earlier, when the modern women's movement was spreading from America to the world, I had joined women wanting to organize in their countries in appealing to the UN to call a world assembly of women. At the first two world women's meetings, in Mexico in 1975 and Copenhagen in 1980, I had seen the beginnings of international networking among women broken up by organized disrupters led by armed gunmen shouting slogans against "imperialism" and "Zionism." I had been appalled at the way the official male delegates from Arab countries and other third-world and Communist nations that control the UN showed contempt for women's rights, using those conferences mainly to launch a new doctrine of religious and ethnic hate, equating Zionism and racism. And I had been repelled by the way the delegates from Western countries, mostly male officials or their wives and female flunkies, let them thereby rob those conferences of the moral and political weight they might have given to the advance of women worldwide. This year, the United States delegation had instructions from President Reagan to walk out if the question of Zionism was included in the conclusions reached at Nairobi.

To my amazement, the women's movement emerged in Nairobi with sufficient strength worldwide to impose its own agenda of women's concerns over the male political agenda that had divided it before. Despite, or because of, the backlash and other problems they face at home, nearly 17,000 women from 159 nations assembled, some 14,000 having paid their own way or been sent by volunteer, church or women's groups to the unofficial forum that is part of every such UN conference. Some traveled by plane three and four days, or by bus from African villages.

Whole new worlds of women's skills, strength, expertise and a new confidence in themselves and each other became visible in 1800 workshops at the unofficial world forum on the Nairobi University campus. Women in saris and African kangas, blue jeans and summer dresses, overflowed into the corridors, discussing "New Dimensions of Women's Spirituality," "Women as the Driving Force in Development," "The Economic Value of Women's Unpaid Work," "Getting Benefits for Part-Time Workers," "Female Sexuality in Different Religious Traditions." The new women lawyers and jurists from Asia, Africa and Latin America used international law, backed up by the media skills of black and white veterans of American civil rights and women's movements, to force the Kenyan government to let us double up and stay in the hotel rooms from which they were going to evict us because of the unexpected numbers of official delegates and journalists. The scholars from centers of women's studies that now exist in 32 nations got beyond "defining everything in terms of our subordination to men" to new feminist thinking, based on women's own experience, "embracing rather than denying biological differences between the sexes," as a brilliant woman scholar from Trinidad put it. New women theologians compared notes in the way their scriptures (Bible, Talmud, Koran) have been distorted by the fundamentalists trying to use every religion's authority to put women down. Across the lines of capitalism, communism, socialism and different levels of "development, we found common roots of economic discrimination against women in the unpaid and undervalued housework and child care which women everywhere are still expected to do on top of paid work, for which women everywhere are still paid less than work of comparable value done by men.

There was a bypassing, or bridging, of the old, abstract ideological conflicts that had seemed to divide women before —a moving beyond the old rhetoric of career versus family, equality versus development, feminism versus socialism, religion versus feminism, or feminism as an imperialist capitalist arrogance irrelevant to poor third-world women. What took the place of all this was a discussion of concrete strategies for women to acquire more control of their lives. Third-world revolutionaries, Arab and Israeli women, as well as Japanese, Greeks and Latins, gathered under a baobab tree where, every day at noon, like some African tribal elder, I led a discussion on "Future Directions of Feminism."

We shared common concerns about how to move ahead

and earn a living in a man's world—as women, even in African villages, now have to do—without losing, even using, one's best values and strengths as women. We talked about how to keep forging ahead as women when other questions—like the Israeli-Arab conflict or the superpowers' nuclear-arms race—are preoccupying our nations and using up their resources. We shared ideas on how to keep advancing, even underground, when fundamentalist groups try to take away a woman's right to control her own body or to move independently in the world, as they are doing in Egypt and the United States and have done in Iran.

When the black-veiled Iranian women, in their chadors and with their armed male guards, occupied my tree one day, we moved to another, and when they occupied both trees, we carried on our dialogue in the sun. "That's the way women have to move now everywhere in the world," I said. "We go forward, we get pushed back, we regroup. It's not a win-lose battle, to be finished in any year." "And we don't waste energy on nonessentials," said an African teacher.

At the official UN conference in Nairobi, American women delegates, mainly Republicans led by Maureen Reagan, the President's daughter, were working the hall for consensus on forward-looking strategies on equality that included things American feminists hardly dare dream of in Reagan's Washington—parental leave, child care, family planning and an economic value for women's work in home and field counted in a nation's GNP as well as equal pay for work of comparable value. Many of the other delegations from European, Latin American, African and Asian nations were now led by or included women who had been fighting for women's rights at home. Ninety percent of the world's governments have set up national bodies for the advancement of women, most of them in this last decade, while ours in the United States have been dismantled. While we were losing our battle for ERA, women won equal political rights with men in all but three nations. We Americans were humbled to learn that everywhere in the world now, women are using their new rights, using laws and civil action to get rights for wives in marriage and divorce, even under polygamy, to protest dowry burnings and murders in India, and to end the practice of female circumcision in Africa.

At Nairobi, when Arab and Communist delegations engaged, as usual, in "anti-Zionist" and "anti-imperialist" rhetoric, these strong women delegates, especially the Africans, kept warning that the women of the world would condemn those who blocked consensus on equality. And they forced the male diplomats to negotiate round the clock until they deleted that anti-Zionist expression of hate that has been ritual at every UN conference since 1975. To the amazement of experts, a program involving forward-looking strategies to advance women to equality was adopted by consensus of the nations of the world, calling on the UN to implement them and to report back to another world assembly of women before the year 2000.

I and other Americans—as many black as white among the 2,000 of us at Nairobi—went home strengthened, resolved not to accept backward-nation status for American women. For though we had gone to Nairobi subdued by our own setbacks and sophisticated enough not to offer Western feminism as the answer to the problems of women of the third world, it was truly humiliating to discover that we are no longer the cutting edge of modern feminism or world progress toward equality. Even Kenya has an equal rights clause in its Constitution!

How can we let the women's movement die out here in America when what we began is taking hold now all over the world? I would like to suggest ten things that might be done to break the blocks that seem to have stymied the women's movement in America:

1. Begin a new round of consciousness-raising for the new generation. These women, each thinking she is alone with her personal guilt and pressures, trying to "have it all," hav-

ing second thoughts about her professional career, desperately trying to have a baby before it is too late, with or without husband, and maybe secretly blaming the movement for getting her into this mess, are almost as isolated, and as powerless in their isolation, as those suburban housewives afflicted by "the problem that had no name" whom I interviewed for "The Feminine Mystique" over 20 years ago. Those women put a name to their problem; they got together with other women in the new feminist groups and began to work for political solutions and began to change their lives.

That has to happen again to free a new generation of women from its new double burden of guilt and isolation. The guilts of less-than-perfect motherhood and less-than-perfect professional career performance are real because it's not possible to "have it all" when jobs are still structured for men whose wives take care of the details of life, and homes are still structured for women whose only responsibility is running their families. I warned five years ago that if the women's movement didn't move into a second stage and take on the problems of restructuring work and home, a new generation would be vulnerable to backlash. But the movement has not moved into that needed second stage, so the women struggling with these new problems view them as purely personal, not political, and no longer look to the movement for solutions.

Putting new names to their problems, they might stop feeling guilty for not being able to conduct their professional lives just like men, might give each other support in new patterns of professional advance and parenting, might together demand new political solutions of parental leave and child care from company or profession or community, or even, once again, from government. They might, then, find new energy to save the rights they now take for granted or even secretly resent, because they are so hard to live with.

2. Mobilize the new professional networks and the old established volunteer organizations to save women's rights. We

can't fight fundamentalist backlash with backward-looking feminist fundamentalism. Second-stage feminism is itself pluralistic, and has to use new pluralist strengths and strategies. The women who have been 30 and 40 percent of the graduating class from law school or business school and 47 percent of the journalism school classes, the ones who've taken women's studies, the women who grew up playing Little League baseball and cheered on those new champion women athletes, the new professional networks of women in every field, every woman who has been looking to those networks only to get ahead in her own field, must now use her professional skills to save the laws and executive orders against sex discrimination in education and employment. They must restore the enforcement machinery and the class-action suits that opened up all these opportunities to her in the first place.

The last time the ladies with briefcases went to Washington from the "new girl" networks like Women's Forum was to get the deadline for ERA extended, nearly a decade ago. The dismantling of the laws on sex discrimination shows how much we need that Constitutional underpinning. But new symbolic marches for ERA are not what we need now but urgent, immediate concrete strategies to save the laws themselves. And this can't be left to the few professional lobbyists on feminist organization payrolls. The new worlds of professionals which the women's movement has created, including the women students in law schools and colleges and those athletes, form part of a new untapped grassroots constituency. Its numbers are strengthened by women in the pink collar service jobs, who have been fighting for equal pay for work of comparable value in the state of Washington, in the cities of Los Angeles and Minneapolis, in the Yale strike, and in the big city hospitals. And, finally, there are the millions of women in the big establishment volunteer organizations, the Junior League and YWCA and Girl Scouts and Churchwomen United, the League of Women Voters, the American Association of University Women, and Business and Professional Women, the nuns and Hadassah members, as well as the Black and Hispanic Women's Political Caucuses, and the Salvation Army, who fought together, finally, for ERA, and worked together in Nairobi, and who speak a common feminist language in America now. All of you have to take on the new job of consciousness-raising and mobilize your own grassroots machinery to save those laws. Because those worried women are right—if companies or institutions are told they don't have to worry about promoting more women or giving them athletic training in a period of budget cuts and general economic dislocation, what's to make them?

The volunteer organizations, it became clear in Nairobi, have been given new goals and gumption and professional expertise by the women's movement, despite the old stereotype of feminism in opposition to volunteerism. Let NOW heal its internal wounds and join with these other groups, as it did in the ERA struggle, to face the current emergency, rather than indulge in wishful thinking about refighting the ERA battle.

America's first movement for women's rights died out after winning the vote, four generations ago, because women didn't tackle the hard political tasks of restructuring home and work so that women who married and had children could also earn and have their own voice in the decision-making mainstream of society. Instead, those women retreated behind a cultural curtain of female "purity," focusing their energies on issues like prohibition, much like the pornographic obsession of some feminists today.

3. Get off the pornography kick and face the real obscenity of poverty. No matter how repulsive we may find pornography, laws banning books or movies for sexually explicit content could be far more dangerous to women. The pornography issue is dividing the women's movement and giving the impression on college campuses that to be a feminist is to be against sex. More important, it is diverting energies that

need to be spent in saving the basic rights now being destroyed and in facing the new problems of economic and emotional survival, for young women and old. And feminists joining forces with the Far Right to outlaw pornography are strengthening the Right's campaign to weaken constitutional protections of all our freedoms and rights, including women's basic right to control her own body.

Karen DeCrow, who once was elected president of NOW on the slogan "Out of the mainstream, into the revolution," wrote a recent article entitled "Strange Bedfellows" for Penthouse. She pointed out that the new feminist-supported proposals to make pornography an illegal violation of the civil rights of women have an unlooked-for effect. They aid the Far Right agenda that would also ban the teaching of evolution in schools, prohibit a woman's right to choose abortion, cut government funding for textbooks that portray women in nontraditional roles, and repeal federal statutes against spouse and child abuse. Reactionary campaigns have already banned books like *Huckleberry Finn*, *The Wizard of Oz*, Kurt Vonnegut's *Slaughterhouse Five*, and my own *Feminine Mystique* as pornographic in public libraries in states, and have eliminated the sale of pornography in some cities in Georgia, Ohio and Florida. "The real question should be whether the status of women has been improved in those cities," she insists. "Have more women received tenure in the colleges and universities? Are there more women judges? Are women in the factories getting the same jobs as men, and the same pay for doing them? Are women in the law firms becoming partners? The time is long overdue to be rid of the myth that if one believes in equality between the sexes, one is against erotic literature. Being a feminist means you are against sexism, not against sex."

What is behind some women's obsession with pornography? Women's sexuality has been distorted and suppressed in almost every society, we learned at Nairobi, and that suppression has gone hand in hand with a general attempt to deny women freedom to control their own lives, to move and earn independently in society. Pornography, and also the crusade to suppress pornography, reduce women to a single dimension, defining them as only passive sex objects, not people who can run their own lives.

But I think the secret this obsession with pornography may mask for women alone, for aging women, and for women still more economically dependent on men than they would like, is fear of poverty, which is the ultimate obscenity for Americans. I sat at a dinner table recently with several women, who I know are struggling personally with these problems, and could not believe their venom against the young rock star Madonna. I suggested that teen-agers identified with her gutsiness, strength and independence as well as with her not-at-all-passive sexuality, which to me was not a retreat from women's liberation, but a celebration of it. Whoever said that feminism shouldn't be sexy!

They were women in their forties, fifties and sixties, and they virtually spat in disgust. Perhaps an unspoken reason so many women are protesting sexually explicit materials is that their own sexuality is denied by society. But I suspect that as long as sex is distorted by women's economic dependence, or fear of it, it can't be truly, freely enjoyed. The obscenity that not even many feminists want to confront in personal terms is the sheer degradation of being poor in opulent, upwardly mobile America. Of course, the women's movement in America, like all such revolutions everywhere, has been mainly a middle-class movement, but the shameful secret it has never really dealt with is the fact that more and more middle-class women are sinking into poverty.

4. Confront the illusion of equality in divorce. Economists and feminists have been talking a lot lately about "the feminization of poverty" in theoretical terms, but the American women's movement has not developed concrete strategies that get at its root cause. It's not just a question of women earning less than men—though as long as women do not get equal pay for work of comparable value, or earn Social Secu-

rity or pensions for taking care of children and home, they are both economically dependent on marriage and motherhood and pay a big economic price for it. And this is as true for divorced aging yuppies as for welfare mothers. Not many women or men want to face the fact that the overwhelming majority of the truly poor in this country, regardless of race, religion or husband's economic status, are women alone, and children in families headed by women.

A startling new book by the sociologist Lenore J. Weitzman, *The Divorce Revolution: The Unexpected Social and Economic Consequences for Women and Children in America*, reveals that in the 1970s, when 48 states adopted "no-fault" divorce laws treating men and women "equally" in divorce settlements— laws feminists originally supported—divorced women and their children suffered an immediate 73 percent drop in their standard of living, while their ex-husbands enjoyed a 42 percent rise in theirs. The legal profession, including women lawyers, sought and won passages in those laws that merely enjoined the judge to "equitable" distribution of property, requiring the wife to "prove" that her contribution was equal to her husband's. (Feminists like myself were almost alone then in demanding truly equal division.)

In dividing "marital property," Lenore Weitzman reports, judges have systematically overlooked the major assets of many marriages—the husband's career assets that the wife helped make possible, his professional education that she may have helped support, the career on which he was able to concentrate because she ran the home, and his salary, pension, health insurance and earning power that resulted. They have also ignored the wife's years of unpaid housework and child care (not totally insured by Social Security in the event of divorce) and her drastically diminished job prospects after divorce. And, for most, the "equal" division of property means the forced sale of the family home—which used to be awarded to the wife and children. Child support, which has often been inadequate, unpaid and uncollectable, usually ends when the child is 18, just as college expenses begin.

Thus the vicious cycle whereby an ever-increasing majority of the truly poor in America are families headed by women.

When those "no fault" divorce "reform" laws were first passed, feminists in the first brave flush of "independence" repudiated women's need for alimony; a generation of "displaced housewives" paid a bitter price.

A new generation of feminist lawyers and judges has now drafted, and must get urgent grass-roots political support for, the kind of law needed, a law that treats marriage as a true economic partnership—and includes fairer standards of property division, maintenance and child support. It should be a law that does not penalize women who have chosen family over, or even together with, professional career.

5. Return the issue of abortion to the matter of women's own responsible choice. I think feminists have been so traumatized by the fundamentalist crusade against abortion and all the talk of fetuses and when life begins that they are in danger of forgetting the values that made abortion a feminist issue in the first place. Those pictures of revived fetuses raise new moral questions. And, in fact, hard new thinking is being done in the medical and religious communities about the use of technology to keep unwanted life alive at both extremes of the life cycle. New, hard thinking is required here of feminist theorists and leaders generally, as well as the new women doctors and midwives.

It's significant that the "Right to Life" forces at Nairobi tried to disrupt not only family planning sessions but workshops on ratifying the UN Covenant against all Forms of Discrimination Against Women. "The forces at play are after something much broader than just stopping abortions," a Latin American feminist warned. "They want to limit the ability of women to make decisions about their reproductive life, because that empowers them to participate in social and economic activity. Their real goal is to put women back into a position of dependency, where they can be controlled."

Underneath the hysteria, poll after poll shows that the

great majority of women in this nation, and most men, still want to decide when and whether to have a child in accordance with their own conscience. This includes women of faith, including the majority of Catholic women. Attacks on the Pope and picketing the churches, as some desperate or deranged male and female abortion champions have lately proposed, would play right into the hands of our "right to life" enemies, who love to paint feminists as satanic opponents of God and family. We must not surrender family values and religious principles to the Far Right. Let the new women theologians and feminist women of faith in every church take on the fundamentalist preachers.

I think women who are young, and those not so young, today must be able to choose when to have a child, given the necessities of their jobs. They will indeed join their mothers, who remember the humiliations and dangers of back-street butcher abortions, in a march of millions to save the right of legal abortion. I certainly support a march for women's choice of birth control and legal abortion. NOW has called for one in the spring of 1986.

6. **Affirm the differences between men and women.** New feminist thinking is required if American women are to continue advancing in a man's world, as they must, to earn their way, and yet "not become like men." This fear is heard with more and more frequency today from young women, including many who have succeeded, and some who have failed or opted out of male-defined careers. More books, like Carol Gilligan's *In a Different Voice*, and consciousness-raising sessions are needed. First-stage feminism denied real differences between women and men except for the sexual organs themselves. Some feminists still do not understand that true equality is not possible unless those differences between men and women are affirmed and until values based on female sensitivities to life begin to be voiced in every discipline and profession, from architecture to economics, where, until recently, all concepts and standards were defined by men. This

is not a matter of abstract theory alone but involves the restructuring of hours of work and patterns of professional training so that they take into account the fact that women are the people who give birth to children. It must lead to concrete changes in medical practice, church worship, the writing of history, standards of ethics, even the design of homes and appliances.

7. Work for a breakthrough for older women. Though the great majority of Americans living vitally now through their sixties, seventies and eighties are women (men still die prematurely, part of the price they seem to pay for machismo dominance), the women's movement has never put serious energy into the job that must be done to get women adequately covered by Social Security and pensions, especially those women now reaching sixty-five who spent many years as housewives and are ending up alone. The need for more independent and shared housing for older women now living alone in suburban houses they can't afford to sell, or lonely furnished rooms—and the need for services and jobs or volunteer options that will enable them to keep on living independent, productive lives—has never been a part of the women's movement agenda. But that first generation of feminist mothers, women now in their sixties, is a powerful political resource for the movement as these women retire from late or early professional or volunteer careers. Women in their fifties and sixties are shown by the polls to be more firmly committed than their daughters to the feminist goals of equality. Let the women's movement lead the rest of society in breaking the spell of the youth cult and drawing on the still enormous energies and the wisdom that may come to some of us in age. Or will we have to start another movement to break through the age mystique, and affirm the personhood of women and men who live beyond that dread ceiling of sixty-five—my own next birthday!

8. Bring in the men. It's passé, surely, for feminists now to see men only as the enemy, or to contemplate separatist models for emotional or economic survival. Feminist theorists like Barbara Ehrenreich cite dismal evidence of the "new men" opting out of family responsibilities altogether. But in my own life I seem to see more and more young men, and older ones—even former male chauvinist pigs—admitting their vulnerability and learning to express their tenderness, sharing the care of the kids, even though most of them may never share it equally with their wives.

And as men let down their masks of machismo, and admit their dependence on the women in their lives, women may admit a new need to depend on men, without fear of sinking back into the old abject subservience. After all, even women who insist they are not, and never will be, feminists have learned to defend themselves against real male brutality. Look at Charlotte Donahue Fedders, the wife of that Security and Exchange commissioner, who testified in divorce court about his repeated abuse—his repeated beatings caused black eyes and a broken eardrum. At one time, a woman in her situation would have kept that shame a secret. The Reagan Administration had to ask him to resign, because wife-beating is no longer politically acceptable, even in conservative America in 1985.

I don't think women can, or should try to, take the responsibility for liberating men from the remnants of machismo. But there has to be a new way of asking what do men really want, to echo Freud, a new kind of dialogue that breaks through or gets behind both our masks. Women cannot restructure jobs or homes just by talking to themselves. As a movement, we have to figure out a new kind of second stage consciousness-raising and a new kind of political organization that bring men in as organic partners.

9. Continue to fight for real political power. Feminists do not now, and in fact never really did support a woman just be-

cause she is a woman. In the '82 elections, NOW actually opposed Millicent Fenwick's Senate race in New Jersey and Margaret Heckler in Massachusetts because, though they had supported ERA, they went along with Reagan's nuclear missile buildup and cuts in social programs and legal protections for women. The "gender gap" that emerged in American politics, when women, for the first time voting independently of men, defeated governors, senators and congressmen who seemed to threaten their values of peace and social concerns, did not operate as strongly in '84 against Reagan as it did in '80, despite the presence of Ferraro on the ticket. Did the onslaught of the bishops and the attempt to tarnish her for collusion in her husband's brutally exposed business dealings rule her out as an embodiment of women's hopes? Did she fail to raise that "different voice" for women in that disastrous campaign? Or did the male backlash against Democratic values prevail also, or sufficiently, among women to offset what had seemed to be her stunning significance.

There is no substitute for having women in political offices that matter. Women are discovering that they have to fight, as men do, in primaries where victory is not certain, and not just wait for an "open seat." After the ERA's defeat, feminists and their supporters raised money nationally to run women candidates in virtually every district in Illinois, Florida and North Carolina where legislators voted against the amendment. And in that single election they increased sizably women's representation in those state legislatures. "If women ruled the world," Bella Abzug put the question to 18 women parliamentarians from Sweden, Ghana, the Soviet Union, Israel, Egypt, Canada, Brazil and others at Nairobi: "Would it make a difference?" "Not if they followed the male model," most of the parliamentarians answered, conceding that most women rulers so far have followed the male model: Indira Gandhi, Golda Meir, Margaret Thatcher. If women are truly "more concerned with real life than the games men play for power in politics and war," as a Kenyan woman

insisted under my African tree, maybe they have to reach
critical political mass for that "different voice" to be heard.

That world women's conference in Nairobi was one of
the few so far anywhere in the world where women were
more than 50% of the delegates. Significantly, it became the
first UN body since 1975 to eliminate that ritual anti-Zionist
expression of religious hate, in the interests of achieving
world consensus on those concrete strategies to advance
women to equality.

10. Move beyond single-issue thinking. Even today, I do not
think women's rights are the most urgent business for American women. The important thing is somehow getting together with men who also put the values of life first to break
through the paralysis that fundamentalist backlash has imposed on all our movements. It is not only feminism that is
becoming a dirty word in America, but also liberalism, humanism, pluralism, environmentalism and civil liberties. The
very freedom of political dissent that enabled the women's
movement to start here has been made to seem unsafe for
today's young men as well as young women. I think the yuppies are afraid to be political.

Women may have to think beyond "women's issues" to
join their energies with men to redeem our democratic tradition and turn our nation's power to the interests of life instead of the nuclear arms race that is paralyzing it. I've never,
for instance, seen the need for a separate women's peace
movement. I'm not really sure that women, by nature, are
more peace-loving than men. They were simply not brought
up to express aggression the way men do (they took it out
covertly, on themselves and on their men and children, psychologists would say). But the human race may not survive
much longer unless women move beyond the nurture of
their own babies and careers to political decisions of war and
peace, and unless men who share the nurture of their children take responsibility for ending the arms race before it

destroys all life. In that sense, I think the women's movement is only a particular moment in human evolution, and once its job is *really* done, then it can and should be allowed to fade away, honorably discharged.